THINK LIKE DA VINCI

Leonardo Da

THINK
LIKE
DA VINCI

7 EASY STEPS TO BOOSTING
YOUR EVERYDAY GENIUS

MICHAEL GELB

This book presents nutrition and exercise information which may or may not be right for you. In view of the complex, individual and specific nature of health and fitness problems, this book is not intended to replace professional medical advice. Every individual is different. Before starting any diet or exercise programme, get your doctor's approval. The publisher and the author expressly disclaim any responsibility for any loss or risk incurred as a consequence of the application of the contents of this book.

HarperElement
An Imprint of HarperCollins*Publishers*
77–85 Fulham Palace Road,
Hammersmith, London W6 8JB

www.harpercollins.co.uk

and *HarperElement* are trademarks of
Harpercollins*Publishers* Ltd

First published as *How to Think Like Leonardo
Da Vinci* by Delacorte Press 1998
This edition 2009

2

©Michael J. Gelb 1998

Michael J. Gelb asserts the moral right to
be identified as the author of this work

The terms *High Performance Learning* and *Mind Mapping* are
registered trademarks used with the permission of Michael J. Gelb
and the Buzan Organization, respectively.

"I think continually of those who were truly great" from *Selected Poems*
by Stephen Spender. Copyright 1934 and renewed 1962 by Stephen Spender.
Reprinted by permission of Random House, Inc., and Peters Fraser & Dunlop Group Ltd.

A catalogue record for this book
is available from the British Library

ISBN 978-0-00-732382-1

Printed and bound in Great Britain by
Clays Ltd, St Ives plc

Mixed Sources
Product group from well-managed
forests and other controlled sources
www.fsc.org Cert no. SW-COC-1806
© 1996 Forest Stewardship Council

FSC is a non-profit international organization established to promote the
responsible management of the world's forests. Products carrying the FSC
label are independently certified to assure consumers that they come
from forests that are managed to meet the social, economic and
ecological needs of present and future generations.

Find out more about HarperCollins and the environment at
www.harpercollins.co.uk/green

*This book is dedicated to
the Da Vincian Spirit manifested in
the life and work of Charles Dent.*

ACKNOWLEDGMENTS

Grazie to all who participated in the evolution of the Da Vincian exercises and to the readers who offered valuable feedback on the evolving manuscript: Ann-Marie Botton, Jolie Barbiere, Stacy Forsythe, Michael Frederick, Ruth Kissane, John Ramo, Dr. Dale Schusterman, and Sylvia Tognetti.

Grazie to the "cognoscenti" of music appreciation: Audrey Elizabeth Ellzey, Dr. Roy S. Ellzey, Joshua Habermann, Murray Horwitz, Dr. Elain Jerdine, and Stacy Forsythe.

Grazie to Professor Roger Paden for repeatedly raiding his faculty library on my behalf.

Grazie to my clients and friends who keep the Da Vincian spirit alive in their organizations, especially Ed Bassett, Bob Ginsberg, Dave Chu, Peter Cocoziello, Jim D'Agostino, Marv Damsma, Doug Durand, Gerry Kirk, Delano Lewis, Nina Le Savoy, and Harvey Sanders.

Grazie molto to my parents, Joan and Sandy Gelb, who inspired my Da Vincian approach to life. To Joan Arnold for incisive editing and constructive feedback. To Sir Brian Tovey for sharing his insights on Florence and the Renaissance. To my wonderful literary agent, Muriel Nellis, and her staff, especially Jane Roberts. And to Tom Spain for his Da Vincian vision and brilliant editing, and his team at Delacorte, especially Mitch Hoffman and Ellen Cipriano.

Grazie mille to four people who made exceptional contributions to this book:

Nusa Maal for her contributions to the Drawing Course, her magnificent illustrations, and for championing the principles of multi-sensory intelligence.

To the modern *uomo universale* Tony Buzan for creating mind maps, the Da Vincian thinking tool.

Grand master Raymond Keene, O.B.E., for sharing his profound knowledge of history and genius.

Audrey Elizabeth Ellzey for invaluable support in research and administration and for her Da Vincian fealty to truth.

Contents

PART ONE

PART TWO

PART THREE

PREFACE: "BORN OF THE SUN"

Think of your greatest heroes and heroines, your most inspirational role models. Maybe, if you are very lucky, the list includes your mom or dad. Perhaps you are most inspired by great figures from history. Immersing yourself in the life and work of great artists, leaders, scholars, and spiritual teachers provides rich nourishment for the mind and heart. Chances are, you picked up this book because you recognize Leonardo as an archetype of human potential and you are intrigued by the possibility of a more intimate relationship with him.

When I was a child, Superman and Leonardo da Vinci were my heroes. While the "Man of Steel" fell by the wayside, my fascination with Da Vinci continued to grow. Then, in the spring of 1994, I received an invitation to visit Florence to speak to a prestigious and notoriously demanding association of company presidents. The group chairman asked, "Could you prepare something for our members on how to be more creative and balanced, personally and professionally? Something that will point them in the direction of becoming Renaissance men and women?" In a heartbeat I responded with my dream: "How about something on thinking like Leonardo da Vinci?"

It was not an assignment I could take lightly. My students would already have paid substantial fees to attend the six-day "university," one of several opportunities the society offers its members each year to meet in the world's great cities to explore history, culture, and business while pursuing personal and professional development. Given the chance to choose among several concurrent classes – mine was running at the same time as five others, including one taught by former Fiat president Giovanni Agnelli – members were invited to rate each speaker on a scale of one to ten and were encouraged to walk out of any presentation they didn't like. In other words, if they don't like you, they chew you up and spit you out!

Despite my lifelong fascination with my new topic, I knew I had work to do. In addition to intensive reading, my preparation included a Da Vinci pilgrimage, beginning with a visit to Leonardo's *Portrait of Ginevra De' Benci* at the National Gallery in Washington, D.C. In New York, I caught up with the traveling "Codex Leicester" exhibit sponsored by Bill Gates and Microsoft. Then to London to see the manuscripts in the British Museum, *The Virgin and Child with St. Anne* at the National Gallery, and to the Louvre in Paris to spend a few days with *Mona Lisa* and *St. John the Baptist*. The highlight of this pilgrimage, however, was visiting the château of Cloux near Amboise, where Da Vinci spent the last few years of his life. The château is now a Da Vinci museum, with amazing replicas of some of Leonardo's inventions crafted by engineers from IBM. Walking the grounds that he walked, sitting in his study and standing in his bedroom, looking out his window, seeing the view that he gazed at every day, I felt my heart overflow with awe, reverence, wonder, sadness, and gratitude.

Of course, I went on to visit Florence, where, eventually, I gave my talk to the presidents. The fun began when the person introducing me confused her notes on my biography with the paper I had submitted on Da Vinci. She said – and I am not, to quote Dave Barry, making this up – "Ladies and gentlemen, I am extremely privileged today to introduce to you an individual whose background surpasses anything I have ever encountered: anatomist, architect, botanist, city planner, costume and stage designer, chef, humorist, engineer, equestrian, inventor, geographer, geologist, mathematician, military scientist, musician, painter, philosopher, physicist and raconteur … Ladies and gentlemen, allow me to present … Mr. Michael Gelb!"

Ah, if only …

Well, the talk was a success (no one walked out), and it gave birth to the book you hold in your hands.

Before that unforgettable introduction, one of the members approached me and said, "I don't believe that anyone can learn to be like Leonardo da Vinci, but I'm going to your lecture anyway." You may be thinking something similar: Is the premise of this book that every child is born with the capacities and gifts of Leonardo da Vinci? Does the author really believe that we can all be geniuses of Da Vinci's stature? Well, actually, no. Despite decades devoted to discovering the full scope of human potential and how to awaken it, I side with Da Vinci's disciple Francesco Melzi, who wrote on the occasion of the maestro's death: "The loss of such a man is mourned by all, for it is not in the power of Nature to create another." As I learn more about Da Vinci, my sense of awe and mystery multiplies. All great geniuses are unique, and Leonardo was, perhaps, the greatest of all geniuses.

But the key question remains, Can the fundamentals of Leonardo's approach to learning and the cultivation of intelligence be abstracted and applied to inspire and guide us toward the realization of our own full potential?

Of course, my answer to *this* question is: Yes! The essential elements of Leonardo da Vinci's approach to learning and the cultivation of intelligence are quite clear and can be studied, emulated, and applied.

Is it hubris to imagine that we can learn to be like the greatest of all geniuses? Perhaps. It's better to think of his example guiding us to be more of what we truly are.

The beautiful words of the poet Sir Stephen Spender provide the perfect preface to launch our flight through history's loftiest mind:

I THINK CONTINUALLY OF THOSE WHO WERE TRULY GREAT

I think continually of those who were truly great.
Who from the womb, remembered the soul's history
Through corridors of light where the hours are suns,
Endless and singing. Whose lovely ambition
Was that their lips, still touched with fire,
Should tell of the spirit clothed from head to foot in song.
And who hoarded from the spring branches
The desires falling across their bodies like blossoms.
What is precious is never to forget
The delight of the blood drawn from ageless springs

Breaking through rocks in worlds before our earth;
Never to deny its pleasure in the simple morning light,
Nor its grave evening demand for love;
Never to allow gradually the traffic to smother
With noise and fog the flowering of the spirit.

Near the snow, near the sun, in the highest field
See how those names are feted by the wavering grass,
And by the streamers of white cloud,
And whispers of wind in the listening sky;
The names of those who in their lives fought for life,
Who wore at their hearts the fire's centre.
Born of the sun they traveled a short while towards the sun.
And left the vivid air signed with their honor.

We live in a world of unprecedented noise, fog, and traffic. But you too are born of the sun, and traveling towards it. This is a guidebook, inspired by one of history's great souls, for that journey. An invitation to breathe the vivid air, to feel the fire in your heart's centre, and the full flowering of your spirit.

Michael J. Gelb
January 1998

PREFACE TO THE NEW EDITION

On July 15, 2003, I had the delightful opportunity to speak with the audience at the 2nd Stage Theater in New York City following a sold-out performance of Mary Zimmerman's brilliant play *The Notebooks of Leonardo da Vinci*. One of the questions from the audience may reflect something in your mind as you hold this book in your hands: "How can the scope and depth of Leonardo's genius be understood and why does his influence seem to be growing?"

We can speculate about the origins of Leonardo's unparalleled genius, but the more we learn about him the more the mystery seems to grow. And so does his influence, even in popular culture. In the opening scene of the major motion picture *The Italian Job* rapper turned actor Mos Def walks along the canal in Venice reading this book. Def shows it to one of his partners in crime, played by Jason Statham, and explains why Leonardo is so "cool." The maestro also stars in Dan Brown's best-selling mystery novel *The Da Vinci Code*, and makes cameo appearances in various episodes of *Star Trek* as a holographic adviser to the captain of the *Enterprise*.

This universal fascination with the supreme man of the Renaissance reflects a more personal, intuitive inkling about our own possibilities for creative expression. Beyond all his stellar achievements, Leonardo da Vinci serves as a global archetype of human potential. Since this book was first published in 1998, it's been translated into 18 languages and I've heard from enthusiasts around the world. A Polish elementary school teacher uses the seven principles to organize her class curriculum. The head of strategy for a major London-based consulting firm discovered that Leonardo was an invaluable ally in helping his multi-national clients solve some of their most important business problems. And a 32-year-old father from Tennessee commented, "This book gave me everything I always wanted to teach my children but didn't have the words to say."

One of my favorite bits of feedback came from renowned anthropologist, visionary, author and shaman Jean Houston. A modern Renaissance woman, Jean serves as an adviser to world leaders on accessing the essential wisdom of the universal archetypes expressed in diverse cultures and traditions. About a year after *Think Like Da Vinci* was first published I was invited to speak to a group of 500 psychotherapists in Washington, D.C. After the presentation, Jean, who was also there to address the conference, appeared and whispered in my ear, "Leonardo is very pleased."

It's easy to imagine Leonardo's pleasure when Ricardo Muti conducted Beethoven's Fifth in tribute to him at La Scala in September of 1999. The celebration took place exactly 500 years after the day when the model for Leonardo da Vinci's magnificent 24-foot-tall equestrian sculpture was destroyed by invading French troops. Now, the "Lost Horse" was being resurrected in Milan, and after leaving the concert one could almost see the smile in the eyes of the statue of Leonardo which graces the center of the La Scala square.

The rebirth of the Horse began in the imagination of a former airline pilot and art collector, Charles Dent, to whom this book is dedicated. Although he died in 1994, Dent's work continued through the non-profit organization he founded. Honoring a promise made to Dent on his deathbed, the board of Leonardo da Vinci's Horse, Inc. led a coalition of donors, artists, metallurgists, volunteers and scholars in fulfilling this dream. Sculpted by Nina Akamu, the majestic Horse stands proudly in Milan with a second full size casting in the Fredrik Meijer Gardens in Grand Rapids, Michigan. Smaller scale bronze replicas also adorn Leonardo's hometown of Vinci, Italy and the Dent family hometown of Allentown, PA.

The rebirth of this lost masterpiece is a testament not only to the maestro's artistic genius but also to his embodiment and expression of the human creative spirit. This spirit was also alive in October of 2001 when Queen Sonja of Norway dedicated a bridge linking her country and

Sweden. Built based on an original design sketched in 1502 by Leonardo da Vinci, the bridge was originally intended for the Turkish Sultan Bejazet II. But, the Sultan declined to proceed with the project because its revolutionary pressed-bow engineering and 720-foot span seemed "too fantastic." In 1996, Norwegian artist Vebjørn Sand saw Leonardo's sketch and, moved by its graceful beauty and powerful symbolism, dreamed of recreating it. After six years of fundraising and testing, in cooperation with the Norwegian Transportation Ministry, Sand's Leonardo Bridge was unveiled just outside Oslo. Spanning the highway connecting Norway to neighboring Sweden, it is the first civil engineering project in history based on an actual Da Vinci design. Sand imagines a Leonardo Bridge on every continent as a global tribute to the remarkable life and genius of Leonardo da Vinci and his inspiration for all of us to express our own creative potential.

Sand and Dent's nephew Peter were both present at the opening reception of the amazing exhibition of Da Vinci drawings at New York's Metropolitan Museum of Art in the spring of 2003. Over flutes of prosecco we shared our reflections on the maestro's drawings and his vivifying presence. We agreed that if God could draw this is what it might look like. Sand then laughed as he shared the story of one municipal council committee that had declined to proceed with the building of a Leonardo bridge because they felt that the design was "too futuristic." Dent explained that having helped fulfill his uncle's vision to create Leonardo's Horse, his organization was now merging with the Discovery Center of Science and Technology, with a mission to bring Leonardo's inspiration to science education for children around the world. The Center's educational mission is expressed in the seven principles for thinking like Leonardo that you will learn in the pages that follow.

One of Leonardo's favorite images was the rippling circles of water that flow out from the center when a stone is dropped into a pool of water. Leonardo's life was a gem tossed into a pool of time that became known as the Renaissance and his genius ripples on and on into eternity. The art critic Bernhard Berenson summed it up when he said of Leonardo,

"Everything he touched turned to eternal beauty." My wish for you is that you will allow the principles for thinking like Leonardo to bring a touch of that rippling beauty to your life every day.

Michael J. Gelb
September 2003

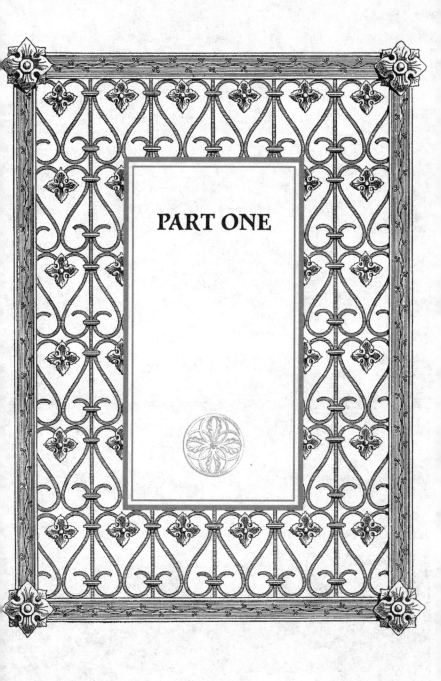

PART ONE

Introduction:

Your Brain Is Much Better than You Think.

lthough it is hard to overstate Leonardo da Vinci's brilliance, recent scientific research reveals that you probably underestimate your own capabilities. You are gifted with virtually unlimited potential for learning and creativity. Ninety-five percent of what we know about the capabilities of the human brain has been learned in the last twenty years. Our schools, universities, and corporations are only beginning to apply this emerging understanding of human potential. Let's set the stage for learning how to think like Leonardo by considering the contemporary view of intelligence and some results of the investigation into the nature and extent of your brain's potential.

Most of us grew up with a concept of intelligence based on the traditional IQ test. The IQ test was originated by Alfred Binet (1857–1911) to measure, objectively, comprehension, reasoning, and judgment. Binet was motivated by a powerful enthusiasm for the emerging discipline of psychology and a desire to overcome the cultural and class prejudices of late nineteenth-century France in the assessment of children's academic potential. Although the traditional concept of IQ was a breakthrough at the time of its formulation, contemporary research shows that it suffers from two significant flaws.

The first flaw is the idea that intelligence is fixed at birth and immutable. Although individuals are endowed genetically with more or less talent in a given area, researchers such as Buzan, Machado, Wenger, and many others have shown that IQ scores can be raised significantly through appropriate training. In a recent statistical review of more than two hundred studies of IQ published in the journal *Nature*, Bernard Devlin concluded that genes account for no more than 48 percent of IQ. Fifty-two percent is a function of prenatal care, environment, and education.

The second weakness in the commonly held concept of intelligence is the idea that the verbal and mathematical reasoning skills measured by IQ tests (and SATs) are the sine qua nons of intelligence. This narrow view of intelligence has been thoroughly debunked by contemporary psychological research. In his modern classic, *Frames of Mind* (1983), psychologist Howard Gardner introduced the theory of multiple intelligences, which posits that each of us possesses at least seven measurable intelligences (in later work Gardner and his colleagues catalogued twenty-five different subintelligences). The seven intelligences, and some genius exemplars (other than Leonardo da Vinci, who was a genius in all of these areas) of each one, are:

+ **Logical-Mathematical** – Stephen Hawking, Isaac Newton, Marie Curie
+ **Verbal-Linguistic** – William Shakespeare, Emily Dickinson, Jorge Luis Borges
+ **Spatial-Mechanical** – Michelangelo, Georgia O'Keeffe, Buckminster Fuller
+ **Musical** – Mozart, George Gershwin, Ella Fitzgerald
+ **Bodily-Kinesthetic** – Morihei Ueshiba, Muhammad Ali, F. M. Alexander
+ **Interpersonal-Social** – Nelson Mandela, Mahatma Gandhi, Queen Elizabeth I
+ **Intrapersonal (Self-knowledge)** – Viktor Frankl, Thich Nhat Hanh, Mother Teresa

The theory of multiple intelligences is now accepted widely and when combined with the realization that intelligence can be developed throughout life, offers a powerful inspiration for aspiring Renaissance men and women.

In addition to expanding the understanding of the nature and scope of intelligence, contemporary psychological research has revealed startling truths about the extent of your potential. We can summarize the results with the phrase: Your brain is much better than you think. Appreciating your phenomenal cortical endowment is a marvelous point of departure for a practical study of Da Vincian thinking. Contemplate the following: your brain

- is more flexible and multidimensional than any supercomputer.
- can learn seven facts per second, every second, for the rest of your life and still have plenty of room left to learn more.
- will *improve* with age if you use it properly.
- is not just in your head. According to renowned neuroscientist Dr. Candace Pert, "… intelligence is located not only in the brain but in cells that are distributed throughout the body … The traditional separation of mental processes, including emotions, from the body is no longer valid."
- is unique. Of the six billion people currently living and the more than ninety billion people who have ever lived, there has never, unless you are an identical twin, been anyone quite like you. Your creative gifts, your fingerprints, your expressions, your DNA, your dreams, are unprecedented and unique.
- is capable of making a virtually unlimited number of synaptic connections or potential patterns of thought.

What happens to your brain as you get older? Many people assume that mental and physical abilities necessarily decline with age; that we are, after age twenty-five, losing significant brain capacity on a daily basis. Actually, the average brain can improve with age. Our neurons are capable of making increasingly complex new connections throughout our lives. And, our neuronal endowment is so great that, even if we lost a thousand brain cells every day for the rest of our lives, it would still be less than 1 percent of our total (of course, it's important not to lose the 1 percent that you actually use!).

This last point was established first by Pyotr Anokhin of Moscow University, a student of the legendary psychological pioneer Ivan Pavlov. Anokhin staggered the entire scientific community when he published his research in 1968 demonstrating that the minimum number of potential thought patterns the average brain can make is the number 1 followed by 10.5 million kilometers of typewritten zeros.

Anokhin compared the human brain to "a multidimensional musical instrument that could play an infinite number of musical pieces simultaneously." He emphasized that each of us is gifted with a birthright of virtually unlimited potential. And he proclaimed that no man or woman, past or present, has fully explored the capacities of the brain. Anokhin would probably agree, however, that Leonardo da Vinci could serve as a most inspiring example for those of us wishing to explore our full capacities.

LEARNING FROM LEONARDO

Baby ducks learn to survive by imitating their mothers. Learning through imitation is fundamental to many species, including humans. As we become adults, we have a unique advantage: we can choose whom and what to imitate. We can also consciously choose new models to replace the ones we outgrow. It makes sense, therefore, to choose the best "role models" to guide and inspire us toward the realization of our potential.

Leon Battista Alberti (1404–1472) was the original *uomo universale* and one of Leonardo's "role models." Architect, engineer, mathematician, painter, and philosopher, Alberti was also a gifted athlete and musician.

So, if you want to become a better golfer, study Ben Hogan, Jack Nicklaus, and Tiger Woods. If you want to become a leader, study Winston Churchill, Abraham Lincoln, and Queen Elizabeth I. And if you want to be a Renaissance man or woman, study Leon Battista Alberti, Thomas Jefferson, Hildegard von Bingen, and best of all, Leonardo da Vinci.

In *The Book of Genius* Tony Buzan and Raymond Keene make the world's first objective attempt to rank the greatest geniuses of history. Rating their subjects in categories including "Originality," "Versatility," "Dominance-in-Field," "Universality-of-Vision," and "Strength and Energy," they offer the following as their "top ten."

10. Albert Einstein
 9. Phidias (architect of Athens)
 8. Alexander the Great
 7. Thomas Jefferson
 6. Sir Isaac Newton
 5. Michelangelo
 4. Johann Wolfgang von Goethe
 3. The Great Pyramid Builders
 2. William Shakespeare

And the greatest genius of all time, according to Buzan and Keene's exhaustive research? Leonardo da Vinci.

As Giorgio Vasari wrote of Leonardo in the original version of his *The Lives of the Artists,* "Heaven sometimes sends us beings who represent not humanity alone but divinity itself, so that taking them as our models and imitating them, our minds and the best of our intelligence may approach the highest celestial spheres. Experience shows that those who are led to study and follow the traces of these marvelous geniuses, even if nature gives them little or no help, may at least approach the supernatural works that participate in his divinity."

Our evolving understanding of the multiplicity of intelligence and the capacities of the brain suggests that nature gives us more help than we might have imagined. In *Think Like Da Vinci* we will "study and follow the traces" of this most marvelous of all geniuses, bringing his wisdom and inspiration to your life, every day.

A PRACTICAL APPROACH TO GENIUS

In the pages that follow you will learn a practical approach, tested in experience, for applying the essential elements of Leonardo's genius to enrich your life. You will discover an exhilarating, original way of seeing and enjoying your world as you develop powerful strategies for creative thinking and new approaches to self-expression. You'll learn proven techniques for sharpening your senses, liberating your unique intelligence, and harmonizing body and mind. With Leonardo as your inspiration, you will make your life a work of art.

Although you may already be familiar with Da Vinci's life and work, you'll finish this book with a fresh perspective and a deeper appreciation for this most enigmatic figure. Looking at the world from his point of view, you may also get a taste of the loneliness genius brings. But I guarantee that you'll be uplifted by his spirit, inspired by his quest, and exalted by your association with him.

The book begins with a capsule review of the Renaissance and its parallels with our time, followed by a biographical sketch of Leonardo and a summary of his major accomplishments. The heart of the book is the discussion of the Seven Da Vincian Principles. These principles are drawn from an intensive study of the man and his methods. I've named them in Leonardo's native Italian. The good news is that Leonardo's

---

Giorgio Vasari (1511–1574), architect of Florence's Uffizi and a pupil of Michelangelo's, originally published his *The Lives of the Artists* in 1549. He was credited by scholars with effectively inventing the discipline of art history with that book. *Lives* remains the most important source on Italian Renaissance art. With uncanny flair Vasari profiles the lives and work of almost two hundred painters, sculptors, and architects, including Giotto, Masaccio, Brunelleschi, Donatello, Botticelli, Verrocchio, Raphael, Michelangelo, Titian, and, of course, Leonardo.

principles will probably be intuitively obvious to you. You do not have to try to invent them in your life. Rather, like much of common sense, they need to be remembered, developed, and applied.

The Seven Da Vincian Principles are:

Curiosità – An insatiably curious approach to life and an unrelenting quest for continuous learning.

Dimostrazione – A commitment to test knowledge through experience, persistence, and a willingness to learn from mistakes.

Sensazione – The continual refinement of the senses, especially sight, as the means to enliven experience.

Sfumato (literally "Going up in Smoke") – A willingness to embrace ambiguity, paradox, and uncertainty.

Arte/Scienza – The development of the balance between science and art, logic and imagination. "Whole-brain" thinking.

Corporalita – The cultivation of grace, ambidexterity, fitness, and poise.

Connessione – A recognition of and appreciation for the inter-connectedness of all things and phenomena. Systems thinking.

Having read this far, you are already applying the first Da Vincian principle. Curiosità – the quest for continuous learning – comes first because the desire to know, to learn, and to grow is the powerhouse of knowledge, wisdom, and discovery.

If you are interested in thinking for yourself and freeing your mind from limiting habits and preconceptions, then you are on track for the second principle: Dimostrazione. In his search for truth, Da Vinci insisted on questioning conventional wisdom. He used the word *dimostrazione* to express the importance of learning for oneself, through practical experience.

Pause for a few moments, and recall the times in the past year when you felt most vividly alive. Chances are, your senses were heightened. Our third principle – Sensazione – focuses on sharpening the senses, consciously. Leonardo believed that refining sensory awareness was the key to enriching experience.

Portrait of the Maestro.

As you sharpen your senses, probe the depths of experience, and awaken your childlike powers of questioning, you will encounter increasing uncertainty and ambiguity. "Confusion endurance" is the most distinctive trait of highly creative people, and Leonardo probably possessed more of that trait than anyone who has ever lived. Principle number four – Sfumato – guides you to be more at home with the unknown, to make friends with paradox.

For balance and creativity to emerge from uncertainty requires principle number five – Arte/Scienza – or what we now call whole-brain thinking. But Da Vinci believed that balance was more than just mental. He exemplified and affirmed the importance of principle number six – Corporalita – the balance of body and mind. And if you appreciate patterns, relationships, connections, and systems – if you seek to understand how your dreams, goals, values, and highest aspirations can be integrated into your

> "We respect him by learning from him."
> – FREUD ON DA VINCI

daily life – then you are already applying principle number seven: Connessione. Connessione ties everything together.

Each principle is highlighted by excerpts from the maestro's notebooks and illustrated with his sketches or paintings. This illumination is followed by some questions for reflection and self-assessment. These questions are designed to stimulate your thinking and inspire your application of the principles. The questions are followed by a program of practical exercises for cultivating a personal and professional Renaissance. To get the most benefit from *Think Like Da Vinci,* read the whole book first, without doing the exercises. Just contemplate the questions for reflection and self-assessment. After this preview, review the explanation of each principle and then do the exercises. Some of the exercises are easy and fun, while others require challenging inner work. All are designed to bring the spirit of the maestro to your daily life. In addition to the exercises, you will find an annotated reading and resource list to guide you in exploring and applying each principle. The reading list includes recommendations on the Renaissance, the history of ideas, the nature of genius, and, of course, the life and work of Leonardo.

In the final section of the book you will discover "The Beginner's Da Vinci Drawing Course," and you'll also learn how you can participate in a history-making project that embodies the essence of the Da Vincian spirit.

The Renaissance,
Then and Now

Just across the Arno River, a bit off the well-trodden Florentine tourist track, you'll find the church of Santa Maria del Carmine. Enter, make a left and then another quick left, and you are in the Brancacci Chapel, surrounded by the frescoes of Masolino and Masaccio. The first fresco on the left is Masaccio's evocation of Adam and Eve being expelled from the garden. And it is here that the Renaissance begins: Instead of having the two-dimensional otherworldliness of medieval paintings, Masaccio's Adam and Eve look like real human beings. Their slumping postures and downcast faces express real emotion. Portrayed in three dimensions, with their feet solidly on the ground, Masaccio's figures herald a new era of human promise and potentiality.

To appreciate this new era, and to get the most from our study of Leonardo da Vinci, we must first gain some insight into the preceding period. In *A World Lit Only by Fire: The Medieval Mind and the Renaissance,* William Manchester claims that pre-Renaissance Europe was characterized by "a mélange of incessant warfare, corruption, lawlessness, obsession with strange myths, and an almost impenetrable mindlessness." Describing the period from the fall of the Western Roman Empire to the dawn of the Renaissance, Manchester writes, "In all that time nothing of real consequence had either improved or declined. Except for the introduction of water wheels in the 800s and windmills in the 1100s, there had been no inventions of significance. No startling new ideas had appeared, no new territories outside Europe had

---

Masaccio's "expulsion" is an ironic theme for what may be the first true Renaissance painting. Both Michelangelo and Leonardo spent many hours studying it. Leonardo commented, "Masaccio showed by the perfection of his work how those who are inspired by a model other than nature, a mistress above all masters, are laboring in vain."

been explored. Everything was as it had been for as long as the oldest European could remember. The center of the Ptolemaic universe was the known world – Europe with the Holy Land and North Africa on its fringes. The sun moved round it every day. Heaven was above the immovable Earth, somewhere in the overarching sky; hell seethed far beneath their feet. Kings ruled at the pleasure of the Almighty; all others did what they were told to do … The church was indivisible, the afterlife a certainty; all knowledge was already known. And nothing would ever change."

The word *Renaissance* comes from the combination of the French verb *renaître*, meaning "to revive," and the noun *naissance*, meaning birth. The Italians call it Rinascimento. After centuries of serfdom and superstition, the ideal of human power and potentiality was reborn. The revival of this classical ideal was presaged by Giotto, initiated by Brunelleschi, Alberti, and Masaccio, and reached full expression through Leonardo, Michelangelo, and Raphael. This dramatic transformation of worldview from the medieval era went hand in hand with a number of discoveries, innovations, and inventions, including:

+ **The printing press** – Made knowledge available to vast numbers of people beyond the clergy and ruling elites. In 1456 there were fewer than sixty extant copies of Gutenberg's bible, the first book printed in Europe. By the turn of the century there were over fifteen million printed books in circulation.

+ **The pencil and inexpensive paper** – Made writing, note-taking, and therefore the recording of learning accessible to the common citizen.

+ **The astrolabe, the magnetic compass, and the large sailing ship** – Resulted in a tremendous expansion of ocean traffic, international trade, and exchange of information. As Columbus and Magellan proved that the world is not flat, much of traditional wisdom was rendered flat.

+ **The long-range cannon** – Although catapults, mangonels, and small cannons were in use for many years, they were not able to breach fortress walls. The powerful long-range cannon was pioneered by a Hungarian engineer named Urban in the mid-1400s. As the new technology spread, the feudal fortress, and therefore feudalism, soon lost its impregnability. The stage was set for the birth of the modern nation-state.

✦ **The mechanical clock** – Stimulated commerce by allowing people to experience time as a controllable commodity. In the Middle Ages people had no concept of time as we understand it. The vast majority of people didn't know what year it was or even what century they lived in.

Many of these innovations and most of the great art masterpieces of the period were fueled by the entrepreneurial spirit, the spreading desire for consumer goods, and a rush to capital. In *Worldly Goods: A New History of the Renaissance,* Lisa Jardine shows, with magnificent illustrations and incisive, detailed text, how the cultural and intellectual transformations of the Renaissance were driven by expanding capitalism. She suggests that "those impulses which today we disparage as 'consumerism' " were present in the Renaissance mind-set that produced the works and advances we treasure today. Even commercialism played a role: "A painter's reputation rested on his ability to arouse commercial interest in his works of art, not on some intrinsic criteria of intellectual worth."

This extraordinary burgeoning awareness of human capability was delightfully reflected by changes in the rules of chess. Prior to the Renaissance, the queen moved only one square at a time; but as the perception of human horizons and potential expanded, she was granted the wide-ranging powers she maintains to this day.

Still, the question remains why the Renaissance took place when it did. For one thousand years prior, European accomplishments in the realms of science and exploration were negligible. Throughout the Middle Ages, the vast majority of human intellectual energy and effort was diverted to questions of doctrinal minutiae and "holy" war. Instead of exploring new lands, innovations, and ideas, the best minds engaged in debates on how many angels could fit on the head of a pin, and the church rarely hesitated to torture anyone who questioned its dogma. This, of course, put something of a damper on independent thinking.

The seminal event that led to the Renaissance, my colleague Raymond Keene and I believe, occurred in the fourteenth century when the Black Plague swept through Europe. Almost one half of the population was destroyed in a rapid and hideous fashion. Priests, bishops, nobles, and knights died in the same proportion as peasants, serfs, harlots, and tradesmen. Devotion, piety, and loyalty to the church provided no protection, shaking the faith of people from all walks of life. Moreover, wealthy families had their ranks thinned almost overnight, concentrating wealth in the hands of the lucky survivors. While they would previously have spent this wealth on the church, the wealthy began to hedge their bets after the plague and began to invest in independent scholarship. In what was at first an almost imperceptibly subtle shift of consciousness, answers were sought outside of prayer and dogma. Surging intellectual energy, dammed for a millennium in ecclesiastical reservoirs, began to flow through the pestilence-inspired breach.

Five hundred years after the Renaissance, at a time when nations and corporations rival the church in their claims to people's loyalties, the world is experiencing an even more dramatic expansion of knowledge, capitalism, and interconnection. Air travel – the fulfillment of one of Da Vinci's dreams and prophecies – telephones, radio, television, motion pictures, facsimile machines, personal computers, and now the Internet combine to weave an increasingly complex web of global information exchange. Revolutionary advances in agriculture, automation, and medicine are taken for granted. We've landed men on the moon and machines on Mars, unleashed the power of the atom, deciphered the genetic code, and unlocked many of the secrets of the human brain. These dramatic developments in communication and technology stimulate the energies of capitalism and free society and the erosion of totalitarianism.

You can't help but notice that change is accelerating. How these changes will affect you personally and professionally, nobody knows. But, like the thinkers at the end of the cataclysmic change caused by the

Black Death, we owe it to ourselves to ask if we can afford to let the authorities of our time – whether church, government, or corporation – think for us.

It is safe to say, however, that accelerating change and increasing complexity multiply the value of intellectual capital. The individual's ability to learn, adapt, and think, independently and creatively, is at a premium. During the Renaissance, individuals with a medieval mind-set were left behind. Now, in the Information Age, medieval- and industrial-era thinkers are threatened with extinction.

The Renaissance was inspired by the ideals of classical antiquity – awareness of human power and potentiality, and a passion for discovery – but it also transformed them to meet the challenges of the time. Now we can draw inspiration from Renaissance ideals, transforming them to meet our own challenges.

Perhaps, like many of my friends, you feel that your greatest challenge is living a balanced, fulfilling life in the face of increasing stress from every direction. As we noted, our medieval ancestors had no concept of time; we, on the other hand, are in danger of being controlled by the clock. In the Middle Ages, information was unavailable to the average person, and the few books that existed were in Latin, which was taught only to the elite. Now we are awash in an unprecedented, unrelenting overflow of data. In five hundred years we've moved from a world where everything was certain and nothing changed to a world where nothing seems certain and everything changes.

Accelerating change has inspired a never-before-seen burgeoning of interest in personal growth, soul awakening, and spiritual experience. The sheer availability of information about the world's esoteric traditions has launched a tsunami of seeking. (A hundred years ago you would have had to have climbed a mountain in India to learn how to meditate; today you can take a course at the Y, download information from the Internet, or choose from hundreds of volumes at your local bookstore.) At the same time, the information glut contributes to pervasive cynicism, fragmentation, and a sense of helplessness. We have more possibilities, more freedom, more options than any people who have ever lived. Yet

THE MODERN RENAISSANCE MAN OR WOMAN

The ideal of the Renaissance man or woman, or *uomo universale*, has always suggested a well-rounded, balanced person, comfortable with both art and science. The liberal arts curriculum of universities around the world originated as a reflection of this ideal. In an age of increasing specialization, attaining balance requires going against the grain. In addition to possessing a good knowledge of the classical liberal arts, the modern *uomo universale* is also:

- **Computer literate:** Although even Leonardo may have had trouble programming a VCR, the modern Renaissance man or woman is attuned to developments in information technology and is increasingly at home on the World Wide Web.
- **Mentally literate:** As discussed earlier, 95 percent of what we know about the human brain has been learned in the last twenty years. *Mental literacy* is a term, coined by Tony Buzan, to express a practical familiarity with this evolving understanding of the workings of the human mind. It begins with an appreciation of the vast potential of the brain and the multiplicity of intelligences, and includes the development of the accelerated learning and creative thinking skills that will be introduced in the following pages.
- **Globally aware:** In addition to appreciating the global links in communication, economies, and ecosystems, the modern *uomo universale* is comfortable with different cultures. Racism, sexism, religious persecution, homophobia, and nationalism are viewed as vestiges of a primitive stage of evolution. Modern Renaissance people in the West cultivate a particular appreciation for Eastern culture and vice versa.

there is more junk, more mediocrity, more garbage to sort through than ever too.

For seekers who wish to cut through the dross, to find deeper levels of meaning, beauty, and quality of life, Leonardo da Vinci – the patron saint of independent thinkers – beckons you onward.

The Life of Leonardo da Vinci

f you have ever filled out a job application or written your résumé, then you can particularly appreciate the letter that Leonardo wrote in 1482 to Ludovico Sforza, regent of Milan. Da Vinci composed what is perhaps the most outstanding employment application letter of all time:

"I wish to work miracles…"

– LEONARDO DA VINCI

Most illustrious Lord, having now sufficiently seen and considered the proofs of all those who count themselves master and inventors of instruments of war, and finding that their invention and use of the said instruments does not differ in any respect from those in common practice, I am emboldened without prejudice to anyone else to put myself in communication with your Excellency, in order to acquaint you with my secrets, thereafter offering myself at your pleasure effectually to demonstrate at any convenient time all those matters which are in part briefly recorded below.

1. I have plans for bridges, very light and strong and suitable for carrying very easily …
2. When a place is besieged I know how to cut off water from the trenches, and how to construct an infinite number of … scaling ladders and other instruments …
3. If because of the height of the embankment, and the strength of the place or its site, it should be impossible to reduce it by bombardment, I know methods of destroying any citadel or fortress, even if it is built on rock.

Self-portrait in red chalk.

4. I have plans for making cannon, very convenient and easy of transport, with which to hurl small stones in the manner almost of hail …

5. And if it should happen that the engagement is at sea, I have plans for constructing many engines most suitable for attack or defense, and ships which can resist the fire of all the heaviest cannon, and powder and smoke.

6. Also I have ways of arriving at a certain fixed spot by caverns and secret winding passages made without any noise even though it may be necessary to pass underneath … a river.

7. Also I can make covered cars, safe and unassailable, which will enter the serried ranks of the enemy with artillery, and there is no company of men at arms so great as not to be broken by it. And behind these the infantry will be able to follow quite unharmed and without any opposition.

8. Also, if need shall arise, I can make cannon, mortars, and light ordnance, of very beautiful and useful shapes, quite different from those in common use.

9. Where it is not possible to employ cannon, I can supply catapults, mangonels, traps, and other engines of wonderful efficacy not in general issue. In short, as the variety of circumstances shall necessitate, I can supply an infinite number of different engines of attack and defense.

10. In time of peace I believe that I can give you as complete satisfaction as anyone else in architecture, in the construction of buildings both public and private, and in conducting water from one place to another.

11. Also I can execute sculpture in marble, bronze, or clay, and also painting, in which my work will stand comparison with that of anyone else whoever he may be.

12. Moreover, I would undertake the work of the bronze horse, which shall endure with immortal glory and eternal honor the auspicious memory of the Prince your father and of the illustrious house of Sforza.

And if any of the aforesaid things should seem impossible or impracticable to anyone, I offer myself as ready to make trial of them in your park or in whatever place shall please your Excellency, to whom I commend myself with all possible humility.

He got the job. Although, according to Giorgio Vasari, it was probably his courtly charms along with his talents as a musician and party planner that were mostly responsible for his positive reception. It's amazing to imagine a genius of Da Vinci's stature devoting his time to the design of pageants, balls, costumes, and other ephemerae, yet as Kenneth Clark points out, "This was expected of Renaissance artists between Madonnas."

Thirty years earlier, according to a document prepared by his grandfather, Leonardo was born at 10:30 P.M. on Saturday, April 15, 1452. His mother, Caterina, was a peasant from Anchiano, a tiny village near the small town of Vinci, about forty miles away from Florence. His father, Ser Piero da Vinci, who was not married to his mother, was a prosperous accountant and notary for the city of Florence. Young Leonardo was taken from Caterina at age five and raised in the home of his grandfather, also a notary. Because children born out of wedlock were disqualified from membership in the Guild of Notaries, Leonardo was not eligible to follow in the footsteps of his father and grandfather. But for this quirk of fate he could have been the greatest accountant of all time!

In quattrocento Florence, it was a common practice for a master to allow one of his more gifted students to complete some of the details of a painting. Domenico Ghirlandajo, Pietro Perugino, and Lorenzo di Credi were some of Leonardo's fellow apprentices in Verrocchio's workshop.

Fortunately, he was sent instead to be an apprentice in the studio of the master sculptor and painter Andrea del Verrocchio (1435–1488). Verrocchio's name translates from the Italian as "true eye," a name he was given to recognize the penetrating perceptiveness of his work and a perfect title for the teacher of Leonardo (Verrocchio's masterpiece is the equestrian monument of General Colleoni in Venice, although he is most

Da Vinci biographer Serge Bramly, author of the brilliant Discovering the Life of Leonardo da Vinci, *comments on the difference between the young Leonardo's work and that of his teacher: "When the* Baptism of Christ *is X-rayed, the difference between his [Leonardo's] technique and Verrocchio's emerges quite staggeringly. Whereas the master still indicated relief by highlighting contours with white lead (which blocks the X rays and therefore shows up clearly on them), Leonardo superimposes very thin layers of paint, unmixed with white; his application is so smooth and fluid there are no brush strokes to be seen. The X rays go straight through his section; the angel's face shows up completely blank."* As though he really created an angel.

popularly known for his *Putto with a Dolphin* in the courtyard of the Palazzo Vecchio in Florence and his statue of David in the Bargello). The first painting known to be by Da Vinci's hand is the angel and a bit of the landscape in the lower left-hand corner of Verrocchio's *Baptism of Christ.*

In *The Lives of the Artists,* Giorgio Vasari records that when Verrocchio saw the delicate, exquisite, and numinous quality of his pupil's work, he vowed "never to touch colors again." Although this may sound like reverential humility or despair at his own limitations, it is most likely that

Verrocchio made a business decision to delegate more painting commissions to his gifted apprentice and to concentrate his own talents instead on the profitable practice of sculpture.

Leonardo's precocious talents drew the attention of Verrocchio's prime patron, Lorenzo de' Medici, Il Magnifico. Leonardo was introduced to the extraordinary milieu of philosophers, mathematicians, and artists cultivated by Lorenzo. There is some evidence that during the period of his apprenticeship, the young Leonardo lived in the Medici home.

After six years with Verrocchio, Leonardo was admitted to the Company of St. Luke, a guild of apothecaries, physicians, and artists headquartered in the Ospedale Santa Maria Nuova, in 1472. It is likely that he took the opportunity, provided through the location of the guild,

Verrocchio's bust of Lorenzo de' Medici, Il Magnifico.

The Annunciation *by Leonardo da Vinci. The misty background, detailed botanical studies, and luminous curly hair are early trademarks of the maestro's style.*

to deepen his study of anatomy. The most educated guessers assign his anatomically outstanding evocation of St. Jerome in the Vatican Gallery and his *Annunciation* in the Uffizi to this period.

We can imagine Leonardo in his late teens and early twenties, strolling the streets of Florence in his silk leggings, his long auburn-blond curls cascading over the shoulders of his rose-colored velvet tunic. Vasari extolled "the splendor of his appearance, which was extremely beautiful, and made every sorrowful soul serene." Renowned for his physical grace, beauty, and talents as a storyteller, humorist, conjurer, and musician, Leonardo probably spent a fair amount of his youthful time enjoying life. But this lighthearted period came to an abrupt close when shortly before his twenty-fourth birthday, he was arrested and brought before a committee of the Florentine government to answer charges of sodomy. One can imagine the traumatic effect upon someone so sensitive of being accused of what was then a capital crime and being held in jail. As he noted, "The greater the sensibility the greater the suffering … much suffering."

Although the charges were eventually dismissed due to insufficient evidence, the seeds of Leonardo's departure from Florence had been sown. Nevertheless, he did receive a number of commissions in the next few years including a few from the Florentine government. By far his most significant work of this first Florentine period is *The Adoration of the Magi* for the monks of San Donato a Scopeto.

In 1482 Leonardo moved to Milan. Working under the patronage of Ludovico "the Moor" Sforza, Leonardo created his masterpiece, *The Last Supper*. Painted on the wall of the refectory of Santa Maria delle Grazie from 1495 to 1498, Leonardo's *Last Supper* captures, with stunning psychic force, the moment that Christ proclaims, "One of you shall betray me." Christ sits alone, resigned and serene, at the center of the table as the

St. Jerome *by Leonardo da Vinci. This painting was discovered in the nineteenth century. It was in two pieces, one of which was being used as a tabletop.*

Bernard Berenson, the art critic who introduced the word connoisseur *into the English language, called Leonardo's* Adoration of the Magi *(left) "truly a great masterpiece" and added, "Perhaps the quattrocento produced nothing greater." Preparatory work for the* Adoration *below.*

The Last Supper *by Leonardo da Vinci. Imagine looking at this painting through the eyes of the monks who commissioned it. "Never before," comments art historian E. H. Gombrich, "had the sacred episode appeared so close and so lifelike."*

disciples explode in turmoil around him. Yet in a geometrically perfect composition, the disciples counterbalanced – left and right, higher and lower – in four groups of three, Leonardo brings the uniqueness of each soul to life. Christ's tranquillity, conveyed through Leonardo's seamless sense of order and perspective, contrasts with the surrounding human emotion and chaos to yield a moment of transcendence unparalleled in the history of art. Although the painting has deteriorated considerably, despite, and in some cases because of, attempts at restoration, it remains, in the words of art historian E. H. Gombrich, "one of the great miracles of human genius."

When he wasn't charming Ludovico's court or creating transcendent paintings, Leonardo was busy with studies of anatomy, astronomy, botany, geology, flight, and geography and plans for inventions and

Leonardo da Vinci: Study for the Sforza equestrian monument.

military innovations. He also received an important commission from the Moor to build an equestrian monument honoring his father, Francesco Sforza, the previous grand duke of Milan. After exhaustive researches into the anatomy and movement of horses, Da Vinci crafted a plan to create what critics agree would have been the greatest equestrian statue ever produced. After more than a decade of work Leonardo constructed a model twenty-four feet high. Vasari wrote that "there was never a more beautiful thing or more superb." Leonardo calculated that casting this masterpiece would require more than eighty tons of melted bronze. The bronze, unfortunately, was not forthcoming, as Ludovico needed it to build cannons to stave off invaders. He failed, and in 1499 the French overwhelmed Milan and drove Sforza into exile. In a historical act of bad taste and barbarism that ranks with the Ottoman army's blowing the nose off the Sphinx, and the Venetian fleet's landing a mortar projectile on the Parthenon, the

"About the horse I will say nothing for I know the times." – From Leonardo's letter to Ludovico on learning that the bronze for the monument would not be supplied.

French archers destroyed the model horse by using it for target practice.

Ludovico's defeat meant that Leonardo was without a patron or a home. He found his way to Florence in 1500 and the next year he unveiled his preparatory drawing for *The Virgin and Child with St. Anne and the Infant St. John,* commissioned by the Servite Friars. Describing the public reaction, Vasari writes that the painting "not only filled every artist with wonder, but when it was set up … men and women, young and old, flocked for two days to see it, as if in festival time, and they marveled exceedingly." Although Leonardo never completed the painting for the Servites, his drawings formed the basis of a later work, the exquisitely tender *Virgin and Child with St. Anne,* now in the Louvre.

In 1502 Leonardo shifted his attention from the sublime evocation of divine femininity to take up an appointment as chief engineer to the

Ludovico "the Moor" Sforza, regent of Milan and patron of Leonardo.

Leonardo's Drawing of The Virgin and Child with St. Anne.

infamous commander of the papal armies, Cesare Borgia. He traveled extensively for the next year, making six remarkably accurate maps of central Italy for his new patron. Despite his access to Leonardo's maps and military innovations, Cesare saw his battlefield fortunes wane. The Signoria of Florence sent Niccolò Machiavelli to advise Borgia in his struggles, but the great strategist was unable to prevent the collapse of Borgia's forces. Machiavelli did, however, befriend Leonardo during this period, a friendship that set the stage for the maestro to receive an important commission from the Signoria of Florence after his return in April 1503.

During the same period that he was struggling with *The Battle of Anghiari,* Leonardo painted a portrait, according to Vasari, of the third wife of a Florentine nobleman, Francesco del Giocondo. Madonna Elisabetta, nicknamed Mona Lisa, was to be immortalized in history's

Peter Paul Rubens's rendition of The Battle of Anghiari *by Leonardo da Vinci.*

most famous and mysterious painting. Leonardo took the painting with him when he returned to Milan, this time in the service of Louis XII's viceroy, Charles d'Amboise. During his second stay in Milan, Leonardo focused on studies in anatomy, geometry, hydraulics, and flight while designing and decorating palaces, planning monuments, and building canals for his patron. Leonardo also managed to paint his St. John and Leda and the Swan.

In 1512 Lodovico's son Maximilian drove the French out of Milan and established a short reign before being deposed. Leonardo fled to Rome, where he sought the patronage of Leo X, the new Medicean pope, whose brother arranged for him to receive a stipend and lodging at the Vatican. Although the pope was an art lover, he was too preoccupied with the commissions he had already granted Michelangelo and Raphael to pay much attention to the sixty-year-old Da Vinci. Leonardo rarely held a paintbrush during this time, concentrating primarily on studies of anatomy, optics, and geometry. He did, however, meet and profoundly influence the young Raphael.

The lukewarm support he received from the Vatican disappeared altogether with the death of his sponsor in 1516. As Leonardo noted before leaving Rome in disappointment, "The Medici made me and destroyed me."

William Manchester comments on Da Vinci's lack of papal support: ". . . of all the great Renaissance artists, Da Vinci alone was destined to fall from papal grace. . . . In a larger sense he was a graver menace to medieval society than any Borgia. Cesare merely killed men. Da Vinci, like Copernicus, threatened the certitude that knowledge had been forever fixed by God, the rigid mind-set that left no role for curiosity or innovation. Leonardo's cosmology . . . was, in effect, a blunt instrument assaulting the fatuity which had, among other things, permitted a mafia of profane popes to desecrate Christianity."

Niccolò Machiavelli. Machiavelli's The Prince, *a masterpiece of pragmatism, is one of the most influential books in the Western canon.*

Cesare Borgia. A study of the Borgia family makes the most scandalous modern soap opera look tame.

Ladies and gentlemen, let's get ready to rumble! Welcome to the Sala del Gran Consiglio of the Palazzo Vecchio for the All-Time Heavyweight Painting Championship of the World. On the wall to the right with the scruffy smock and broken nose, the challenger, Michelangelo Buonarroti, will paint The Battle of Cascina, and on the opposite wall, wearing his trademark rose-colored tunic and carefully groomed blond, curly beard, the champion, Leonardo da Vinci, will paint The Battle of Anghiari.

It really happened, thanks largely to Machiavelli's influence. The Battle of the Battles is the quintessentially Florentine event, expressing the competitive, sharp-edged attitude of that city's fathers, eyes focused clearly on their legacy. Sadly, we know both works only through sketches, copies, and written description. Leonardo attempted an experiment for fixing the paint on the wall that failed; he left the unfinished work as it began to deteriorate, returning to Milan in 1506. Michelangelo was called to Rome by Pope Julius II, leaving only sketches behind. Nevertheless, these two unfinished works had a profound influence on the future of art. According to Kenneth Clark, "The battle cartoons of Leonardo and Michelangelo are the turning point of the Renaissance . . . they initiate the two styles which 16th century painting was to develop – the Baroque and the Classical."

Who won the battle of the battles? Clark marvels at Leonardo's baroque design and extols his unsurpassed depiction of horses and individual human faces while emphasizing that their contemporaries probably favored Michelangelo because of the incomparable beauty of his classical nudes. We know that Michelangelo copied parts of Da Vinci's design in his notebook and that Leonardo was influenced by his younger rival to give his own nudes a more heroic pose. We'll call it a draw.

François I, king of France and patron of Leonardo.

Accompanied by his small entourage of pupils and assistants, Leonardo wound his way through Milan to Amboise in the Loire Valley, knowing he would not return to the land of his birth. The last few years of his life were spent there under the patronage of François I, king of France. Although Da Vinci had many patrons and admirers throughout his days, the French king was perhaps the only one who came close to recognizing and appreciating the singular nature of Da Vinci's genius. François provided Leonardo with a lovely château and a generous stipend and left the great master free to think and work as he pleased. Although his official title was "painter, engineer, and architect of the king," Da Vinci's primary obligation was to converse, to muse, and to philosophize with his majesty. According to Benvenuto Cellini, François "affirmed that never had any man come into the world who knew so much as Leonardo, and that not only in sculpture, painting, and architecture, for in addition he was a great philosopher."

Under King François's patronage Leonardo persevered in his studies, but time was running out. Years of exile had sapped his vitality. Then a severe stroke cost him the use of his right hand. Leonardo saw that he would die without fully realizing his dream of unifying all knowledge.

His last days, like much of his life, are shrouded in mystery. He once wrote, "As a day well spent brings blessed sleep, so a life well lived brings a blessed death." Yet elsewhere he noted, "It is with the greatest reluctance that the soul leaves the body, and its sorrow and lamentations are not without cause." Vasari tells us that as death approached, Leonardo, never religious but always deeply spiritual, "desired scrupulously to be informed of Catholic practice and the good and holy Christian religion."

Leonardo Da Vinci died at the age of sixty-seven on May 2, 1519. Vasari claims that in his final days Leonardo was filled with repentance and apologized to "God and man for leaving so much undone." Yet toward the end Leonardo also wrote, "I shall continue" and "I never tire of being useful." Vasari records that Leonardo was observing and describing, in scientific detail, the nature of his illness and symptoms as he died in the arms of the French king. Although some scholars claim that documents prove that François was elsewhere at the time of Da Vinci's death, the evidence is inconclusive, and Vasari may be right. It is easy to believe, however, that the maestro would, even at the moment of death, continue his process of learning and study.

The life of Leonardo da Vinci is a mysterious tapestry, woven in paradox, dyed in irony. No one has ever attempted so much in so many areas, and yet much of his work was left unfinished. He never completed *The Last Supper, The Battle of Anghiari,* or the Sforza horse. Only seventeen of his paintings exist, a number of which are incomplete. Although his notebooks contained wondrous information, he never organized and published them as he intended.

Scholars have offered a range of social, political, economic, and psychosexual explanations for Da Vinci's leaving so many works

Leonardo's sketch of the Arno River valley, dated August 5, 1473, is brimming with the forces of nature.

incomplete. Some have even branded him a failure because he left so much unfinished. Professor Morris Philipson argues convincingly, however, that this is somewhat like criticizing Columbus for not discovering India.

Philipson and other scholars all seem to agree, however, that more important than any of his specific accomplishments is the example of the man himself. Leonardo offers the supreme inspiration for reach to exceed grasp.

MAJOR ACCOMPLISHMENTS

It would take an encyclopedia to begin to do justice to the full scope of Leonardo's accomplishments. We can get a glimpse of some of his most notable achievements through the categories of art, invention, military engineering, and science.

Leonardo *the artist* transformed the direction of art. He was the first Western artist to make landscape the prime subject of a painting. He pioneered the use of oil paints and the application of perspective, chiaroscuro, contrapposto, sfumato, and many other innovative and influential methods.

Leonardo's *Mona Lisa* and *The Last Supper* are recognized universally as two of the greatest paintings ever produced. They are certainly the most famous. Leonardo also created other wonderful paintings including *The Virgin of the Rocks, The Madonna and Child with St. Anne, The Adoration of the Magi, St. John the Baptist,* and his portrait of Ginevra de' Benci that hangs in the National Gallery in Washington, D.C.

In a sentiment echoed later by Freud, biographical novelist Dmitry Merezhkovsky, author of *The Romance of Leonardo da Vinci*, compared Leonardo to "a man who wakes too early, while it is still dark and all around him are still sleeping."

Although Leonardo's paintings are few in number, his drawings are abundant and equally magnificent. Like the *Mona Lisa*, Leonardo's *Canon of Proportion* has become a universally familiar icon. His studies for *The Madonna and Child with St. Anne* and the heads of the apostles in *The Last Supper,* along with his drawings of flowers, anatomy, horses, flight, and flowing water, are unmatched.

Leonardo was also renowned as an architect and a sculptor. Most of his architectural work focused on general principles of design, although he

The figure of Plato, king of philosophers, in Raphael's masterpiece The School of Athens *is believed to be based on Leonardo.*

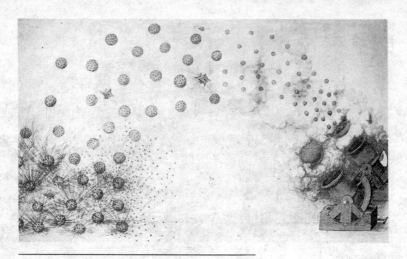

Leonardo's design for a mortar is bursting with creativity.

did consult on a number of practical projects including cathedrals in Milan and Pavia, and the French king's château at Blois. While he is believed to have contributed to a number of sculptures, scholars agree that the only existing sculptures definitely touched by the maestro's hand are three bronzes on the north door of the Baptistery in Florence. The *Saint John the Baptist Preaching to a Levite and a Pharisee* was created in collaboration with the sculptor Rustici.

Leonardo *the inventor* made plans for a flying machine, a helicopter, a parachute, and many other marvels including the extendable ladder (still in use by fire departments today), the three-speed gear shift, a machine for cutting threads in screws, the bicycle, an adjustable monkey wrench, a snorkel, hydraulic jacks, the world's first revolving stage, locks for a canal system, a horizontal waterwheel, folding furniture, an olive press, a number of automated musical instruments, a water-powered alarm clock, a therapeutic armchair, and a crane for clearing ditches.

More than any single invention, Leonardo deserves credit for pioneering the concept of automation. He designed myriad machines that could save labor and increase productivity. Although some were fanciful and impractical, others, like his automated looms, were portents of the Industrial Revolution.

As a *military engineer* Da Vinci made plans for weapons that would be deployed four hundred years later, including the armored tank, machine gun, mortar, guided missile, and submarine. As far as we know, however, nothing he designed was ever used to injure anyone during his lifetime. A man of peace, he referred to war as *"pazzia bestialissima* – beastly madness," and found bloodshed "infinitely atrocious." His instruments of war were designed "to preserve the chief gift of nature, which is liberty," he wrote. At times he shared them reluctantly, accompanying one design with a written glimpse of his ambivalence: "I do not wish to divulge or publish this because of the evil nature of men."

Leonardo *the scientist* is the subject of considerable scholarly debate. Some scholars suggest that if Leonardo had organized his scientific thoughts and published them, he would have had a massive influence on the development of science. Others argue that he was so far ahead of his time that his work would not have been appreciated even if it was formulated in comprehensible general theories. While Leonardo's science

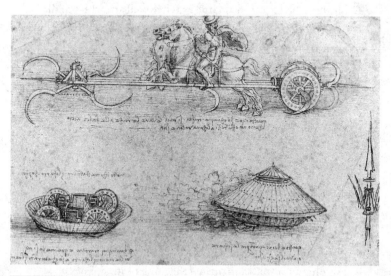

Scythed chariot and "tank".

may best be appreciated for its intrinsic value as an expression of his quest for truth, most scholars agree that he can be credited with significant contributions to several disciplines:

Anatomy

+ He pioneered the discipline of modern comparative anatomy.
+ He was the first to draw parts of the body in cross section.
+ He drew the most detailed and comprehensive representations of humans and horses.
+ He conducted unprecedented scientific studies of the child in the womb.
+ He was the first to make casts of the brain and the ventricles of the heart.

Botany

+ He pioneered modern botanical science.
+ He described geotropism (the gravitational attraction of the earth on some plants) and heliotropism (the attraction of plants toward the sun).
+ He noted that the age of a tree corresponds to the number of rings in its cross section.
+ He was the first to describe the system of leaf arrangement in plants.

Geology and Physics

+ He made significant discoveries about the nature of fossilization, and he was the first to document the phenomenon of soil erosion. As he wrote, "Water gnaws at mountains and fills valleys."
+ His physics studies anticipated the modern disciplines of hydrostatics, optics, and mechanics.

Leonardo's investigations led him to anticipate many great scientific discoveries including breakthroughs by Copernicus, Galileo, Newton, and Darwin.

40 years before Copernicus – Da Vinci noted, in large letters for emphasis, "IL SOLE NO SI MUOVE," "The sun does not move." He added, "The earth is not in the center of the circle of the sun, nor in the center of the universe."

60 years before Galileo – He suggested that "a large magnifying lens" should be employed to study the surface of the moon and other heavenly bodies.

200 years before Newton – Anticipating the theory of gravitation, Leonardo wrote, "Every weight tends to fall towards the center by the shortest possible way." And elsewhere he added that because "every heavy substance presses downward, and cannot be upheld perpetually, the whole earth must become spherical."

400 years before Darwin – He placed man in the same broad category as monkeys and apes and wrote, "Man does not vary from the animals except in what is accidental."

More valuable than any of his specific scientific achievements, Leonardo's approach to knowledge set the stage for modern scientific thinking.

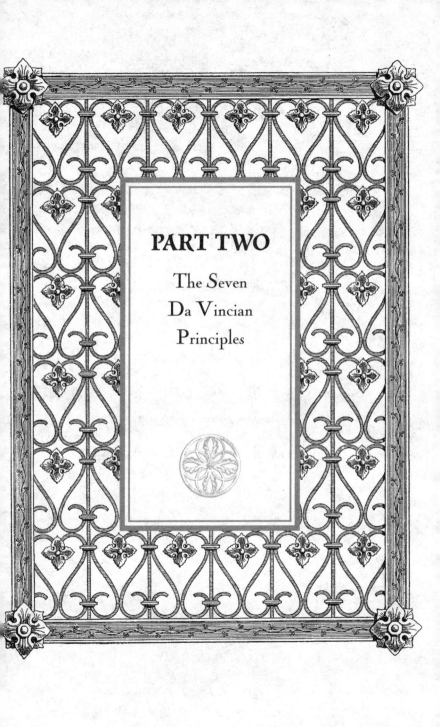

PART TWO

The Seven
Da Vincian
Principles

Curiosità

*An Insatiably Curious
Approach to Life and an
Unrelenting Quest for
Continuous Learning.*

*A*ll of us come into the world curious. Curiosità builds upon that natural impulse, the same impulse that led you to turn the last page – the desire to learn more. We've all got it; the challenge is using and developing it for our own benefit. In the first years of life our minds are engaged in an unquenchable thirst for knowledge. From birth – and some would argue, even before – the baby's every sense is attuned to exploring and learning. Like little scientists, babies experiment with everything in their environment. As soon as they can speak, children start articulating question after question: "Mommy, how does this work?" "Why was I born?" "Daddy, where do babies come from?"

> *"The desire to know is natural to good men."*
> – Leonardo da Vinci

As a child, Leonardo possessed this intense curiosity about the world around him. He was fascinated with nature, showed a remarkable gift for drawing, and loved mathematics. Vasari records that the young Leonardo questioned his mathematics teacher with such originality that "he raised continuous doubts and difficulties for the master who taught him and often confounded him."

Great minds go on asking confounding questions with the same intensity throughout their lives. Leonardo's childlike sense of wonder and insatiable curiosity, his breadth and depth of interest, and his willingness to question accepted knowledge never abated. Curiosità fueled the wellspring of his genius throughout his adult life.

What were Leonardo's motives? In his book *The Creators: A History of Heroes of the Imagination,* Pulitzer prize-winner Daniel Boorstin tells us what they were not. "Unlike Dante, he had no passion for a woman. Unlike Giotto, Dante, or Brunelleschi, he seemed to have had no civic loyalty. Nor devotion to church or Christ. He willingly accepted commissions from the Medici, the Sforzas, the Borgias, or French kings – from the popes or their enemies. He lacked the sensual worldliness of a Boccaccio or a Chaucer, the recklessness of a Rabelais, the piety of a Dante, or the religious passion of a Michelangelo." Leonardo's loyalty, devotion, and passion were directed, instead, to the pure quest for truth and beauty. As Freud suggested: "He transmuted his passion into inquisitiveness."

Leonardo's inquisitiveness was not limited to his formal studies; it informed and enhanced his daily experience of the world around him. In a typical passage from the notebooks Da Vinci asks: "Do you not see how many and how varied are the actions which are performed by men alone? Do you not see how many different kinds of animals there are, and also of trees and plants and flowers? What variety of hilly and level places, of springs, rivers, cities, public and private buildings; of instruments fitted for man's use; of diverse costumes, ornaments and arts?"

Elsewhere he adds, "I roamed the countryside searching for answers to things I did not understand. Why shells existed on the tops of mountains along with the imprints of coral and plants and seaweed usually found in the sea. Why the thunder lasts a longer time than that which causes it, and why immediately on its creation the lightning becomes visible to the eye while thunder requires time to travel. How the various circles of water form around the spot which has been struck by a stone, and why a bird sustains itself in the air. These questions and other strange phenomena engage my thought throughout my life."

Leonardo's intense desire to understand the essence of things led him to develop an investigative style equally noteworthy for its depth of study as for its range of topics. Kenneth Clark, who called him "undoubtedly the most curious man who ever lived," describes Da Vinci's uncompromising quest in accessibly contemporary terms: "He wouldn't take Yes for an answer." In his anatomic investigations, for example, Leonardo dissected each part of the body from at least three different angles. As he wrote:

Three views of a flower by Leonardo da Vinci.

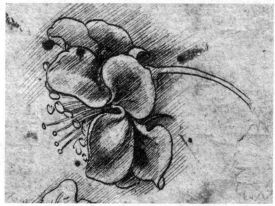

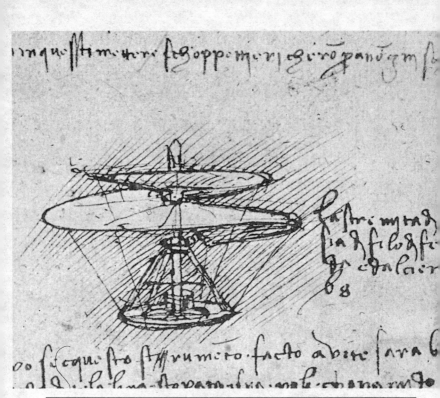

In addition to his helicopter (above) and other flying machines, Leonardo also developed a parachute: "If a man has a tent made of linen, of which the apertures have all been stopped up, and it be twelve cubits across and twelve in depth, he will be able to throw himself down from any great height without sustaining injury." Leonardo's work on the parachute is particularly amazing. No one was yet able to fly, and he designed a means for safely exiting a flying machine. And, incredibly, Leonardo's proportions for a parachute were the only ones that actually work.

This depicting of mine of the human body will be as clear to you as if you had the natural man before you; and the reason is that if you wish thoroughly to know the parts of the man, anatomically, you, or your eye, require to see it from different aspects, considering it from below and from above and from its sides, turning it about and seeking the origin of each member … Therefore by my drawings every part will be known to you, and by all means of demonstrations from three different points of view of each part.

But his curiosity didn't stop there: Da Vinci studied everything with the same rigor. If multiple perspectives yielded a deeper understanding of the body, for example, they would also help him evaluate his attempts to share that understanding. The result: layer upon layer of rigorous examination, all designed to refine not only his understanding but its expression, as he explains in his *Treatise on Painting:*

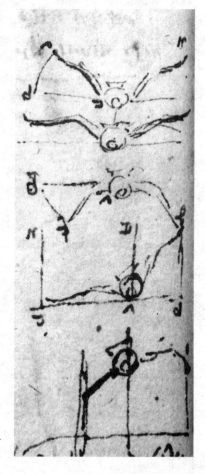

Study of flying birds by Leonardo da Vinci.

We know well that mistakes are more easily detected in the works of others than in one's own … When you are painting you should take a flat mirror and often look at your work within it, and it will then be seen in reverse, and will appear to be by the hand of some other master, and you will be better able to judge of its faults than in any other way.

Not content with just one strategy for assessing his work objectively, he adds: "It is also a very good plan every now and then to go away and have a little relaxation; for when you come back to the work your judgement will be surer, since to remain constantly at work will cause you to lose the power of judgement."

"For in truth great love is born of great knowledge of the thing loved."
– LEONARDO DA VINCI

And finally, he suggests: "It is also advisable to go some distance away, because then the work appears smaller, and more of it is taken in at a glance, and a lack of harmony or proportion in the various parts and the colors of the objects is more readily seen."

His inexhaustible quest for truth also inspired him to look at reality from unusual and extreme perspectives. It took him under the water (he designed a snorkel, diving equipment, and a submarine) and into the sky (he designed a helicopter, a parachute, and his famous flying machine). He plunged into unfathomed depths and sought previously unimaginable heights in his passion to understand.

Leonardo's fascination with flight – his studies of the atmosphere, wind, and especially the movements of birds – offers a compelling metaphor for his life and work. A page of his notebooks depicts a bird in a cage with the caption "The thoughts turn towards hope." He observes poetically that a mother goldfinch, seeing her children caged, feeds them a bit of a poisonous plant, noting, "Better death than to be without freedom."

Giorgio Vasari informs us that in the course of his frequent strolls through the streets of Florence, Leonardo often encountered merchants selling caged birds. It was Da Vinci's custom to stop, pay the requisite price, and then open the door of the cage, releasing the prisoners to the endless blue sky. For Leonardo, the quest for knowledge opened the door to freedom.

CURIOSITÀ AND YOU

Great minds ask great questions. The questions that "engage our thought" on a daily basis reflect our life purpose and influence the quality of our lives. By cultivating a Da Vinci-like open, questing frame of mind, we broaden our universe and improve our ability to travel through it.

Have you opened your door to freedom? The exercises that follow are designed to help you do so. But first take a moment to reflect on how frequently and effectively you are already putting your Curiosità to work – and how you might benefit from doing so more often.

Consider the role of Curiosità in your life today. Ask yourself how curious you are. When was the last time you sought knowledge simply for the pursuit of truth?

Written backward, Leonardo's notes are designed to be read in a mirror. Scholars debate the purpose of this "mirror writing." Some suggest it was to protect the privacy of his thoughts, while others argue that it was simply a matter of convenience for a left-hander.

What did you gain from this effort? Think of the people you know. Do any of them strike you as embodying the ideals of Curiosità? How are their lives enriched by this?

Your Curiosità can be developed and put to use more easily than you may have thought. First complete the self-assessment checklist on the next page; your answers will tell you how you are already using it – and where there is room for improvement. Then try your hand at cultivating your own Curiosità through the simple exercises that follow.

Curiosità:
Self-Assessment

- ❑ I keep a journal or notebook to record my insights and questions.
- ❑ I take adequate time for contemplation and reflection.
- ❑ I am always learning something new.
- ❑ When I am faced with an important decision, I actively seek out different perspectives.
- ❑ I am a voracious reader.
- ❑ I learn from little children.
- ❑ I am skilled at identifying and solving problems.
- ❑ My friends would describe me as open-minded and curious.
- ❑ When I hear or read a new word or phrase, I look it up and make a note of it.
- ❑ I know a lot about other cultures and am always learning more.
- ❑ I know or am involved in learning a language other than my native one.
- ❑ I solicit feedback from my friends, relations, and colleagues.
- ❑ I love learning.

CURIOSITÀ: APPLICATION AND EXERCISES

KEEP A JOURNAL OR "NOTEBOOK"

Leonardo da Vinci carried a notebook with him at all times so that he could jot down ideas, impressions, and observations as they occurred. His notebooks (seven thousand pages exist; most scholars estimate that this is about one half of the amount he left to Francesco Melzi in his will) contained jokes and fables, the observations and thoughts of scholars he admired, personal financial records, letters, reflections on domestic problems, philosophical musings and prophecies, plans for inventions, and treatises on anatomy, botany, geology, flight, water, and painting.

Notes on different subjects are frequently scribbled on the same page, and many observations appear more

"This is to be a collection without order, taken from many papers, which I have copied here, hoping afterwards to arrange them according to the subjects of which they treat; and I believe that I shall have to repeat the same thing several times; for which, O reader, blame me not ..."
– FROM THE FRONT PAGE OF ONE OF LEONARDO'S MANUSCRIPTS ON PHYSICS

than once, in different sections. And, of course, the pages are filled with glorious sketches, doodles, and illustrations. Although he expressed an intention to organize and publish them someday, he never got around to it. He was too busy searching for truth and beauty. For Da Vinci, the process of recording questions, observations, and ideas was of great importance.

You can, like Leonardo, facilitate Curiosità by keeping a notebook or journal. Get a bound notebook or journal filled with blank pages. You can use anything from the eighty-nine-cent K mart version to a fancy one with an inspiring image on the front cover. The important thing is to carry it with you everywhere and write in it regularly. Supplement your notebook with scrapbooks or files on diverse areas of interest. Cut out and collect newspaper and magazine articles, or download information from the Internet, on any subject you fancy – science, art, music, food, health …

As Leonardo did, use your notebook to record your questions, observations, insights, jokes, dreams, and musings (mirror writing is optional).

Busy lives and job responsibilities tend to drive us toward hard conclusions and measurable results, but the exploratory, free-flowing, unfinished, nonjudgmental practice of keeping a Da Vincian notebook encourages freedom of thought and expansion of perspective. In the manner of the maestro, don't worry about order and logical flow, just record.

Try the following Curiosità exercises in your notebook:

A Hundred Questions

In your notebook, make a list of a hundred questions that are important to you. Your list can include *any kind of question* as long as it's something you deem significant: anything from "How can I save more money?" or "How can I have more fun?" to "What is the meaning and purpose of my existence?" and "How can I best serve the Creator?"

Do the entire list in one sitting. Write quickly; don't worry about spelling, grammar, or repeating the same question in different words (recurring questions will alert you to emerging themes). Why a hundred questions? The first twenty or so will be "off the top of your head." In the next thirty or forty themes often begin to emerge. And, in the latter part of the second half of the list you are likely to discover unexpected but profound material.

When you have finished, read through your list and highlight the themes that emerge. Consider the emerging themes without judging them. Are most of your questions about relationships? Business? Fun? Money? The meaning of life?

Top Ten Questions

Review your list of a hundred questions. Choose the ten that seem most significant. Then rank them in importance from one to ten. (Of course, you can add new questions or change the order at any time.) Do not attempt to answer them right now; you've done enough just putting them in writing in a place where you can easily find them.

Ten Power Questions

The following questions are drawn from different people's "top ten." These questions are powerful catalysts to personal growth and fulfillment. Copy them in your notebook for contemplation:

"Feathers shall raise men even as they do birds, toward heaven; that is by letters written with their quills."

– LEONARDO DA VINCI

- When am I most naturally myself? What people, places, and activities allow me to feel most fully myself?
- What is one thing I could stop doing, or start doing, or do differently, *starting today* that would most improve the quality of my life?
- What is my greatest talent?
- How can I get paid for doing what I love?
- Who are my most inspiring role models?
- How can I best be of service to others?
- What is my heart's deepest desire?
- How am I perceived by: my closest friend, my worst enemy, my boss, my children, my co-workers, etc.?
- What are the blessings of my life?
- What legacy would I like to leave?

How Does a Bird Fly?

Choose one of the following topics inspired by Da Vinci's passionate questioning: a bird in flight, flowing water, the human body, a landscape, reflected light, a knot or braid. And in your journal, ask at least ten questions about it. Again, there's no need to write answers; in Curiosità, we focus on the questions. For example: How does a bird fly?

- Why does it have two wings?
- Why does it have feathers?
- How does it "take off"?
- How does it slow down?
- How does it accelerate?
- How high can it fly?
- When does it sleep?
- How good is its eyesight?
- What does it eat?

Then *choose a topic from your personal or professional life and do the same exercise* – ask ten questions about your career, your relationship, your health. Record the questions in your journal – no answers yet, just questions.

THEME OBSERVATION

Working with a theme is a powerful tool for focusing your Curiosità. Choose a theme for the day and record observations in your notebook. You can jot down your thoughts throughout the day, or just make mental notes to be recorded in your notebook at a quiet time before sleep. Aim to make accurate, simple observations. Speculation, opinion, and theory are fine, but actual observation offers the richest resource.

Your list of a hundred questions, or the power questions, will provide plenty of themes for this exercise. Additionally, you can choose any of the following or make up your own. Some favorite themes include: Emotions, Seeing, Listening, Touch, Aesthetics, and Animals. Do this exercise on your own or choose a theme with a friend and compare notes at the end of the day.

CONTEMPLATION EXERCISE

In an age of sound bites, contemplation is becoming a lost art. Attention spans grow shorter and the soul suffers. To *contemplate*, as defined by Webster, is "to look at with continued attention, to meditate on." It comes from the root *contemplari*, which means "to mark out a temple" (con, "with"; *templum*, "temple") or "to gaze attentively."

A Sample Theme Exercise

My friend Michael Frederick is a theater director, acting coach, and teacher of the Feldenkrais Method, the Alexander technique, and yoga. He has been doing theme work for more than twenty-five years. He graciously agreed to share the following unedited sample from his notebook:

January 10, 1998. Theme: Contact with Material Objects

1) 7:40 a.m. Noticed the quality and sense of my feet first touching the floor. That the contact with the floor was supporting me and allowing me to continue lengthening through my body as I stood up for the first time today.

2) 8:20 a.m. As I brushed my teeth, I saw how I was holding my toothbrush too tight in my right hand and this tension spread up through my arm and shoulder causing neck tension. Then I looked in the mirror and noticed I was slumping.

3) 11:30 a.m. Holding the telephone with a vise grip and with my head cocked to the right side causing a pain in my arm and shoulder. Similar to my toothbrush observation. Holding on to objects with an over-effort … "for dear life."

4) 4:30 p.m. While eating a sandwich in a hurry, I saw how I would gobble the food down without paying attention to what I was eating. Speed was important and this made me lose contact with the taste and even knowing exactly what the sandwich consisted of.

5) 5:30 p.m. I also noticed the sunset today and the warmth of the sun contacting my face allowed me to slow down and see what was in front of me (i.e., bringing me more into the present moment).

6) 9:30 p.m. Sorting through today's mail. Having to take time with the junk mail (i.e., junk material objects). Felt like my life was/is taken up with sorting & filing & fixing & handling material objects. I become a "caretaker" of these objects!

7) 10:30 p.m. As I hold this pen in my hand, I'm noticing how little effort is required to actually write. The pen works very well without the extra effort of pushing.

Choose any question from the previous exercises – for example: What people, places, and activities allow me to feel most fully myself? – and hold it in your mind for a sustained period, at least ten minutes at a time. A good way to do this is to take a large sheet of paper and write the question out in big, bold letters. Then:

+ Find a quiet, private place and hang it on the wall in front of you.
+ Relax, breathe deeply, allowing extended exhalations.
+ Just sit with your question.
+ When your mind starts to wander, bring it back by reading the question again, out loud. It is particularly valuable to do this contemplation exercise before going to sleep, and again upon waking. You will find that if you practice it sincerely, your mind will "incubate" insights overnight.

STREAM OF CONSCIOUSNESS EXERCISE

A powerful complement to contemplation, stream of consciousness writing is a marvelous tool for plumbing the depths of your questions. Choose any question, and working in your notebook, write your thoughts and associations as they occur, without editing.

Devote at least ten minutes to writing your responses. The secret of effective stream of consciousness writing is to *keep your pen moving;* don't lift it away from the paper or stop to correct your spelling and grammar – just write continuously.

Stream of consciousness writing yields lots of nonsense and redundancy but can lead to profound insight and understanding. Don't worry if you seem to be writing pure gibberish; this is actually a sign that you are overriding the habitual, superficial aspects of your thought process. As you persevere, keeping your pen on the paper and moving it continuously, you'll eventually open a window through which your intuitive intelligence will shine.

+ Take a break after each stream of consciousness session.
+ Go back to your notebook and read aloud what you have written.
+ Highlight the words or phrases that speak to you most strongly.
+ Again, look for themes, the beginnings of poems, and more questions.
+ Contemplate the metaphor of the poet's motto: "Write drunk, revise sober."

The contemplation and stream of consciousness exercises are excellent tools for personal and professional problem solving. Let's consider the role of Curiosità in problem solving a bit further.

CURIOSITÀ AND CREATIVE
PROBLEM SOLVING

Think back to your school days. We all remember what curiosity did to the cat. But what happened to the kids who asked too many questions? A common refrain from overworked, beleaguered teachers was "We don't have time for all these questions; we've got to get through the curriculum." Now persistent question askers are diagnosed with Attention Deficit Disorder or "hyperactivity" and treated with Ritalin and other drugs. If the young Leonardo were alive today and attending grade school, he would probably be on medication.

Although we all started life with a Da Vinci-like insatiable curiosity, most of us learned, once we got to school, that answers were more important than questions. In most cases, schooling does not develop curiosity, delight in ambiguity, and question-asking skill. Rather, the thinking skill that's rewarded is figuring out the "right answer" – that is, the answer held by the person in authority, the teacher. This pattern holds throughout university and postgraduate education, especially in a class where the professor wrote the text. (In a classic study at a top university, summa cum laude graduates were given their same final exams one month after graduation, and they all failed. Researcher Leslie Hart summarized the results: "Final exams are final indeed!") The authority-pleasing, question-suppressing, rule-following approach to education may have served to provide society with assembly-line workers and bureaucrats, but it does not do much to prepare us for a new Renaissance.

Why is the sky blue? Leonardo's answer: "I say that the azure that the air makes us see is not its proper color, but this color comes from warm, damp air, evaporated into minuscule and imperceptible particles, which, being struck by the light of the sun, become luminous below the obscurity of the mighty darkness which covers them like a lid."

Leonardo da Vinci's life was an exercise in creative problem solving of the very highest order. The principle of Curiosità provides the primary key to his method. It begins with intense curiosity and an open mind, and proceeds with a stream of questions asked from different perspectives.

You can increase your problem-solving skills, at work and at home, by honing your question-asking ability. For most people this requires shifting the initial emphasis away from focusing on "the right answer" and toward asking "Is this the right question?" and "What are some different ways of looking at this problem?"

> "First, there are questions about the construction of certain machines, then, under the influence of Archimedes, questions about the first principles of dynamics; finally, questions which had never been asked before about winds, clouds, the age of the earth, generation, the human heart."
>
> – KENNETH CLARK ON LEONARDO'S NOTEBOOKS

Successful problem solving often requires replacing or reframing the initial question. Questions can be framed in a wide variety of ways, and the "framing" will dramatically influence your ability to find solutions. Psychologist Mark Brown offers the example of an evolution in questioning that resulted in a major transformation of human societies. Nomadic societies were based on the question "How do we get to water?" They became agrarian and stable cultures, Brown says, when they began asking "How do we get the water to come to us?"

Some people like to muse on the philosophical conundrum "What is the meaning of life?" But more practical philosophers ask, "How can I make my life meaningful?"

FINDING THE QUESTION

How can you sharpen your question-asking skills so that solutions will start to come to you? Begin by asking the simple, "naive" questions that sophisticated people are prone to overlook. Da Vinci's questioning was often striking in its simplicity, as when he wrote: "I ask why the hammer blow causes the nail to jump out" or "Why is the sky blue?"

Ask awkward questions like: Why is the emperor naked? Why is this a problem? Is this the real issue? Why have we always done it this way? Aim to raise questions that have not been asked before.

In your notebook, write out a problem or question that you are concerned with in your personal or professional life, and ask: What? When? Who? How? Where? and Why?

What is the problem? are the underlying issues? preconceptions, prejudices, or paradigms may be influencing my perception? will happen if I ignore it? possibilities may exist that I haven't yet considered? problems may be caused by solving this problem? metaphors from nature can I use to illuminate it?

When did it start? does it happen? doesn't it happen? will the consequences of it be felt? must it be resolved?

Finding illustrative metaphors in nature was one of Leonardo's favorite techniques. When he designed the magnificent spiral staircase for the French king's château at Blois, for example, he was inspired by the twisting shells of the conchs that he had collected along Italy's northwestern shore many years before. His design for musical pipes, similar to the recorder, was drawn from his study of the human larynx. More recently, Alexander Graham Bell was inspired to invent the telephone by modeling the ear; the little burrs that stick to your trousers when you walk through the woods inspired the inventor of the Velcro fastener; and the inventor of the pull-tab top for aluminum cans was inspired by asking himself the question "What, in nature, opens easily?" A picture of a banana popped into his mind, leading him to ask, "How can the design of the banana serve as a model for the task at hand?"

Who cares about it? is affected by it? created it? perpetuates it? can help solve it?

How does it happen? can I get more objective information? can I look at it from unfamiliar perspectives? can it be changed? will I know that it has been solved?

Where does it happen? did it begin? haven't I looked? else has this happened?

Why is it important? did it start? does it continue? Ask why, why, why, why, why … to get to the bottom of an issue.

CURIOSITÀ AND CONTINUOUS LEARNING

Leonardo knew the importance of continuous learning: "Just as iron rusts from disuse, and stagnant water putrefies, or when cold turns to ice, so our intellect wastes unless it is kept in use." The continuous quest for learning is the powerhouse of the Da Vincian spirit. It is, of course, that spirit that inspires you to read this book. And although it may be impractical for most of us to attempt to master all knowledge, we can further embrace the Da Vincian spirit by learning a new discipline.

Over the last twenty years, I've asked thousands of people what they would learn if they could learn anything at all. The most common answers: to play a musical instrument; a new language (Leonardo taught himself Latin when he was forty-two); scuba diving, sailing, or skydiving; to play tennis or golf; to draw, paint, or sculpt; to act in a play; to sing in a choir; to write poetry or novels; to study dancing, yoga, or martial arts. I call these "ideal" or "dream" hobbies and find that the people who pursue them passionately live richer, more fulfilling lives.

Over the years I've encouraged thousands of people to begin their ideal hobby. During that time I've encountered all sorts of excuses for not doing it – and have developed responses for each. When they say "I'll never be good enough," I tell them to get over it – that Da Vinci wasn't satisfied with his work either. When they say "I'm too busy with my spouse and kids," I suggest that they try getting them involved. When they say "The lessons and equipment are too expensive," I tell them to start saving for it today, creating a special account for their hobby, or to volunteer to assist a master teacher of the discipline they would like to learn. When they claim "I'm much too busy at work. I'll start when things settle down," I point out that things are not going to settle down – and on their death bed, they will be glad that they spent more time following their dreams. And when they say "I'm too old; I should have started when I was young," I remind them that it's never too late. Our learning power can improve with age if we awaken the power of Curiosità.

REALIZE YOUR IDEAL HOBBY

Working in your notebook, map out a strategy for realizing your ideal hobby, now. Make a list of your ideal hobbies (if you are not sure what they are, make some up). Choose one and ask:

+ How, specifically, will I benefit from this pursuit?
+ What are my goals?
+ What resources will I need?
+ Where can I find a good teacher?
+ How much time will I devote to it?
+ What obstacles must I overcome?
+ The most creative and fulfilled people I know also find answers to the following question: How can I get paid for pursuing my ideal hobby?

Making the "ideal hobby" an integral part of your life is a simple but profound way to contribute to your own personal Renaissance. Find a great teacher or coach; schedule ten lessons and pay for them in advance. This tends to prevent last-minute excuses and the inertia of habit from interfering with your intention. By pursuing passionately an area of interest, besides work and family, you broaden your perspective in a way that enriches all aspects of your life. You are, in Joseph Campbell's words, "following your bliss."

LEARN A NEW LANGUAGE

Learning a new language is a popular ideal hobby and a wonderful way to cultivate Curiosità. Like Leonardo, you can learn a new language at any age. We all know that babies are the best learners. Their openness, energy, and playfulness allow them to learn languages with ease. A baby raised in a home where three languages are spoken will learn all three without difficulty. The good news is that if you are willing to adopt key aspects of the baby's learning strategy, you can progress with similar ease and delight. And as an adult, you can take advantage of resources that can help *you learn even faster than a baby*.

Let's say, for example, that you wanted to learn *la bella lingua* (the beautiful language): Italian. Here are a few tips for accelerating your language learning:

+ Be willing to make lots of mistakes. Bambinos do not worry about looking cool or instantly achieving perfect pronunciation and grammar; they just dive in and speak. Your progress in learning will correlate directly with your willingness to play and to embrace feelings of unfamiliarity and foolishness.
+ Have you ever noticed how babies will find a word or phrase and repeat it over and over? Do the same: repetition is the simplest secret of recall.

+ If possible, start your learning process with an "immersion course." Just as a rocket needs most of its energy to launch and fly out of our atmosphere, you will get the most from your learning if you launch your efforts with a concentrated program. Your "intensive" will "jump-start" your brain circuitry to start rewiring for your new language.
+ If you can't find a formal immersion course, then create your own by listening to audiocassettes, watching Italian-language movies with subtitles, learning the lyrics of great Italian songs like "Rondini al Nido" and "Santa Lucia," singing along to Pavarotti recordings, sitting in Italian espresso bars and just listening to people talking, and going to real Italian restaurants and ordering in the native tongue. If you tell the waiter that you are trying to learn the language and ask for help, you will usually get a free Italian lesson, even better service, and sometimes extra antipasto!

- Learn words and phrases related to areas of passionate interest. Many language programs are a bit boring because they focus on necessary but mundane matters such as "Where is the station?" and "Here is my passport." In addition to these everyday matters, aim to learn the language of romance, sex, poetry, art, fine food, and wine.
- Put Italian translation Post-it notes on everything in your house.
- Most important, open yourself to the feeling of the language and culture. When you speak, pretend you are an Italian (I recommend Marcello Mastroianni or Sophia Loren, for starters). Adopt the expressive gestures and facial expressions that go with the language; you will have more fun and learn much faster.

Try this little experiment: Say the phrase "the beautiful language" out loud. Now say it again and notice where the sound resonates in your body. Okay, this time say it in Italian, as if you were an Italian: *"la bella lingua."* Does it resonate differently? Most people find that English resonates a bit higher, in the throat and the front of the palate, and that Italian resonates farther back in the palate, lower in the throat, and most strongly, in the heart.

BUILD YOUR OWN LEXICON

Another marvelous way to practice continuous learning is to build your own lexicon. In the Codex Trivulzianus and elsewhere, Leonardo noted and defined words that were of particular interest to him. Arranged in columns, the lists include new vocabulary, foreign terms, and neologisms.

One list included words such as:

arduous – difficult, painful
Alpine – of the region of the Alps
archimandrite – a leader of a group

After defining over nine thousand words, he commented, with a delightful blend of pride and humility, "I possess so many words in my native language that I ought rather to complain of not understanding things than of lacking for words to express my thoughts properly."

> "His interest in everything was equaled by his spontaneous originality in response to everything that interested him."
>
> – PROFESSOR MORRIS PHILIPSON

This practice is a simple, powerful way to model the maestro and nurture Curiosità. A powerful vocabulary correlates significantly with academic and professional success and offers a delightful expansion of your options for self-expression. Every time you discover an unfamiliar word or phrase, look it up and note it in your journal. Then take every opportunity to use it in your writing and everyday conversation.

NURTURE YOUR "EMOTIONAL INTELLIGENCE"

In addition to strengthening his verbal/linguistic intelligence by teaching himself Latin and creating his own lexicon, the maestro also cultivated his emotional intelligence. His Curiosità was as acute in observing his fellow humans as it was in his study of horses, birds, water, and light. As he wrote, "Oh, that it may please God to let me also expound the psychology of the habits of man in such fashion as I am describing his body!" Leonardo's deep interest in people from all walks of life is the source of the profound depth of character he illuminated in the subjects of his drawings and paintings. He counseled: "When you are out for a walk, see to it that you watch and consider other men's postures and actions as they talk, argue, laugh or scuffle; their own actions, and those of their supporters and onlookers: and make a note of these with a few strokes in your little notebook which you must always carry with you."

Leonardo's acute observations led him to practical understanding of the art of getting along with others, and he complemented his interpersonal intelligence with a lifelong commitment to developing his intrapersonal intelligence (self-knowledge). In addition to profound contemplation and reflection, Leonardo cultivated self-knowledge by seeking feedback, advising his readers to "be desirous of hearing patiently the opinion of others, and consider and reflect carefully whether he who censures you has reason for his censure."

You can strengthen Curiosità and deepen self-knowledge by asking your spouse, children, friends, clients, co-workers, boss, and employees for regular feedback. In words that are natural to you, ask questions such as:

+ What are my weaknesses, blind spots, and areas for improvement?
+ What are my strengths, my best qualities?
+ What can I do to be more effective, helpful, or sensitive?

When you ask for feedback, be sure to listen carefully to the responses you receive, especially if they are not what you wanted or expected to hear; don't explain, justify, or argue. It's best not to comment at all; just listen. Record the feedback in your notebook for contemplation.

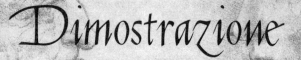

Dimostrazione

*A Commitment to Test
Knowledge through
Experience, Persistence,
and a Willingness to Learn
from Mistakes.*

T hink of the best teachers you have ever had. What makes a teacher great? More than anything else, it is the ability to help the student learn for himself. The finest teachers know that experience is the source of wisdom. And the principle of Dimostrazione is the key to making the most of your experience. Leonardo made the most of his experiences in the studio of the master painter and sculptor Andrea del Verrocchio, whom Da Vinci biographer Serge Bramly refers to as "a one-man university of the arts." The training the young Leonardo received as an apprentice in Verrocchio's studio emphasized experience more than theory. He learned to prepare canvases and paints and was introduced to the optics of perspective. The technical secrets of sculpture, bronze casting, and goldsmithing were part of the curriculum, and he was encouraged to study, through direct observation, the structure of plants and the anatomy of animals and humans. Thus he grew up with a profoundly practical orientation.

Leonardo's practical orientation, penetrating intelligence, curiosity, and independent spirit led him to question much of the accepted theory and dogma of his time. In the course of his geologic investigations, for example, he discovered fossils and seashells on mountain peaks in Lombardy. In the Codex Leicester he advances decisive arguments against the prevailing view that these were deposits of the biblical flood, based not on theology but on his logical thinking and real-world experience. Disputing each assumption on which conventional wisdom was based, he finally concludes that "such an opinion can not exist in brains of any extensive powers of reasoning …"

In his studies of geology, Leonardo walked the hills of Lombardy and held fossils in his hands. When he wanted to learn anatomy, he dissected more than thirty human bodies and countless animal corpses. Like his research on fossilization, his anatomic work was a direct challenge to the accepted authorities of the time. As he wrote: "Many will think that they can with reason blame me, alleging that my proofs are contrary to the authority of certain men held in great reverence by their inexperienced judgements, not considering that my works are the issue of simple and plain experience which is the true mistress."

Throughout his life he proudly referred to himself as *uomo senza lettere* ("man without letters") and *discepolo della esperienza* ("disciple of experience"). He wrote, "To me it seems that those sciences are vain and full of error which are not born of experience, mother of all certainty, first hand experience which in its origins, or means, or end has passed through one of the five senses."

Leonardo championed originality and independence of thought. He urged, "No one should imitate the manner of another, for he would then deserve to be called a grandson of nature, not her son. Given the abundance of natural forms, *it is important to go straight to nature* …" His willingness to reject imitation, question authority, and think for himself would be remarkable in any age; but it becomes truly amazing when one considers that he was heir to an era that assumed, as William Manchester emphasizes, that "all knowledge was already known."

In addition to being one of the least pious thinkers of his time, Leonardo was also one of the least superstitious. He saw the popular attention to alchemy and astrology as the enemy of experience and independent thought and desired the day "when all astrologers will be castrated."

Although critical of the scholastic and academic traditions, Leonardo did not throw out the baby with the bathwater. For example, he taught himself Latin in 1494 at the age of forty-two to gain a deeper knowledge of the classics. And Leonardo maintained his own library. His collection included the Bible, Aesop, Diogenes, Ovid, Pliny the Elder, Dante, Petrarch, Ficino, and texts on agriculture, anatomy, mathematics, medicine, and warfare. Da Vinci scholar Professor Edward MacCurdy emphasizes that "he was in the habit of studying all classical and medieval authorities obtainable on the subjects in which he was interested."

Leonardo consorted with other great minds including Bramante, Machiavelli, Luca Pacioli, and Marcantonio della Torre. He viewed the work of others as "experience by proxy" to be studied carefully and critically and ultimately to be tested through his own experience.

Leonardo saw how preconceptions and "bookish prejudices" limited scientific inquiry. He knew that learning from experience also meant learning from mistakes. He wrote, "Experience never errs; it is only your judgement that errs in promising itself results as are not caused by your experiments."

Although generally recognized as the greatest genius of all time, Leonardo made many colossal mistakes and staggering blunders. Among his most notable faux pas were tragically unsuccessful experiments in fixing paint for *The Battle of Anghiari* and *The Last Supper;* disastrous and hugely wasteful attempts, sponsored by the Signoria of Florence, to divert the Arno River; and a flying machine that never got off the ground. There was also a particularly hilarious failed scheme to automate Ludovico Sforza's kitchen. Asked to preside as head chef for a major banquet, Leonardo created a grand plan for sculpting each course to be served to the more than two hundred guests. The dishes were designed as miniature works of art. Leonardo built a new, more powerful stove and a complex system of mechanical conveyor belts to move plates around the kitchen. He also designed and installed a massive sprinkler system in case of fire. On the day of the banquet everything that could go wrong did. Ludovico's regular kitchen staff weren't capable of the fine carving that Leonardo required, so the maestro invited more than a hundred of his artist friends to help out. In the vastly overcrowded kitchen, the conveyor system failed, and then fire broke out. The sprinkler system worked all too well, causing a flood that washed away all the food and a good part of the kitchen!

Despite mistakes, disasters, failures, and disappointments, Leonardo never stopped learning, exploring, and experimenting. He demonstrated Herculean persistence in his quest for knowledge. Next to a drawing of a plow in his notebook Leonardo proclaimed, "I do not depart from my furrow." Elsewhere he noted, "Obstacles do not bend me" and "Every obstacle is destroyed through rigor."

Martin Kemp, author of *Leonardo da Vinci: The Marvellous Works of Nature and Man,* comments: "There is no doubt which principle Leonardo considered as defining the true direction for the furrow he wished to plow. That principle was what he termed 'experience.'"

DIMOSTRAZIONE AND YOU

The real significance of the Renaissance was the transformation of fundamental assumptions, preconceptions, and beliefs. Leonardo's willingness to challenge the dominant world view, through application of the principle of Dimostrazione, placed him in the vanguard of this revolution. He realized that one challenges the world view by first challenging one's own view, cautioning that "the greatest deception men suffer is from their own opinions." Learning to think like Leonardo requires the eye-opening work of questioning our own opinions, assumptions, and beliefs.

Are you ever deceived by your own opinions? Are your opinions and beliefs truly your own? The exercises that follow are designed to help you think with more freedom and originality. But first take some time to consider the role that Dimostrazione plays in your life today and how you might strengthen it further. Evaluate your own independence: Are you an independent thinker? When was the last time you changed a deeply held belief? What did it feel like?

Think of your friends and colleagues. What sources do they rely on to determine their beliefs and opinions? Who is the most independent, original thinker you know? What makes that person an original?

Think for a moment of the way you have learned what you know. Do you learn more from your successes or failures, from good times or bad? We all know that good judgment comes from experience. But we also know that we often gain experience through bad judgment. Do you make the most of your mistakes?

Contemplate the self-assessment checklist on the next page. These are challenging questions, but your honest reflection will help you focus on getting the most from the exercises that follow.

Dimostrazione:
Self-Assessment

- ❏ I am willing to acknowledge my mistakes.
- ❏ My closest friends would agree that I am willing to acknowledge my mistakes.
- ❏ I learn from my mistakes and rarely make the same one twice.
- ❏ I question "conventional wisdom" and authority.
- ❏ When a celebrity I admire endorses a product, I am more likely to buy it.

- ❏ I can articulate my most fundamental beliefs and the reasons I hold them.
- ❏ I have changed a deeply held belief because of practical experience.
- ❏ I persevere in the face of obstacles.
- ❏ I view adversity as an opportunity for growth.
- ❏ I am sometimes susceptible to superstition.
- ❏ In considering new ideas my friends and associates would say that I am
    a) gullible and "New Agey,"
    b) a closed-minded cynic, or
    c) an open-minded skeptic.

DIMOSTRAZIONE:
APPLICATION
AND EXERCISES

EXAMINE EXPERIENCE

An hour spent with these questions can yield a lifetime's reflection on how experience has determined your attitudes and behaviors. Working with your notebook, explore the following questions:

What are the most influential experiences of your life? Take about twenty to thirty minutes and list at least seven, along with a one-sentence summary of what you learned from each experience.

Now spend a few minutes reflecting on how you *apply* what you have learned from these most influential experiences on an *everyday* basis.

Next look at your list of significant experiences and ask, What is the single most influential experience of my life? (For some people this is an easy question to answer; for others, there isn't one experience that jumps out. If nothing jumps out for you, choose any experience from your list.)

Then spend a few minutes asking yourself, How has this experience colored my attitudes and perceptions? Aim to note down, in a sentence or two, the effects of the experience on your view of the world.

Finally ask yourself, Can I rethink some of the conclusions drawn at the time? Avoid answering this last question too quickly; just hold it in your mind and heart for a while and let it "marinate."

CHECK YOUR BELIEFS AND SOURCES

Many of us are unaware of the sources we use to obtain and verify information. We know that we have opinions, assumptions, and beliefs about a wide variety of topics: human nature, ethics, politics, ethnic groups, scientific truth, sexuality, religion, medicine, the meaning of life, art, marriage, parenting, history, other cultures, etc. But do you know how you found those beliefs? Or where you got the information on which they're based?

Start by choosing any three of the above areas; for example, you might choose human nature, politics, and art. Then, in your notebook, write down at least three ideas, opinions, assumptions, or beliefs that you hold in the areas you have chosen to consider. For example:

Human Nature
+ "I believe that people are basically good."
+ "I believe that behavior is predominantly determined by genetics."
+ "It's human nature to resist change."

After you have listed at least three beliefs about each of your chosen areas, ask yourself:

+ How did I form this idea?
+ How firmly do I believe it?
+ Why do I maintain it?
+ What would make me change my belief?
+ Which of my beliefs inspire the strongest emotions?

Then look at each of your beliefs in the three areas you have chosen to examine and consider the role of the following sources in its formation:

✦ **Media:** books, the Internet, television, radio, newspapers, and magazines.
✦ **People:** family, teachers, physicians, religious leaders, bosses, friends, and associates.
✦ Your own experience.

What criteria do you use for assessing the validity of information you receive? Do most of your ideas come from books? Or are you primarily influenced by family? How much of what you read in the newspaper or see on television do you believe? Aim to determine, through reflection and contemplation, the dominant source of your information and the underpinnings of your beliefs and opinions. See if you hold any beliefs for which you have no experiential verification. Is there a way you could test your convictions in experience?

THREE POINTS OF VIEW

In your notebook write out a statement of the belief that, in the previous exercise, generated the strongest emotion.

In the Curiosità chapter we learned that when Leonardo was questing for objective knowledge – dissecting a corpse or assessing one of his paintings – he viewed his subject from at least three different perspectives. Do the same with your beliefs and opinions. Just as the maestro used a mirror to see his paintings in reverse, try making the strongest possible argument *against* your belief.

Leonardo also sought perspective by reviewing his paintings from a distance. Try reviewing your belief "from a distance" by asking yourself, Would my views on this change if I: lived in a different country; came from another religious, racial, economic, or class background; was twenty years older/younger or was a member of the opposite gender?

Finally, seek out friends or acquaintances who you suspect might offer perspectives different from your own. Interview your friends, aiming to see the issue from another point of view.

PRACTICE INTERNAL ANTICOMMERCIAL MARTIAL ARTS

As you read this book, thousands of exceptionally creative, highly focused advertising executives are marshaling budgets in the billions to influence your values, self-image, and buying habits. Preying on sexual insecurities or Walter Mitty fantasies or just bludgeoning with pure repetition, advertisers are very good at reaching their demographic targets. Maintaining independence of thought in the face of this onslaught requires a discipline similar to that developed through martial arts training. Try the following "self-defense" exercises:

◆ Go through your favorite magazine and analyze the strategy and tactics of each advertisement.
◆ Do the same analysis with the commercials from your favorite television and radio programs.

- Note which advertisements affect you most strongly and why.
- How did advertising affect you when you were a child?
- Make a list of the three best advertisements you have ever seen. What made them so good?
- Identify ten purchases you have made over the last few months, and ask yourself if you were influenced, in any way, by advertising.
- Try a stream of consciousness writing session on the topic "The role of advertising in the formation of my values and self-image."

One of the most clever and cynical tactics of advertisers is expressed in the attempt to co-opt the image of independent thinking and individualism. Witness attempts to identify with "the Rebel" and "the Individualist" through such revolutionary gestures as driving an off-road vehicle, smoking a fifteen-dollar cigar, or wearing a particular brand of jeans or sneakers or a baseball cap turned backward. Record examples of this phenomenon in your notebook. Some that you may have noticed include:

- The Marlboro Man and the Virginia Slims Lady.
- The chain of steak houses whose motto is "No rules, just right" or the hamburger franchise that reminds us, "Sometimes you gotta break the rules." (Try testing these by violating the implicit rule "Pay for your steak or burger.")
- Even the beloved Dilbert, symbol of rebellion to inane bureaucracy, has become co-opted. He is now a mass-market phenomenon, used to sell more advertising and generate more cubicles.

LEARN FROM MISTAKES AND ADVERSITY

Explore your attitude toward mistakes by contemplating the following questions and recording your reflections in your notebook:

✦ What did you learn at school about making mistakes?
✦ What did your parents teach you about making mistakes?
✦ What is the biggest mistake you ever made?
✦ What did you learn from it?
✦ What mistakes do you repeat?
✦ What role does the fear of making mistakes play in your daily life, at work and at home?
✦ Are you more likely to make mistakes of commission or omission?

Try a stream of consciousness writing session on the topic "What I would do differently if I had no fear of making mistakes."

Leonardo made many mistakes and experienced tremendous adversity in his quest for truth and beauty. In addition to false accusations, invasions, exile, and the wanton destruction of one of his greatest works, the maestro's most significant adversity was probably the sheer loneliness of being so far ahead of his time.

Although he experienced self-doubt and questioned the value of his efforts, he never gave up. Leonardo's courage and persistence in the face of adversity are tremendously inspiring. He strengthened his will to continue his work through affirmations that he wrote in his notebook, such as:

"I do not depart from my furrow."
"Obstacles do not bend me."
"Every obstacle is destroyed through rigor."
"I shall continue."
"I never tire of being useful."

CREATE AFFIRMATIONS

Long-term studies by Dr. Martin Seligman and many others show that the critical determinant of success in business and life is resilience in the face of adversity. Awareness, deep contemplation, and a sense of humor are your best friends in attempting to learn from difficult experiences. You can also, like Leonardo, strengthen your resilience by creating your own affirmations. In your notebook, write out at least one affirmation to inspire you in dealing with each of your greatest challenges.

Many people use affirmations beginning with the phrase "I am ..." Such as "I am patient with myself" or "I am becoming more patient with myself." Although "I am" affirmations can be helpful, they tend to elicit a primarily intellectual, cognitive response. You can get your affirmations to work at a deeper level by framing them in a more emotional, heart-centered way. The following experiment shows how:

Repeat the following affirmation: *I am patient with myself.* Notice your response.

Now try it this way: *I feel patient with myself.* Again, notice your response. When you tell yourself how you feel, not just how you are, you are more likely to feel what you say, allowing your affirmations to take hold on a deeper level.

The following affirmations, written in collaboration with my friend Dr. Dale Schusterman, are designed to help you access your heart center so that deeper changes can emerge.

Relationships

+ I feel willing to allow another person into my heart.
+ I feel curious what I might change in myself that would help my partner.
+ I feel the difference between my father and my husband (mother/wife).
+ I honor the feminine nature in my wife (girlfriend).

Spirituality

+ My connection to the divine (Christ, Higher Self, Buddha, etc.) is my top priority (say this while visualizing work, relationships, money, expectations, parents, stressful events from the past, etc.).
+ I feel the presence of the divine within me.
+ In my heart, I feel a divine will working in my life.
+ I acknowledge the lessons my soul needs to learn from (say the name of a person or an experience).

Money

+ I feel the difference between my desires and my needs.
+ I feel curious how to allow abundance to enter my life.
+ I feel willing for abundance to enter my life.
+ I feel worthy of abundance in my life.

+ I acknowledge that abundance already exists in my life.

Learning
+ The brilliance of my mind manifests in ways that surprise me.
+ I acknowledge my ability to learn intuitively.
+ I feel curious how to (solve this problem, learn this subject).
+ I trust the knowledge to be here when I need it.

Career
+ I feel worthy in my contribution to the world.
+ I feel connected to my inner strength when others view my work.

+ I feel curious how to manifest my inner purpose in the world.
+ I feel willing to manifest my inner purpose in the world.

Joy of Life
+ I feel joy within myself in all situations (say this as you visualize a stressful situation).
+ I feel deserving of happiness.
+ I feel joy in the happiness of others.
+ My joy and happiness come from within me.

Self-actualization
+ I trust my inner self.
+ I feel the presence of the divine within me.
+ I allow myself to feel my feelings.
+ I acknowledge my feelings about myself.

DIMOSTRAZIONE FOR PARENTS

How do you raise a child who thinks for himself, learns from mistakes, and perseveres in the face of adversity? As with most aspects of parenting, the answers aren't easy. But one key is to nurture your child's confidence. The word confidence comes from the roots fidere, "to trust," and con, "with." Confidence, trust in oneself and one's abilities, is the secret of success, and the experience of success is a key to building confidence. Build your children's confidence by guiding them to success in learning. Break tasks down into simple components so kids get a series of small successes rather than a few big failures.

Nothing builds a child's self-confidence like unconditional love. Let your children know that you love them for who they are, rather than for what they do. Complement unconditional love with enthusiastic encouragement. Shower your children with phrases like "You can do anything you set your mind to," "I believe in you," and "I know you can do it."

Treat mistakes as learning opportunities. When your children do fail, give them gentle, accurate feedback and enthusiastic encouragement. One of the problems with some "self-esteem"-oriented education is that it confuses unconditional love and encouragement with inaccurate feedback. Telling a child that his performance is good or right when it is not undercuts the development of genuine self-esteem. Accurate feedback grounds your child in reality and communicates your respect for his ability to learn.

LEARN FROM "ANTI-ROLE MODELS"

One of the most efficient ways to learn from mistakes is to let someone else make them for you. It is wonderful to have positive role models like Leonardo whom you can strive to emulate. But you can also learn a tremendous amount by studying "anti-role models." For example, I learned most of what I know about coaching and teaching from my worst coaches and teachers. I remember sitting in class while one teacher droned on endlessly; another never listened when someone asked a question; then there was the coach who was fond of humiliating his players. They taught me what *not* to do. I am also grateful to other anti-role models who, by demonstrating exactly what not to do, have helped me avoid getting into debt and having a nervous breakdown.

Make a list of at least three people who have made mistakes that you would like to avoid. How can you learn from *their* mistakes? The tricky thing about this exercise is that sometimes your greatest anti-role models also happen to be positive role models in some areas. Your task, of course, is to accurately discriminate between what you want to emulate and what you want to avoid.

DIMOSTRAZIONE AT WORK

In the business world, senior executives overwhelmingly point to a failure to heed their own experience as the prime cause of their worst decisions. Too often businesspeople allow their better judgment, based on experience, to be overruled by analysts, attorneys, and academic authorities. Mark McCormack, the founder of the International Management Group and author of *What They Don't Teach You at Harvard Business School*, describes the limiting mental set that can be created by academic training: "… A master's in business can sometimes block an ability to master experience. Many of the M.B.A.s we hired were either congenitally naive or victims of their business training. The result was a kind of real-life learning disability – a failure to read people properly or to size up situations and an uncanny knack for forming the wrong perceptions."

The best leaders and managers know, as Leonardo did, that experience is the heart of wisdom.

Sensazione

The Continual Refinement
of the Senses, Especially
Sight, as the Means to
Enliven Experience.

S ight, sound, touch, taste, and smell. If you think like Leonardo, you recognize these as the keys to opening the doors of experience. Da Vinci believed that the secrets of Dimostrazione are revealed through the senses, especially sight. *Saper vedere* (knowing how to see) was one of Leonardo's mottoes, and the cornerstone of his artistic and scientific work. In *The Creators: A History of Heroes of the Imagination,* Daniel Boorstin entitles his chapter on Da Vinci "Sovereign of the Visible World." Da Vinci's sovereignty stemmed from the combination of his open, questioning mind, his reliance on actual experience, and his uncanny visual acuity. Nurtured by a boyhood spent observing and enjoying the natural beauty of the Tuscan countryside and further cultivated by his teacher Verrocchio, "the true eye,"

> *"All our knowledge has its origin in our perceptions."*
> – LEONARDO DA VINCI

Leonardo developed astonishing powers of sight bordering on those of a cartoon superhero. In his "Codex on the Flight of Birds," for example, he recorded minutiae about the movements of feathers and wings in flight that remained unconfirmed and not fully appreciated until the development of slow-motion moving pictures.

Da Vinci was most dramatic and rapturous in describing the power of vision:

He who loses his sight loses his view of the universe, and is like one interred alive who can still move about and breathe in his grave. Do you not see that the eye encompasses the beauty of the whole world: It is the master of astronomy, it assists and directs all the arts of man. It sends men forth to all the corners of the earth. It reigns over the various departments of mathematics, and all its sciences are the most infallible. It has measured the distance and the size of the stars; has discovered the elements and the nature thereof and from the courses of the constellations it has enabled us to predict things to come. It has created architecture and perspective, and lastly, the divine art of painting. O, thou most excellent of all God's creations! What hymns can do justice to thy nobility; what peoples, what tongues, sufficiently describe thine achievements?

Da Vinci's gaze allowed him to capture exquisite and unprecedented subtleties of human expression in his paintings. For the maestro the eye was truly the window of the soul, and as he emphasized repeatedly, "the chief means whereby the understanding may most fully and abundantly appreciate the infinite works of nature."

For Leonardo vision was supreme, and painting was therefore the greatest discipline. Hearing, and therefore music, came next in importance. He wrote, "Music may be called the sister of painting, for she is dependent upon hearing, the sense which comes second ... painting excels and ranks higher than music, because it does not fade away as soon as it is born ..." (In Leonardo's day there were, of course, no audiocassettes, phonograph records, or compact discs.)

"Who would believe that so small a space could contain the images of the whole universe."
– LEONARDO DA VINCI

Among his many extraordinary abilities, Leonardo was a brilliant musician. His popularity at the palaces of his patrons was partly attributable to his playing of the flute, lyre, and other instruments. Vasari tells us that "he sang divinely without any preparation." When he was accepted by his new patron, Ludovico Sforza in Milan, he brought a silver-handled lyre in the shape of a horse's head that he made himself as a gift. In addition to composing, playing, and singing, Leonardo sought musical accompaniment whenever he painted. For the maestro, music was sensory, spiritual nourishment.

Though vision and hearing were at the head of Leonardo's sensory hierarchy, he valued, practiced, and encouraged the refinement of all the senses. He took great care to wear the best clothes he could afford, savoring the feel of fine velvets and silks. His studio was always filled with the scent of flowers and perfumes. He cultivated his senses further through his passion for the culinary arts. Leonardo created, in the West, the concept of small, healthy, exquisitely sculpted portions of food for banquets.

Yet Leonardo reflected sadly that the average human "looks without seeing, listens without hearing, touches without feeling, eats without tasting, moves without physical awareness, inhales without awareness

> *The five senses are the ministers of the soul."*
>
> – LEONARDO DA VINCI

of odour or fragrance, and talks without thinking." His assessment reads, centuries later, as an invitation to improve our senses – and our minds and experiences along the way.

SENSAZIONE AND YOU

What is the most beautiful thing you have ever seen? The sweetest sound you've ever heard? The most exquisitely tender touch? Imagine a sublimely delicious taste and a haunting, delectable aroma. How does your experience of one sense affect all the others?

The questions and exercises in this chapter are sensational fun: You will be tasting chocolate and wine and discovering new ways to appreciate music and art. You will learn to enrich your experience of touch and to make your own cologne, in the manner of the maestro. And you will be introduced to synesthesia, the synergy of the senses, a secret of great artists and scientists. Underlying all the fun and pleasure is the serious purpose of refining sensory intelligence.

In addition to being the conduits of pleasure and pain, your senses are the midwives of intelligence. *Sharp* is a synonym for *smart* and *dull* another word for *dumb;* both refer to sensory acuity. But in a world of traffic, cubicles, beepers, concrete, ringing telephones, artificial ingredients, jackhammers, and Beavis and Butt-Head, it becomes all too easy, as Leonardo said, "to look without seeing." To do so violates the spirit of Leonardo, who made special efforts to nurture his sensory awareness and acuity. Da Vinci biographer Serge Bramly compares Leonardo's program of sensory development and refinement to an athlete's training regimen. He writes, "Just as an athlete develops his muscles, Leonardo trained his senses, educating his observant faculties. We know from his notebooks the kind of mental gymnastics he put himself through." The sense training offered by the delightful sensory gymnastics in this chapter will guide you toward heightened sensory awareness, acuity, and enjoyment. But first reflect on the self-assessment checklists on pages 99–104.

Sensazione: Self-Assessment - Vision

❑ I am sensitive to color harmonies and clashes.
❑ I know the color of all my friends' eyes.
❑ I look out into the far horizon and up to the sky at least once a day.
❑ I am good at describing a scene in detail.
❑ I like doodling and drawing.
❑ Friends would describe me as alert.
❑ I am sensitive to subtle changes in lighting.
❑ I can picture things clearly in my mind's eye.

You can witness an ironic testament to Leonardo's lament when you next visit the Louvre. As you approach the *Mona Lisa*, you will see a number of signs, written in large letters and different languages, reading: "No Flash Photography, Please." As you attempt to take in the subtleties of this most mysterious of all paintings, you'll find yourself almost blinded by the stroboscopic effect of the nonstop camera flashes of the Philistines who never bother to stop and actually *look* at the painting.

Sensazione: Self-Assessment - Hearing

❑ Friends describe me as a good listener.
❑ I am sensitive to noise.
❑ I can tell when someone is singing off-key.
❑ I can sing on key.
❑ I listen to jazz or classical music regularly.
❑ I can distinguish the melody from the bass line in a piece of music.
❑ I know what all the controls on my stereo system are for and can hear the difference when I adjust them.
❑ I enjoy silence.
❑ I am attuned to subtle changes in a speaker's voice tone, volume, and inflection.

Sensazione: Self-Assessment - Smell

- ❑ I have a favorite scent.
- ❑ Smells affect my emotions strongly, for better or worse.
- ❑ I can recognize friends by their scent.
- ❑ I know how to use aromas to influence my mood.
- ❑ I can reliably judge the quality of food or wine by its aroma.
- ❑ When I see fresh flowers, I usually take a few moments to breathe in their aroma.

Sensazione: Self-Assessment - Taste

- ❏ I can taste the "freshness" of fresh foods.
- ❏ I enjoy many different types of cuisine.
- ❏ I seek out unusual taste experiences.
- ❏ I can discern the flavor contributions of different herbs and spices in a complex dish.
- ❏ I am a good cook.
- ❏ I appreciate the pairing of food and wine.
- ❏ I eat consciously, aware of the taste of my food.
- ❏ I avoid junk food.
- ❏ I avoid eating on the run.
- ❏ I enjoy participating in taste tests and wine tastings.

Sensazione: Self-Assessment - Touch

- ❑ I am aware of the "feel" of the surfaces that surround me daily, e.g., the chairs, sofas, and car seats I sit on.
- ❑ I am sensitive to the quality of fabric that I wear.
- ❑ I like to touch and be touched.
- ❑ Friends say I give great hugs.
- ❑ I know how to listen with my hands.
- ❑ When I touch someone, I can tell if he or she is tense or relaxed.

Sensazione: Self-Assessment - Synesthesia

- ❏ I enjoy describing one sense in terms of another.
- ❏ I intuitively understand which colors are "cold" and which are "hot."
- ❏ My response to art is visceral.
- ❏ I am aware of the role of synesthesia in the thinking of great artists and scientists.
- ❏ I can sense which of these sounds – "ooooohhlaaaa," "zip-zip-zip," "ni-ni-ni-ni-ni" – are reflected in the following shapes: ~' ^ ^ ^, vvvvv.

SENSAZIONE: APPLICATION AND EXERCISES

VISION: LOOKING AND SEEING

Leonardo wrote that "the eye encompasses the beauty of the whole world." You can begin to cultivate keener vision – and appreciate more fully the beauty that the world has to offer – with the following practices:

The Eye-palming Exercise

Sit at a desk in a quiet, private place. Keep your feet squarely on the floor and sit so that you are supported by the bones at the bottom of your pelvis. If you wear glasses, take them off; contact lenses are okay. Now rub your palms together vigorously for about twenty seconds. Resting your elbows lightly on the desk, cup your palms and place them over your gently closed eyes; be sure not to touch the eyeball or put pressure on the sides of your nose.

Breathe deeply, in an easy, relaxed fashion, and rest with your eyes closed for three to five minutes. When you are ready to finish, take your palms away from your eyes, but leave your eyes closed for another twenty seconds or so. (Do not rub your eyes!) Then gently open your eyes and look around. You will probably notice that colors seem brighter and that everything seems sharper and more defined. Do this once or twice a day.

"This is Leonardo's description of a sunrise: "At the first hour of the day the atmosphere in the south near to the horizon has a dim haze of rose flushed clouds; toward the west it grows darker, and toward the east the damp vapor of the horizon shows brighter than the actual horizon itself, and the white of the houses in the east is scarcely to be discerned; while in the south, the farther distant they are, the more they assume a dark rose flushed hue, and even more so in the west; and with the shadows it is the contrary, for these disappear before the white houses."

Focus Near and Far

This is a very simple and valuable exercise that you can practice many times each day. Look at something close to you – such as this book or your hand – then change your focus to the farthest horizon. Pick out a specific element of the far horizon and focus on it for a few seconds, then come back to your hand, then look out again to the farthest horizon, focusing on a different element this time. In addition to enlivening your eyes and expanding your perception, this exercise can improve your driving and specifically prevent you from speeding, unknowingly, past state troopers on the freeway.

"Soft Eyes"

Sitting in front of a computer screen and reading reports drives many people toward a habitually hard, narrow focus. Instead, allow a few deep exhalations and try the following exercise: Place your index fingers together at eye level about twelve inches from your face. Looking straight ahead, move your fingers slowly away from each other on the horizontal plane. Stop moving your fingers when you can no longer see them with your peripheral vision. Bring your fingers back to center and do the same exercise with the vertical plane. Exhale. Now "soften" your eyes by relaxing the muscles of your forehead, face, and jaw and allow a receptivity to the broadest possible expanse of vision. Note the way this exercise affects your mind and body.

Describe a Sunrise or Sunset

Look in the newspaper to learn the exact time of the sunrise or sunset. Find a quiet place to sit where you can get a good view. Arrange to arrive at least ten minutes before the official time. Quiet your mind and body with a few deep full breaths, focusing on extended exhalations. Do the palming exercise for three minutes, then focus near and far, accessing soft eyes as you take in the horizon. Describe the details of the experience in your notebook.

Study the Lives and Work of Your Favorite Artists
Make a list of your ten favorite painters. Then devote a set period of time (a week, three months, a year) to immersing yourself in the study of their life and work. Read everything you can. Visit their works. Hang reproductions of your favorite paintings in your bathroom, office, and kitchen.

Here's my top ten list (of painters of the Western world):

1. Leonardo (surprise!)
2. Paul Cézanne
3. Vincent van Gogh
4. Rembrandt van Rijn
5. Michelangelo
6. Jan Vermeer
7. Giorgione
8. Masaccio
9. Diego Velázquez
10. Mary Cassatt

Make the Most of Museums
How can you deepen your appreciation of great art and enhance your capacity for *saper vedere* (knowing how to see)? One simple key is to have a strategy for museum visits. Many very well educated people find themselves overwhelmed by visits to art museums. There is so much to see. Without a positive strategy for viewing and

enjoying an exhibition, one can often come away exhausted and unfulfilled. Audio and docent tours can be excellent, but they vary dramatically in quality.

Try the following: Go to a museum with a friend. Decide in advance which sections of the collection you wish to view. As you enter each room, split up, agreeing to meet at a set time.

Suspend judgments based on all the analytical terms you may have learned in your college art history course. Just look at each painting or sculpture with fresh, innocent eyes. Avoid looking at the name of the artist or the title of the painting until *after* you have taken the time to appreciate it deeply. What appeals to you about a particular work of art? Make notes in your journal on the paintings or sculptures that affect you most profoundly. Then meet with your friend and share your impressions of the most outstanding work in that room. Your focus on articulating what draws you to a particular work will hone your appreciation and enjoyment. And, of course, you get the benefit of your friend's perspective, which can deepen your appreciation not only of particular paintings but also of your friend. When I do this exercise with my friends, they invariably say something like "That was the most fun I've ever had in a museum!"

"Leonardo observed that "the idea or the faculty of imagination [serves] as both rudder and bridle to the senses, inasmuch as the thing imagined moves the sense."

Practice "Subtle Speculation": The Art of Visualization

Visualization is a marvelous tool to sharpen all your senses, improve your memory, and prepare for accomplishing your goals in life. Visualization was an essential element of Leonardo's strategy for learning and creating. As he wrote, "I have found in my own experience that it is of no small benefit when you lie in bed in the dark to go over again in the imagination the outlines of the forms you have been studying or of other noteworthy things conceived by subtle speculation; and this is certainly a praiseworthy exercise and useful in impressing things on the memory." Although intended as advice for painters, it applies equally well to artists of life.

You can practice conscious visualization to improve everything from your golf game and ballroom dancing to your drawing and presentation skills. Visualization seems to be most effective when you are relaxed, so good times to practice include:

+ in the morning upon waking;
+ at night as you fade off to sleep;
+ when you are a passenger in a train, plane, boat, or auto;
+ when taking a break from work;
+ after meditation, yoga, or exercise; or
+ anytime when your body is relaxed and your mind is free.

The ability to visualize a desired outcome is built into your brain, and your brain is designed to help you succeed in matching that picture with your performance. And the more thoroughly you involve all your senses, the more compelling your visualization becomes. To get the most from your visualization practice:

Try the following exercises to enhance the vividness of your multisensory visualization.

Do not imagine the *Mona Lisa* with a mustache! If you failed to carry out this instruction, it is because your power of visualization is so strong that it takes any suggestion, positive or negative, and turns it into an image. And as the maestro emphasized, "the thing imagined moves the sense." Many people, however, are burdened by the mistaken assumption that they "can't visualize." What they usually mean is that they do not see clear, Technicolor internal visual images. It is important to realize that you can get the *full benefits of visualization practice* without "seeing" clear Technicolor images. If you think you cannot visualize, try answering the following questions: What is the model and color of your car? Can you describe your mother's face? What are the markings on a dalmatian dog? Chances are you answered these questions easily by drawing on your internal image data bank, the occipital lobe of your cerebral cortex. This data bank has the potential, in coordination with your frontal lobes, to store and create more images, both real and imaginary, than all the world's film and television production companies combined.

- ✦ Keep your visualization positive – Many people practice unconscious negative visualization, more commonly known as worry. Although the ability to picture what might go wrong is essential to intelligent planning, be careful to avoid fixating on images of failure, disaster, and catastrophe. Instead, visualize your positive response to any challenge.
- ✦ Distinguish between fantasy and visualization – Fantasy can be fun, and the free flow of imagery it inspires can be useful in generating creative ideas. But visualization is different from fantasy. When visualizing, you consciously focus your mind on imagining a desired process and outcome. In other words, you practice disciplined mental "rehearsal." And it is your consistency and intensity of focus, rather than the Technicolor clarity of your visualization, that is most important in making it effective.
- ✦ Make your visualization multisensory – Use all your senses to make your visualization unforgettable and irresistible. Whether you are preparing for a presentation, planning a meal, or training for athletic competition, imagine the sights, sounds, feel, smell, and taste of success.

Picture Your Favorite Scene

Enjoy some deep full breaths and then close your eyes. Create a picture of your favorite place, real or imaginary. Perhaps, for example, you choose a beach. In your mind's eye, look out at the vast expanse of the blue-green ocean, following the forward rush of foamy white wave crests. Listen to the rumbling rhythm of the surf and feel the warm rays of the sun on your back. Breathe in the invigorating smell of the salty air carried by the soft sea breeze and savor the texture of wet sand between your toes. Spy a squadron of six brown pelicans skimming just above the water, suddenly dispersing in all directions. The largest pelican returns and dives straight down to swallow a silver-tailed fish. Grasp a handful of sand. Hold it up to the clear blue sky. Let it fall through your fingers, light dancing off the crystals. Wash your hands in the undertow. Lick your fingers, tasting the salty sea. Continue enjoying your visit to your favorite place, relishing every delightful sensory detail.

> Da Vinci noted two types of visualization:
>
> + "Postimagining – the imagining of things that are past."
> + "Preimagining – the imagining of things that are to be."

Create Your Own Internal Masterpiece Theater

One of the best ways to cultivate the art of visualization is through the visualization of art. Choose any one of the masterpieces of your favorite artist – for example, Leonardo's *The Last Supper* or Van Gogh's *Sunflowers*. Hang a reproduction on your wall and study it for at least five minutes each day for a week. Then as you drift off to sleep each night, aim to re-create the painting in your mind's eye. Visualize the details. Bring all your senses to this exercise: Imagine the sounds around the table in *The Last Supper* or the smell of the sunflowers. Record the changes in your impressions of the work from day to day.

Learn to Draw

The ultimate Da Vincian approach to visual refinement would be to learn to paint. But like that of most artists, Da Vinci's painting is predicated on his drawing. Leonardo emphasized that drawing was the foundation of painting and of learning how to see. He wrote, "… Drawing is as indispensable to the architect and the sculptor as it is to the potter, the goldsmith, the weaver, or the embroiderer … it has given arithmeticians their figures; it has taught geometers the shape of their diagrams; it has instructed opticians, astronomers, machine builders, and engineers."

For Leonardo, drawing was much more than illustration; it was the key to understanding creation. So for aspiring Da Vincians, learning to draw is the best way to begin to learn to see and create. To help you get started, you will find "The Beginner's Da Vinci Drawing Course" on page 262.

> "*The eye encompasses the beauty of the whole world.*"
>
> – LEONARDO DA VINCI

LISTENING AND HEARING

Every sound and every silence provides an opportunity to deepen auditory perspicacity; but city sounds can be overwhelming and cause us to dull our sensitivity. Surrounded by jackhammers, televisions, and airplane, subway, and automobile noises, most of us "tune out" for self-protection. Try the following exercises to "tune up" your auditory sense.

Layered Listening

Once or twice each day pause for a few moments, enjoy a few full deep exhalations, and listen to the sounds around you. First you'll hear the loudest, most obvious sounds – the air conditioner, the clock ticking, the traffic outside, the background noises of people and machinery. Then as that "layer" becomes clarified, begin to notice the next layer down – sounds of your breathing, a gentle breeze, footsteps in the hall, the shifting of your sleeve when you move your hand. Keep moving your awareness deeper into the next layer and then the next until you hear the soft, rhythmic beating of your heart.

Listen for Silence

Practice listening for the spaces between sounds – the pauses in a friend's conversation or your favorite music, and the silences between the notes in the song of a bluebird. Make silence a theme for a day and record your observations in your notebook. Do you have access to a place of complete silence, away from the humming of machines? Try to find such a place. How does it feel to be in a place of complete quiet?

Practice Silence

Experiment with a day of silence. For a whole day, don't talk, just listen. It is best to spend your silent day out in nature, walking in the woods, hiking in the mountains, or strolling by the sea. Immerse yourself in nature's sounds. This "verbal fasting" strengthens your ability to listen deeply and is wonderfully refreshing for your spirit.

Study the Lives and Work of Your Favorite Composers and Musical Artists

Fine music is the most powerful tool for cultivating appreciation of sound and the subtleties of hearing. Leonardo referred to the art of music as "the shaping of the invisible." You can increase your sensitivity and enjoyment by focusing first on what you already know you enjoy. Make a list of your top ten favorites in your chosen style of music – whether they be classical composers, gospel giants, klezmer bands, tango orchestras, crooners, fiddlers, opera or rock stars, shakuhachi flute players, jazz greats, raga masters, or R&B artists. Choose one and immerse yourself in his or her work for a day, week, or month. If you have a CD player in your car, load it up with the works of your artist or composer of the week. Use some of the active-listening techniques offered later in the chapter to develop a richer appreciation for his or her body of work.

Learn the Major Movements of Western Music

The music of the world is amazingly rich, diverse, and wonderful; and a familiarity with and an appreciation for the master works of the Western tradition is a marvelous point of departure for a personal auditory Renaissance. With the expert guidance of composer Audrey Elizabeth Ellzey, noted conductor Joshua Habermann, vocalist Stacy Forsythe, and National Public Radio's Murray Horwitz, I've compiled a brief introduction to the Western tradition for your enjoyment.

Medieval (A.D. 450–1450): The medieval period was characterized by chants in churches and monasteries, and secular songs of wandering minstrels and other entertainers. The human voice was the most important instrument of the time. Most composers of the Middle Ages, like most painters, toiled anonymously. One delightful exception is Hildegard von Bingen. Her prayerful, humble, yet beautifully expressive works are, amazingly, appearing on top ten sales charts around the world.

Renaissance (1450–1600): The most important development in this period was the evolution of polyphony, music with parts that are independent of one another. Musical compositions were printed for the first time, enabling performers to learn and follow multiple parts. Music became more complex. Josquin, Byrd, and Dufay are a few of the notable Renaissance composers whose music survives. Most experts agree, however, that the Italian Palestrina, born shortly after Leonardo's death, is the greatest composer of the period.

Baroque (1600–1750): The music of the Baroque period is dominated by musical counterpoint. In musical counterpoint, individual melodic lines are still independent but more tightly governed by regular harmonic progressions. Baroque music is very consistent, relying on a rigid set of rules for its construction. Music from this period, as in the Renaissance, was written primarily for royal or religious functions. Bach and Handel are supreme exemplars of the Baroque style.

Classical (1785–1820): After a transitional period of thirty-five years (1750–1785), the classical era began. During the classical period counterpoint became less popular as single lines of melody were accompanied by harmony. Baroque rules and rigidity relaxed, and the sonata was born. The sonata form gave composers more freedom and opportunity to reveal an individual style. Although still formal, music from this period is best known for its elegance and finesse. Mozart, Haydn, and Beethoven are the greatest masters of the classical period.

Romantic (1820–1910): During the Romantic period, exotic harmonies and melodic experimentation further expanded musical structures. Yearning for an ideal, the individual gave voice to the expression of emotion. Personal passion and deep feelings came to life in the great instrumental works of Brahms, Chopin, and Schubert, and the majestic opera of Verdi, Puccini, and Wagner.

Twentieth Century (1910–): In the beginning of the twentieth century, composers like Stravinsky, Debussy, Richard Strauss, Mahler, Schoenberg, Shostakovich, and Bartók were blazing new musical trails. Rebelling against the rigidity of the previous eras, modern composers diverged in so many directions that audiences had trouble keeping up. World War II complicated matters further. For example, the music of Stravinsky and Debussy was outlawed in Russia, and Shostakovich was suppressed (as in the later half of this century). Electronic innovations have dramatically influenced both serious and popular music. Modern audio technology has also allowed enthusiasts to listen to great music in their homes and automobiles. Consequently, contemporary audiences often seek out new virtuosos and better recordings of past greats rather than new composers and musical forms.

Study Great Music from the Classical Canon

Through dogged questioning of my experts I managed to wrangle out the beginnings of a rough consensus on ten of the greatest works from the classical canon. Listen to them and decide for yourself.

1. Bach: Mass in B Minor

Profundity of spirit and joyous celebration in one of the most stirring works in the history of sacred music.

"ALL-STAR" LIST MAKING

I asked all my experts for their top ten lists of "greats." Without exception they resisted my request for hierarchical organization, protesting that "art doesn't work that way." Nevertheless, I persisted, asking questions like "If you were stranded on the proverbial desert island and could have only ten classical or ten jazz pieces, what would you choose?" Why do I ask for top ten lists when as Murray Horwitz pointed out, "we are not choosing the NBA all-star team"? The exercise of ordering your favorites, whether in music, painting, or wine appreciation – the discipline of choosing one and eliminating another, ranking one a level higher than another, and then articulating why you chose the way you did – requires a depth and clarity of consideration and comparison that inspires richer appreciation and enjoyment. Comparing your list with a friend's is also a delightful way of expanding your erudition and getting to know your friend. Approach hierarchical list making with appropriate humility and lightheartedness and remember that your all-star team can, of course, be reordered at will.

2. Beethoven: Symphony #9

Transformation of darkness to light with a spectacular finale; Beethoven's setting of Schiller's text celebrating the brotherhood of man is awe-inspiring.

3. Mozart: Requiem

Considered by most to be the supreme work for chorus and orchestra. Ironically, the Requiem was finished by Mozart's student due to his untimely death.

4. Chopin: Nocturnes

These intimate piano compositions will suffuse your soul with moonlight. (Try to find the heavenly recording by pianist Arthur Rubinstein.)

5. Brahms: German Requiem

The scope of expression ranges from monumental echoes of the eternal to extremely personal and comforting.

6. Mahler: Symphony #6

Exploring the depths of emotion as only Mahler can, this symphony celebrates the triumph of hope over despair.

7. R. Strauss: Four Last Songs

These pieces for soprano and orchestra are settings of poems by Hermann Hesse and Joseph von Eichendorff. The lush orchestration forms a rich backdrop for the soprano's soaring melodies. Strauss's depiction of the soul taking flight in "Beim Schlafengehen" is one of the most extraordinary moments in all of Western music.

8. Debussy: Preludes

Each of these jewel-like piano pieces is a unique miniature characterization in an impressionistic style.

9. Stravinsky: "The Rite of Spring"

Explosive, incendiary, and compellingly rhythmic, the audience rioted at its premiere.

10. (tie) Verdi: **Aida** *and Puccini:* **La Bohème**

Everyone agreed that an operatic composition deserved a place in the top ten; but we could not agree on which one. So it's a tie. In live performance, Verdi's *Aida* will give you an unforgettable experience of the opera. For recorded listening, Puccini's *La Bohème* is hard to beat. His beautiful melodies capture the essence of romance. (All of the experts emphasized the importance of seeking out the highest quality recordings by the finest performers and conductors.)

Our very brief introduction to the timeless masterpieces of Western music is incomplete without consideration of American popular song and jazz.

DEVELOP ACTIVE LISTENING

You can add to your music-listening pleasure by taking a more active approach to what doesn't need to be a passive endeavor. Practice the following "active listening" strategies.

Listen for patterns of tension and release: This is one of the simplest and most enjoyable ways to deepen your appreciation and enjoyment of music. All composers, regardless of genre, employ methods that ultimately involve the creation of tension and its subsequent release. By using such techniques as rhythmic variation, key change, rests, and harmonic movement, the composer leads the listener along a path of motion, stillness, and melodic highs and lows, all leading to the raising of musical expectations and fulfillment. Even if the listener is unaware of the process, he is constantly being led to musical plateaus, stair climbing, and release. Listen to several pieces by anyone from Franz Lizst to Lennon and McCartney and see if you can pinpoint the key moments of momentum – building and release. It is as simple as watching a wave in motion.

Appreciate your favorite music in terms of the elements: Leonardo and his contemporaries often viewed the world in terms of the elements: earth, fire, water, and air. This is a delightful way to think about music. What are the dominant elements of the music you enjoy? Experiment with cataloging your favorite composers and artists by dominant element. For example, although all the great composers express all the elements, I think the element of "earth" is best expressed by Brahms and Beethoven; "fire" by Stravinsky and Shostakovich; Ravel and Debussy evoke the essence of "water"; and Mozart and Bach are the supreme expression of "air." Do you agree?

Learn to discriminate: Appreciation deepens with the ability to make discriminations. The simplest level in music is to know one type from another, for example, to distinguish R&B from country or classical from jazz. Then one learns to differentiate between subtypes, distinguishing New Orleans jazz from fusion, or Baroque and Classical from Romantic. Recognition of composers offers another level of appreciation, distinguishing Bach from Brahms and Mozart from Monteverdi. Next one might begin to recognize the characteristics of different soloists, orchestras, conductors, and recordings.

Try listening to the same piece of music played by different orchestras and conductors. For example, listen to Mahler's Sixth Symphony played by the Boston

American Popular Song

Among America's greatest gifts to the world is an amazing body of work produced in a golden age lasting roughly from 1910 to the 1960s. These are the classic American popular songs that resonate with audiences around the world as a deeply emotional evocation and celebration of modern life. At their best, they make up a union of music and lyrics worthy of consideration on the same level as the oratorios of Handel. (My primary criterion for assessing worthiness is the likelihood that the music will still inspire and move people a century from now.)

Among the greatest of the great are:

+ George and Ira Gershwin – George Gershwin wrote what some have called the first American opera, *Porgy and Bess*. The Gershwin synthesis of early jazz, blues, and European music yielded works of great beauty and enduring influence.
+ Richard Rodgers and Oscar Hammerstein – Rodgers and Hammerstein formed a unique team that produced scores for musical gems such as *Oklahoma!* and *The Sound of Music*.
+ Alan Lerner and Frederick Loewe – Another team famous for charming show tunes such as those in *My Fair Lady*.
+ Irving Berlin – He wrote fun, easygoing, quintessentially American songs such as "White Christmas," "Cheek to Cheek," and "Say It Isn't So."
+ Jerome Kern – premiering in 1927, this pioneer of musical theater's landmark production of *Showboat* set the stage for the emergence of the great American musicals.
+ Cole Porter – Porter's lyrics are the epitome of sophistication and wit. Look for the Ella Fitzgerald recording of *The Cole Porter Song Book*, which contains classics such as "I Love Paris," "Too Darn Hot," and "I've Got You Under My Skin."

Jazz

At its best, jazz is a sonic dance between chaos and order, expressing and inspiring the essence of creativity. Murray Horwitz suggests that the three most important names in jazz are Louis Armstrong, Duke Ellington, and Charlie Parker.

Trumpeter and singer Louis Armstrong may be the single most important figure in jazz performance – one of the two or three greatest soloists, the hardest swinger, and the most irresistible personality. Listen to his records with his mentor, Joe "King" Oliver: "Snake Rag," "Dippermouth Blues," etc. And then listen to his own famous "Hot Fives" and "Hot Sevens"; his "West End Blues" and the popular recordings for Decca in the 1940s and '50s such as "Up a Lazy River" and "On the Sunny Side of the Street."

Duke Ellington, Horwitz says, is among the greatest of all American composers, of any genre. His masterpieces include extended suites such as *Harlem, Such Sweet Thunder,* and *Far East Suite.* His shorter pieces are also stunning, especially "Portrait of Ella Fitzgerald," "Black and Tan Fantasy," and "Clothed Woman." Check out the development of his orchestration and compositional approach as it progressed from the 1920s all the way through to the 1970s. You'll discover his unique piano style and delight in his extraordinary collaboration with Billy Strayhorn. Treat yourself to wonderful songs like "Satin Doll," "Solitude," and "Take the 'A' Train."

Many claim that our third jazz immortal, alto saxophonist Charlie "Yardbird" Parker ("Bird" for short), never played an imperfect solo. This claim may seem unbelievable, but it is maintained by dozens of top musicians. In addition to his amazing solos, Parker's collaborative efforts sparkle with verve and originality. Playing with trumpeter Dizzie Gillespie, pianist Thelonious Monk, drummer Kenny Clarke, and others, he pioneered the development of "bebop." Among highlights to look for are the Dial records (including both takes of "Embraceable You"), the famous "Jazz at Massey Hall" concert, and "Charlie Parker with Strings."

In addition to the three titans above, I asked Murray Horwitz to recommend jazz artists, and one or two of their classic pieces, that offer an ideal introduction to this great American musical tradition:

- Benny Goodman ("Sing, Sing, Sing," from the 1938 Carnegie Hall concert)
- Count Basie (almost anything, but especially "April in Paris," and especially the version with Ella Fitzgerald singing)
- Mildred Bailey ("I'll Close My Eyes," "It's So Peaceful in the Country," "Squeeze Me")
- Miles Davis ("Kind of Blue" and "Four and More")
- Coleman Hawkins ("Body and Soul," "Talk of the Town")
- Billie Holiday ("Fine and Mellow," her work with Count Basie, Lester Young, and Buck Clayton, and her late records from the 1950s)
- Dizzy Gillespie (especially his big band recordings from the 1940s)
- Jelly Roll Morton (all of the Red Hot Peppers recordings)
- Nat King Cole ("After Midnight" and the trio recordings)
- Thomas "Fats" Waller ("Valentine Stomp," "Love Me or Leave Me," "Ain't Misbehavin'")
- John Coltrane ("My Favorite Things," "A Love Supreme")

Symphony Orchestra (a top professional orchestra with an annual budget of 49 million dollars) conducted by Seji Ozawa. Then listen to the same Mahler played by the Boston Philharmonic Orchestra (a part-time orchestra composed of a mix of students, amateurs, and a few professionals with an annual budget of $460,000) conducted by Benjamin Zander. Describe the difference in what you hear in your notebook.

You can also listen for different musicians playing the same instrument. Listen to "Snake Rag" by King Oliver all the way through. Then listen again, and aim to distinguish the lead cornet, played by the King, from the cornet contributing the harmony lines, played by Louis Armstrong.

Listen for emotion: Why does a particular piece of music play with your heartstrings? Which compositions, songs, instruments, and voices affect you most profoundly?

Listen to an early recording of Frank Sinatra. What is the emotional quality of his voice? Then listen to a later recording, from the period after his affair with Ava Gardner ("New York, New York" and "My Way" are the great exemplars of this post-Ava phase). How has the emotional quality changed?

Listen to the transition between the third and fourth movement of Beethoven's Fifth Symphony. Listen for the sound of triumph and exuberance. Then listen to the second movement of Beethoven's Third Symphony. Listen for the sound of tragedy, sadness, and gloom. Why do these sounds affect you as they do?

Listen for cultural and historical imprints: Music is a unique hallmark of human culture, imbued with distinctive imprints of the historical period from which it evolved. Choose your favorite composers and styles of music and aim to understand their work through the context from which it emerged. See if rap music, for example, is best appreciated as a poetic evocation of inner-city life, evolving out of the rhythms and storytelling traditions of Africa; or if Bach's highly structured, rule-oriented music communicates the respect for authority, both divine and secular, that characterized Teutonic society in the Baroque period.

Orchestrate Your Life

To get the most from your enjoyment of great music, you will want to take the time to listen deeply without any distractions. Focus your full attention on Beethoven's Ninth, for example, from beginning to end, and then listen again. You will find it is a marvelous treat for the ear, heart, and mind. Of course, you can also enjoy the benefits of what Leonardo called "the shaping of the invisible" as you go about your day. Music affects mood and emotion, alertness and receptivity; it changes your brain-wave patterns (for better or worse) and is used to rally soldiers for war and boxers on their way into the ring. It can help babies sleep, encourage plants to grow, and comfort the sick.

Take advantage of the power of sound by noting down various activities of everyday life and exploring your ideal musical accompaniment. Then orchestrate your life accordingly – say, waking up to Vangelis's "Chariots of Fire," studying to Mozart's violin concertos, or falling asleep to Kitaro's "Silk Road."

AROMATIC AWARENESS

All day, every day, we are confronted with a smorgasbord of smells. Our five million olfactory cells can sniff out one molecule of odor-causing substance in one part per trillion of air. And we take about 23,000 breaths per day processing about 440 cubic feet of scent-laden air.

But most people have a very limited vocabulary for describing aromatic experience: "It stinks" or "That smells good" are the most common references. Aim to increase your discrimination of and appreciation for smell by expanding your olfactory vocabulary. Perfumers categorize smells as floral (roses), minty (peppermint), musky (musk), ethereal (pears), resinous (camphor), foul (rotten eggs), and acrid (vinegar). Use these terms and make up your own descriptors as you explore the following exercises.

Leonardo's recipe for personal cologne: "To make scent: Take fresh rose-water and moisten the hands, then take the flower of lavender and rub it between the hands, and it will be good."

What Do You Smell Right Now?

Describe what you smell, right now, as vividly as you can. Then, in the manner of your most beloved canine acquaintance, explore your immediate environment with your nose. Breathe in the smell of this book, an empty coffee cup, the palm of your hand, the back of your chair. Describe your experience in your notebook.

Make "Smells" a Theme for a Day

Record what you smell and how it affects you through the course of a day. Seek out unusual or intense aromas. Linger in the cheese department of your favorite gourmet store. Drive to the country and walk through a barnyard. Inhale the aroma of all the herbs and spices in your kitchen. How does smell affect your moods? Your

memory? Aim to find and record specific examples of aromas affecting your emotion or recall.

Olfactory Cornucopia

This exercise is easier and more fun to do with friends. Assemble a range of items with distinctive aromas – for example, a rose, a piece of cedarwood, a vanilla bean pod, the recently worn T-shirt of a very close friend, a bit of seaweed, a slice of orange, a handful of soil, a leather jacket, a good cigar, freshly cut ginger. Put on a blindfold and ask a friend to hold each item, in turn, close to your nose for thirty seconds. Describe each smell and your reaction to it.

Make Your Own Perfume

Go to a fragrance shop and sample essential oils: lavender, patchouli, clove, rose, eucalyptus, etc. Invest in as many as you can. How does each fragrance affect you? How does it affect your friends? Experiment with different combinations and make your own favorite scent.

Study Aromatherapy

The aromas of plants and herbs were used for healing by the ancient Egyptians, Hebrews, and Chinese. Popular in classical times and in Leonardo's day, the therapeutic application of natural herbs and scents is enjoying a rebirth. Check your bookstore for any number of books on this fast-growing topic.

All the exercises just described offer rich rewards, but the most delightful way to explore the olfactory sense is in conjunction with good food and fine wine.

You have approximately ten thousand taste buds, each made up of fifty taste cells. Your taste buds are specialized to discern sweet, sour, bitter, and salty. Sweet sensors are located at the tip of your tongue, sourness is registered on the sides, bitterness is at the back, and salty sensors are spread over the surface.

TASTE

For most of us the opportunity to taste presents itself at least three times a day. But in the rush of our lives, it is often difficult to pay attention. It is all too easy to "grab a bite on the run" and to consume an entire meal without really tasting anything. Instead, pause for a few moments before eating. Reflect on the origins of the meal you are about to enjoy. Aim to be 100 percent present as you taste the first bite of your food.

Develop Comparative Tasting

Listening to great music is a marvelous way to develop your hearing; comparing one great performance to another is even more effective. The same is true for taste and smell. Eating fine foods and drinking great wines provides a delightful continuing sensory education, but you can dramatically accelerate the development of your olfactory and gustatory perspicacity through comparative appreciation. Try the following exercises in comparative appreciation:

Buy three kinds of honey (e.g., orange blossom, wildflower, clover), open the jars, and smell each one for thirty seconds. Describe the aromas. Then taste each one in turn; hold half a teaspoonful in your mouth and swirl it around with your tongue. Take a sip of springwater between tastes to clear your palate. Describe the differences in aroma and taste.

Now try the same comparison process with three kinds of olive oil, chocolate, mushrooms, beer, apples, bottled water, smoked salmon, caviar, grapes, or vanilla ice cream.

Explore Wine Tasting

Fine wine is art you can drink. It is the liquid quintessence of the earth's bounty; proof, as Benjamin Franklin observed, that "God loves us and loves to see us happy." Learning to appreciate and enjoy wine is the most powerful and delightful way to refine your sense of smell and taste. (If you choose not to drink alcohol, you can try the following exercises with the nonalcoholic wines produced by Ariel, St. Regis, and others.)

To hold a successful wine tasting, you need: a harmonious, well-lit environment so you can appreciate the color of the wine (purists insist on white tablecloths to highlight the wine's color); a basket of crusty bread and some springwater to clear your palate between tastes of different wines; good wineglasses engineered to optimize aroma and taste (the best are made by Reidel Crystal). And, of course, a corkscrew and some fine wine.

Organize your tasting around a theme. Try, for example, comparing a top-level California chardonnay, pinot noir, or cabernet sauvignon with a similarly priced white burgundy, red burgundy, or Bordeaux from France. Or taste three different vintages of Chianti, from Leonardo da Vinci's homeland, the Tuscan region of Italy. (Try the Antinori Chianti Classico Tenuta Riserva. The Antinori family were established Tuscan winemakers when Leonardo was born in 1452. The 1997, 1999, and 2000 are the best available vintages.)

Although tasting is the central pleasure of wine, all the senses play a role in its full enjoyment. The feel of the bottle in your hand, the perfect sound of the cork's exit, the texture of the cork in your fingers, the gurgle of the wine as it fills your glass. Hold your glass up to the light and gaze at the color of your wine; then swirl the wine

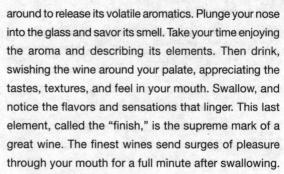

From Leonardo's notebooks: "An Experiment with the Sense of Touch. *If you place your second finger under the tip of the third in such a way that the whole of the nail is visible on the far side, then anything that is touched by these two fingers will seem double, provided that the object touched is round.*"

around to release its volatile aromatics. Plunge your nose into the glass and savor its smell. Take your time enjoying the aroma and describing its elements. Then drink, swishing the wine around your palate, appreciating the tastes, textures, and feel in your mouth. Swallow, and notice the flavors and sensations that linger. This last element, called the "finish," is the supreme mark of a great wine. The finest wines send surges of pleasure through your mouth for a full minute after swallowing.

Describe each stage of the tasting process precisely and poetically.

In addition to using the words employed by experienced tasters, you can enhance your enjoyment and appreciation by making up your own descriptors; the more poetic and fanciful, the better. Offer a prize for the most evocative description (hint: descriptions tend to become increasingly evocative as more wine is consumed). At a recent tasting for the treasurer's department of a major oil company, an accountant, who claimed that he knew nothing about wine, won the prize by describing the taste of an elegant Meursault: "It is like opening a yellow umbrella in a warm rain."

As you gain experience in wine tasting, you'll find that your appreciation for other tastes and smells is heightened. *Salud! Cent'anni!*

TOUCHING AND FEELING

Your brain receives information from more than 500,000 touch detectors and 200,000 temperature sensors. Yet Leonardo lamented that most people "touch without feeling." The secret of sensitive "feeling" touch is an attitude of receptivity, learning to "listen" deeply with

xperienced tasters use hundreds of words to analyze and describe fine wine. Some are self-explanatory; others require elaboration. The following, including some tasting terms in Leonardo's native Italian, are among the most delightful:

amabile	friendly, gentle, slightly sweet
aristocratico	wine from the finest grapes, vintage, soil, and winemakers
balanced	a perfect harmony of yin (acidity) and yang (fruit)
black currants	the classic aroma of cabernet sauvignon
buttery	refers to the texture and "mouth feel" of the wine
carezzevole	caressing, flowing, like the hair of St. Anne
complex	multidimensional; different layers of aroma, flavor, and texture
generoso	easy to appreciate: rich in flavor, extract, and alcohol
rotondo	no rough edges; mellow and full
silky	a smooth, dimensional texture in the palate
stoffa	the right stuff – big, lush complex wines with a strong finish
supple	forthcoming, easy to enjoy
velvety	like "silky," only richer
zing	crisp acidity in white wines – the right acid component provides the structure for appreciating flavor; it also stimulates gastric juices, making good wine an ideal aid to digestion

your hands and whole body, as you'll come to experience in the following exercises.

Touch Like an Angel

Look at the drawing of the angel in Verrocchio's Baptism (page 24) or the face of the Virgin (page 144). Imagine the quality of touch that Leonardo used in applying the gossamer layers of paint. Now, with the exquisite delicacy of the maestro as your inspiration, touch the objects around you. This book, its cover and pages, the fabric of your clothes, your hair, your earlobe, the air at your fingertips. Touch the world around you as though you were experiencing each sensation for the first time.

Bring the same quality of touch to your next intimate encounter. Your partner will become a big fan of the Renaissance.

Blindfold Touch

Invite a friend to share this exercise: Assemble as many of the following objects as you can find: a rubber ball, a silk scarf, a piece of ceramic, a Velcro fastener, a Slinky, a leaf, a bowl of ice, a hammer, a velvet or velour sweater, and anything else you would like to explore. Put on a blindfold and explore them all with receptive, listening hands. Describe the textures, weight, temperature, and other sensations.

Touch Nature

Go outside and explore the textures of nature: the bark and leaves of different trees, grass, the petals of flowers, the earth, the fur of a dog or cat.

Make "Touch" a Theme for the Day

Notice the quality of different people's touch: the firmness of a handshake, the warmth of a hug, the softness of a kiss. Aside from lovemaking, think of the most enjoyable touch you have ever felt. What made it so good? How can you bring more of the quality of touch that you love the most to others? Give a friend a foot massage, and schedule a massage for yourself, to get the most from your theme.

SYNESTHESIA

Synesthesia, the merging of the senses, is a characteristic of great artistic and scientific geniuses.

You can heighten all your powers of Sensazione by cultivating synesthetic awareness. A simple way to begin is to practice describing one sense in terms of the others. Try the following exercises for developing synesthesia:

Draw Music

Listen to your favorite piece of music. As you listen, experiment with expressing your impressions by drawing shapes and colors.

Make Sounds of Color

Look at a reproduction of your favorite painting. Vocalize the sounds inspired by the colors, shapes, and textures on the canvas.

Shape the Invisible

If you were to sculpt a particular piece of music, what materials would you use? What shapes would you make? Which colors would you use? How would the music smell? If you could bite into the music, what would it taste like? Try this imaginary multisensory sculpting exercise with at least two of your favorite pieces of music.

Make Transpositions

Review your list of great artists and composers. Imagine transposing them based on their work, not their personalities. In other words, if Michelangelo were a musician, who would he be? If Mozart were a painter, who would he be? For example, I think that if Michelangelo were a musician, he would be Beethoven; and if Mozart were a painter, he would be Raphael. This is a delightful exercise to do with friends. After everyone has offered a few transpositions, ask each person to explain his or her choices.

Engage in Synesthetic Problem-Solving

Think of a specific question, challenge, or problem. Give it a color, shape, and texture. Imagine what it smells and tastes like. How does it feel? What are the textures, tastes, shapes, colors, and sounds of some possible solutions?

Make Synesthetic Minestrone

Minestrone soup was Leonardo da Vinci's favorite everyday dish. You can sharpen and delight all your senses by preparing the following recipe, adapted from my Grandma Rosa. In addition to being a great Italian cook, Grandma Rosa was a gifted painter. In this exercise, you will make soup like a synesthetic artist.

Ingredients:

- 1 cup cannellini beans (good-quality canned beans, like those from Progresso, are fine)
- 10 oz. Swiss chard (cut into strips)
- 3 medium-size zucchini (quarter-inch slices)
- 2 yellow onions (finely chopped)
- 5 medium-size cloves garlic
- 4 perfect red tomatoes (cut into chunks)
- 2 carrots (diced)
- 4 stalks crisp celery (diced)
- 4 leaves savoy cabbage (cut into strips)
- 3 medium-size potatoes (parboiled, cut into chunks) good olive oil
- 2 cups vegetable, chicken, or beef bouillon the rind of a Parmesan (or pecorino) cheese fresh basil, oregano, black pepper options: arborio rice or fusilli pasta (cooked al dente)

Before you chop, cut, slice, and dice your vegetables, hold each one in your hands and savor its weight, texture, shape, and color. Breathe in the aromas of each ingredient and sing or hum the notes of its essence.

In a large pot, slowly sauté the garlic, celery, carrots, and onions in olive oil (until the onions are translucent). Then add all the other vegetables, one cup of the bouillon, and a touch of freshly ground black pepper, and cook on a low flame. Stir frequently but gently. If you need more liquid, pour in a splash of bouillon. Drop in the rind of Parmesan cheese.

Enjoy the beginnings of the synthesis of colors, textures, and aromas. Sing or hum the sounds of this emerging gustatory and olfactory symphony.

Sensazione for Parents

In a classic study, baby rats were placed in a sensorially deprived environment. Another group was raised in a sensory-rich environment. The sensory-deprived group suffered stunted brain development. They couldn't find their way through a simple maze and were prone to aggressive, violent social behavior. The sensory-rich rodents developed larger, better connected brains. They learned complex mazes quickly and played happily together. Rats are used in experiments like this because their nervous systems show many similarities to ours. So make every effort to create a brain-nourishing environment at home, beginning in the womb. Research by Dr. Thomas Verny and many others shows that your unborn baby will be positively influenced, for example, by listening to Mozart. Once they are born, take every opportunity to create a rich and refined sensory environment for your children. Lots of loving touch and cuddling is particularly important to your growing child's neurological and emotional development. Refinements of smell and taste can wait until they are old enough to appreciate subtleties, but keenness of vision, delight in color, appreciation of sound, and natural synesthetic awareness can be nurtured through drawing, art, and music lessons and daily exposure to beauty.

Simmer for at least 3 hours, until all the ingredients merge.

As you inhale the colors and your senses swim, begin to make beautiful Italianate gestures that express your minestrone experience.

Add the beans, and then the rice or pasta, if you desire, 10 minutes before serving. Sprinkle grated Parmesan or pecorino on top and perhaps a drizzle of olive oil. Garnish with fresh basil or oregano. Serve with fresh-baked Italian bread and a glass of wine or San Pellegrino.

All the separate notes are now blended into harmony. Sing or hum your minestrone song and dance your minestrone dance.

Create Your Own Equivalent to the Maestro's Studio

Building a culture that supports balance and creativity in the workplace is a highly complex task. Creating your own equivalent of the maestro's studio, however, is a simple, concrete step in the right direction. You can use this space for brainstorming, strategizing, and creative problem solving. Companies such as Amoco, DuPont, and Lucent Technologies are successfully applying these ideas. To get started, consider the following elements and resources:

✦ **Room.** Take a conference room, utility room, basement, or empty office, and remove all standard furnishings and telephones. Put a sign on the door that says "Renaissance Room," "Creativity Center," "Leonardo Lab," "Think Tank," etc.

Sensazione at Work

Leonardo emphasized the importance of an aesthetically uplifting working environment. He understood that the sensory impressions from our daily environments act as a kind of food for our brains. Most people in the organizational world, however, suffer from mental malnutrition, the result of a regular "junk-food diet" of sensory impressions. Our workplaces often resemble government offices, hospitals, schools, and prisons, featuring cubicle structures, generic wall color, and fluorescent lights. One wonders if the designs are based on the assumption that sensory deprivation improves productivity.

Ironically, organizations everywhere are issuing urgent calls for greater creativity, innovation, and involvement from all levels. They ask their employees to "think out of the box" while confining them in boxes. As organizations demand greater creativity and innovation from their members, they must provide environments that encourage the behaviors they require.

For many years, psychologists have known that the quality of stimulation provided by the external environment is crucial to brain development in the early years of life.

Recently, however, brain scientists have discovered that the quality of environmental stimulation affects the continuing development of the adult brain. An illustrative story from my own experience offers some insight on how to establish a work environment conducive to a new, more creative, synaptic organization.

In 1982, the Learning Resources Group of a medical equipment company asked for help in solving a training problem. This group was responsible for training customers to use and maintain a machine designed to conduct complex diagnostic tests. To remain cost-effective, training for this machine had to be completed within a week. The problem was that the training often took two or three weeks.

On my first visit to the site, I was impressed with the state-of-the-art interactive training technology. Students attended sophisticated computerized classes and had actual machines to work on. The learning environment, however, was standard cubicle consciousness: generic color walls, fluorescent lights, etc. The only attempt at aesthetics: large pictures of the machine hung just above each machine. The students were given one coffee break in the morning and one in the afternoon.

As an antidote, the thirty-nine members of the learning resources team then spent three days on a training program where they focused on the application of Da Vincian thinking skills to real-life problems. On the first day back in the workplace, the training facilitators experimented by playing Mozart violin concertos during the workday. From that first day onward, they reported that their students were asking at least 50 percent fewer "unnecessary questions." They speculated that the music helped their students relax and focus, freeing them from the need to "get confused" in order to get a break from the monotony.

Among a number of other changes in the learning laboratory, the training facilitators:

+ removed the machine pictures and replaced them with reproductions of their favorite paintings;
+ replaced the fluorescent lights with full-spectrum bulbs;
+ encouraged the students to bring in fresh flowers to make the environment more aesthetically pleasant, fragrant, and "alive";
+ transformed the coffee lounge into a "creative break room," filling it with colored pens and flip charts for doodling; they provided Erector sets, Play-Doh and Slinkies to enliven the sense of touch;
+ encouraged the learners to take up to ten minutes of "brain-break" time every hour.

The Learning Resources Group did its own study on the effects of these changes over the course of a year. The result: Learning effectiveness improved by 90 percent.

- ✦ **Lighting.** Natural lighting is best, so look for a room with windows. Replace standard fluorescent lights with U.V.-radiation-protected full-spectrum fluorescents, halogen lamps, or incandescent bulbs.
- ✦ **Sound.** Install a good-quality stereo system and play jazz or classical music during brainstorming and breaks. (A recent study at the University of California, Irvine, demonstrated that IQ scores rise significantly, although temporarily, when subjects are tested while listening to Mozart.)
- ✦ **Aesthetics.** Hang inspiring art on the walls and perhaps a mobile on the ceiling. Change the art every now and then to keep it fresh. Bring in living green plants and fresh flowers.

- ✦ **Furniture/Equipment.** Bring in a comfortable couch, chairs, overstuffed floor cushions, or even a hammock. Have an ample supply of flip charts (get the extra-large size if possible) and an abundance of colored pens and highlighters (water-based, nontoxic). Add an overhead projector (a good-quality, quiet model) and wall-size dry erase boards.
- ✦ **Fêng Shui.** This is an ancient Chinese system for arranging rooms by placing mirrors, screens, fountains, and furniture to balance the forces of yin and yang and maximize harmony with nature. Western companies such as Chase Manhattan, Citibank, and Morgan Guaranty Trust and innumerable organizations in the East employ fêng shui consultants to create brain-nourishing environments.
- ✦ **Air.** Most indoor environments are stuffy and too hot or too cold. Have a heater/fan available. A

humidifier, dehumidifier, or air purifier (green plants are helpful here) might also be useful. Experiment with aromas – potpourri, incense, or essential oils (e.g., peppermint for alertness, lavender for relaxation).

Sfumato

(Literally "Going up in Smoke") A Willingness to Enbrace Ambiguity, Paradox, and Uncertainty.

As you awaken your powers of Curiosità, probe the depths of experience, and sharpen your senses, you come face to face with the unknown. Keeping your mind open in the face of uncertainty is the single most powerful secret of unleashing your creative potential. And the principle of Sfumato is the key to that openness.

> "To the medieval mind the possibility of doubt did not exist."
> – WILLIAM MANCHESTER

The word *sfumato* translates as "turned to mist" or "going up in smoke" or simply "smoked." Art critics use this term to describe the hazy, mysterious quality that was one of the most distinctive characteristics of Leonardo's paintings. This effect, obtained through the painstaking application of many gossamer-thin layers of paint, is a marvelous metaphor for the man. Leonardo's ceaseless questioning and insistence on using his senses to explore experience led him to many great insights and discoveries, but they also led him to confront the vastness of the unknown and ultimately the unknowable. Yet his phenomenal ability to hold the tension of opposites, to embrace uncertainty, ambiguity, and paradox, was a critical characteristic of his genius.

> *That painter who has no doubts will achieve little."*
> – LEONARDO DA VINCI

The theme of the tension of opposites appears repeatedly in his work and grew in intensity through his lifetime. Writing on the ideal subjects for painters in the *Treatise on Painting,* he conjures up images of profound contrast: "... the essences of animals of all kinds, of plants, fruits, landscapes, rolling plains, crumbling mountains, fearful and terrible places which strike terror into the spectator; and, again pleasant places, sweet and delightful with meadows of many colored flowers bent

The tension of opposites is the central theme of his compelling Virgin of the Rocks, *commissions in 1483. As Bramly comments: "Leonardo composed* The Virgin of the Rocks *around one organizing principle: that of contrast, of opposition. The peaceful group of the mother, the children, and the almost smiling angel is surrounded by a confused background that suggests the end of the world ... The plants are flowering from a barren rock. The Immaculate Conception, Leonardo seems to be saying, paves the way for the agony of the cross. What ought to be a source of joy carries the seeds of Calvary."*

by the gentle motion of the wind which turns back to look at them as it floats on …"

Leonardo's search for beauty led him to explore ugliness in many forms. His sketches of battles, grotesques, and deluges often appear next to sublime evocations of flowers and beautiful youths. When he spotted a deformed or freakish character on the street, he would often spend the entire day following that person to record the details. On one occasion he held a dinner party for the most grotesque-looking people in town. He regaled them with joke after joke until their features became even more contorted through the effect of hysterical laughter. Then when the party ended, he stayed up all night sketching their faces. Kenneth Clark explains Leonardo's curiosity about ugliness by comparing it to "the motives which led men to carve gargoyles on the gothic cathedrals.

Study of a Nutcracker Man and Beautiful Youth by Leonardo da Vinci.

Gargoyles were the complements to saints; Leonardo's caricatures were complementary to his untiring search for ideal beauty."

Leonardo's contemplation of opposition and paradox took many forms. It is expressed in the love of puns, jokes, and humor and in the fascination with riddles, puzzles, and knots recorded throughout his notebooks. His paintings, sketches, doodles, and designs for embroidery, parquet floors, and porcelain tiles frequently express the motif of knots, braids, and scrolls. As Vasari observes,

> Leonardo spent much time on designing a pattern of knots, so interlinked that the thread could be followed from one end to the other, describing a circle. There is an engraving of one of these beautiful and complicated designs, with the inscription "Leonardus Vinci Academia."

Leonardo's fascination with the infinity shape is more than just his delight at the play of words with his name (patterns of knots were known in his day as *fantasie de vinci*). Bramly calls them "symbols of both the infinity and the unity of the world." The knot was Da Vinci's playful expression of the paradox and mystery that emerged as his knowledge deepened.

As he learned more about everything, Leonardo was plunged deeper into ambiguity. And as his awareness of mystery and opposition deepened, his expressions of paradox became more profound. This is strikingly evident in his haunting evocation of Saint John. Kenneth Clark comments:

> St. John the Baptist was the forerunner of the Truth and the Light. And what is the inevitable precursor of truth? A question. Leonardo's St. John is the eternal question mark, the enigma of creation. He thus becomes Leonardo's familiar – the spirit which stands at his shoulder and propounds unanswerable riddles. He has the smile of a sphinx, and the power of an obsessive shape. I have pointed out how this gesture – which itself has the rising rhythm of an interrogative – appears throughout Leonardo's work. Here it is quintessential.

St. John the Baptist *by Leonardo da Vinci.*

Of course, Mona Lisa is Leonardo's supreme expression of paradox. The mystery of her smile has unleashed torrents of ink through the ages. Bramly calls her "a womanly equivalent of Christ." Walter Pater, author of the classic text *The Renaissance,* describes her as "a beauty wrought out from within upon the flesh, the deposit, little cell by little cell, of strange thoughts and fantastic reveries and exquisite passions." Sigmund Freud wrote that the *Mona Lisa* is "… the most perfect representation of the contrasts dominating the love-life of the woman …" Mona Lisa's smile lies on the cusp of good and evil, compassion and cruelty, seduction and innocence, the fleeting and the eternal. She is the Western equivalent of the Chinese symbol of yin and yang.

E. H. Gombrich, author of *The Story of Art,* helps us begin to understand how Leonardo achieved this supreme evocation of the essence

of paradox, Sfumato: "The blurred outline and mellowed colours ...
allow one form to merge with another always leaving something to our
imagination ... Everyone who has ever tried to draw or scribble a face
knows that what we call its expression rests mainly in two features: the
corners of the mouth and the corners of the eyes. Now it is precisely these
parts which Leonardo has left deliberately indistinct, by letting them
merge into a soft shadow. That is why we are never quite certain in what
mood Mona Lisa is really looking at us ..." Gombrich points out the
purposeful discrepancies in the two sides of the portrait and the "almost

miraculous rendering of the living flesh" that add to its uncanny effect.

Of the many mysteries surrounding Mona Lisa perhaps the greatest is the question of her true identity. Is she, as biographer Giorgio Vasari claimed thirty years after Leonardo's death, the wife of Francesco del Giocondo? Is Mona Lisa really Isabella d'Este, marchioness of Mantua, as Dr. Raymond Stites argues in *Sublimations of Leonardo da Vinci*?

Or could she be, as others have suggested, Pacifica Brandano, a companion of Giuliano de' Medici's or perhaps a mistress of Charles d'Amboise's? Or is she a composite of all the women Leonardo had ever known: his mother, the wives and mistresses of noblemen, the peasant women and streetwalkers that he spent hours observing and sketching? Or is she, as some have suggested, an extraordinary self-portrait?

Dr. Lillian Schwartz: Juxtaposition of Leonardo's self-portrait and the Mona Lisa.

Fascinating evidence for this last thesis is offered by Dr. Lillian Schwartz of Bell Laboratories, and author of *The Computer Artists Handbook*. Applying sophisticated computer modeling with precision measurements of scale and alignment, Schwartz compared the *Mona Lisa* with the only extant self-portrait of the artist, drawn in red chalk in 1518. As she describes it, "Juxtaposing the images was all that was needed to fuse them: the relative locations of the nose, mouth, chin, eyes and forehead in one precisely matched the other. Merely flipping up the corner of the mouth would produce the mysterious smile …"

Schwartz concludes that the model for this most famous of paintings is none other than the maestro himself.

Perhaps the *Mona Lisa* was Leonardo's soul portrait. Regardless of Mona Lisa's true identity, she illuminates the essential place of paradox in Da Vinci's worldview.

SFUMATO AND YOU

In the past, a high tolerance for uncertainty was a quality to be found only in great geniuses like Leonardo. As change accelerates, we now find that ambiguity multiplies, and illusions of certainty become more difficult to maintain. The ability to thrive with ambiguity must become part of our everyday lives. Poise in the face of paradox is a key not only to effectiveness, but to sanity in a rapidly changing world.

Rate yourself on a scale of one to ten on tolerance for ambiguity, with one representing complete maniacal need for certainty at all times, and ten representing an enlightened Taoist priest or Leonardo. What behaviors could you change to move up one point on the scale? The exercises that follow are designed to help you strengthen your powers of Sfumato. To get the most from the exercises, spend some time with the self-assessment questions first.

Sfumato:
Self-Assessment

- ❏ I am comfortable with ambiguity.
- ❏ I am attuned to the rhythms of my intuition.
- ❏ I thrive with change.
- ❏ I see the humor in life every day.
- ❏ I have a tendency to "jump to conclusions."
- ❏ I enjoy riddles, puzzles, and puns.
- ❏ I usually know when I am feeling anxious.
- ❏ I spend sufficient time on my own.
- ❏ I trust my gut.
- ❏ I can comfortably hold contradictory ideas in my mind.
- ❏ I delight in paradox and am sensitive to irony.
- ❏ I appreciate the importance of conflict in inspiring creativity.

SFUMATO:
APPLICATION
AND EXERCISES

CURIOSITÀ EQUALS UNCERTAINTY

Return to your list of your ten most important life questions from the Curiosità chapter. Which ones cause you the greatest sense of uncertainty or ambivalence? Are there paradoxes at the heart of any of these questions? Working in your notebook, try your hand at some abstract art. Sketch the feeling of uncertainty generated by a particular question from your Curiosità list. Then experiment with gestures and perhaps an improvisational dance that express that feeling; if you are not sure what to do, then you have got the idea. What music would you choose to accompany your ambiguity dance?

MAKE FRIENDS WITH AMBIGUITY

In your notebook, list and briefly describe three situations from your life, past or present, where ambiguity reigns. You might, for example, remember waiting to hear if you were accepted at the college of your choice, or wondering about the possibility of downsizing in your organization, or considering the future of a significant relationship.

Describe the feeling of ambiguity. Where in your body do you experience it? If ambiguity had a shape, a color, a sound, a taste, a smell, what would they be? How do you respond to feelings of ambiguity? How are ambiguity and anxiety related?

Observe Anxiety

For many people ambiguity equals anxiety; but most people, unless they have worked intensively with a good psychotherapist, do not know when they are anxious. They react to anxiety with some form of automatic avoidance behavior such as talking excessively, pouring a drink, reaching for a cigarette, or having an obsessive fantasy. To thrive with uncertainty and ambiguity, we must learn, first of all, to know when we are anxious. As we become conscious of our anxiety we can learn to accept it, experience it, and free ourselves from limiting compulsions of thought and action.

Describe the feeling of anxiety. Are there different types of anxiety? Where in your body do you experience anxiety? If anxiety had a shape, a color, a sound, a taste, a smell, what would they be? How do you respond to feelings of anxiety? Make "anxiety" a theme for a day. Record your observations in your notebook.

Monitor Intolerance for Ambiguity

Count the number of times per day that you use an absolute, such as "totally," "always," "certainly," "must," "never," and "absolutely."

Note the way you close conversations. Do you usually end with a statement or a question?

CULTIVATE CONFUSION ENDURANCE

The Sfumato principle touches the essence of being. Just as day follows night, our capacity for joy is born in sorrow. We are each the center of a unique and special universe and totally insignificant specks of cosmic dust. Of all the polarities, none is more daunting than life and death. The shadow of death gives life its potential for meaning.

You can develop your Da Vincian powers by nurturing "confusion endurance," sharpening your senses in the face of paradox and embracing creative tension. Practice the Contemplation exercise with any of the following paradoxes:

+ **Joy and Sorrow** – Think of the saddest moments of your life. Which moments were most joyful? What is the relationship between these states? Do you ever feel joy and sorrow simultaneously? Leonardo once wrote, "The highest happiness becomes the cause of unhappiness ..." Do you agree? Is the opposite true?
+ **Intimacy and Independence** – In your closest relationships what is the connection between intimacy and independence? Can you have one without the other? Does this connection ever inspire anxiety?
+ **Strength and Weakness** – List at least three of your strengths as a person. List three or more of your weaknesses. How are the qualities in your lists related?
+ **Good and Evil** – Is it possible to be good without acknowledging and understanding one's own impulses toward evil, what Jung called the "Shadow"? What happens when people are

unconscious of or deny the shadow? How can you recognize and accept your own prejudice, hate, anger, jealousy, envy, greed, pride, and sloth without acting them out?

+ **Change and Constancy** – Note three of the most significant changes you have observed in your lifetime. Note three things that remain constant. Is the idea that "the more things change, the more they remain the same" a valid aphorism or a vapid cliché? Here are some of the maestro's thoughts on the issue: "Constancy may be symbolized by the phoenix which, knowing that by nature it must be resuscitated, has the constancy to endure the burning flames which consume it, and then it rises anew."

+ **Humility and Pride** – Think of the proudest moments of your life. Remember the times you felt most humble. Aim to re-create your most profound feelings of genuine humility and true pride. How are these feelings different? Are there any unexpected similarities between humility and pride? Are these qualities opposites?

+ **Goals and Process** – Think of an important goal that you have accomplished. Describe the process you followed in achieving that goal. Have you ever achieved a success without experiencing fulfillment? How do goal and process, doing and being, relate? Does the end justify the means? To live a successful and fulfilling life, must one: a) be 100 percent committed to achieving clearly defined goals; b) recognize that the process of living every day, the daily quality of life, is of greatest importance; or c) both a and b?

+ **Life and Death** – Make up your own exercise for this one.

Leonardo on life and death: "Behold now the hope or desire of going back to one's own country or returning to primal chaos, like that of the moth to the light, of the man who with perpetual longing always looks forward with joy to each new spring and each new summer ... deeming that the things he longs for are too slow in coming; and who does not perceive that he is longing for his own destruction. But this longing is in its quintessence the spirit of the elements, which, finding itself imprisoned within the life of the human body, desires continually to return to its source. And I have you know that this same longing is in its quintessence inherent in nature ..."

MEDITATE ON MONA

Serge Bramly refers to a Chinese poet of the Sung dynasty who observed that the three most wasteful and disturbing things in the world were to witness poorly educated youths, mishandling of fine tea, and great art go unappreciated. Leonardo's *Mona Lisa* is so familiar that it is rarely seen. Sit with Mona for a while. Wait for your analytical mind to calm down and breathe in her essence. Note your responses. (When you visit Paris, go to the Louvre when it opens at 9:00 a.m. and head straight for a relatively private audience with the real *Mona*.)

EMBODY MONA'S SMILE

Experiment with embodying Mona's facial expression, especially the famous smile. Note how you feel. Responses from people who have tried this exercise include:

+ "I feel like my mind is in two places at once."
+ "When I smile like that, I feel freer inside."
+ "It makes me feel like one of the cognoscenti."
+ "I felt an immediate transformation – everything was suddenly completely different."

Now go back to the most anxiety-producing questions from your Curiosità list. Only this time when you think about each question, embody Mona's smile. Does your thinking change when you look from Mona's perspective? Record your observations in your notebook.

INCUBATION AND INTUITION

Great musicians claim that their art comes to life in the spaces between notes. Master sculptors point to the space around their work as the secret of its power. Similarly, the spaces between your conscious efforts provide a key to creative living and problem solving. These spaces allow perceptions, ideas, and feelings to incubate.

When Leonardo was working on *The Last Supper,* he spent many days on the scaffold, painting from dawn until dusk; then, without warning, he would take a break. The prior of Santa Maria delle Grazie who contracted for his services was not amused. As Vasari noted, "The prior of the church entreated Leonardo with tiresome persistence to complete the work, since it seemed strange to him to see how Leonardo sometimes passed half a day at a time lost in thought, and he would have preferred Leonardo, just like the labourers hoeing in the garden, never to have laid down his brush." Vasari explains that the prior complained to the duke, who questioned Leonardo about his working habits. He tells us that Leonardo persuaded the duke that "the greatest geniuses sometimes accomplish more when they work less."

Clearly, Leonardo didn't underestimate his stature; yet pride in his abilities and confidence in the rhythms of incubation were balanced with

> "The eyes have the lustre and moisture always seen in living people, while around them are the lashes and all the reddish tones which cannot be produced without the greatest care. The eyebrows could not be more natural. . . . The nose seems lifelike with its beautiful pink and tender nostrils. The mouth, with its opening joining the red of the lips to the flesh of the face, seems to be real flesh rather than paint. Anyone who looked very attentively at the hollow of her throat would see her pulse beating."
>
> – GIORGO VASARI ON VIEWING THE *MONA LISA*

humility and delightful humor. Vasari relates that the maestro explained to the duke that he still had two faces to complete: Christ and Judas. The face of Christ, which ultimately was to remain unfinished, was a challenge that Leonardo felt to be beyond his powers, "for he was unwilling to seek a model on earth and unable to presume that his imagination could conceive of the beauty and celestial grace required of the divinity incarnate." As for the face of Judas, Leonardo explained to the duke that it would be a great challenge to find a model for one "so wicked as to betray his Lord the Creator of the World. Nonetheless, he would search for a model for this second face, but if in the end he could not find anything better, there was always the head of the prior."

Although your boss may not accept the idea that "the greatest geniuses sometimes accomplish more when they work less," the art of incubation is, nevertheless, essential to actualizing your creative potential. Almost everyone has experienced "sleeping on a problem" and awakening with a solution. But incubation is most effective when you alternate, as Leonardo did, between periods of intense, focused work and rest. Without periods of intense, focused work, there is nothing to be incubated.

Discovering and learning to trust your incubatory rhythms is a simple secret of accessing your intuition and creativity. Sometimes incubation yields an obvious insight, or Aha! But frequently the fruits of unconscious work are subtle and easy to overlook. The muses demand attention to the delicate nuances of thought, listening for the faint whispers of shy inner voices.

Neuroscientists estimate that your unconscious database outweighs the conscious on an order exceeding ten million to one. This database is the source of your creative potential. In other words, a part of you is much smarter than you are. The wisest people regularly consult that smarter part. You can, too, by making space for incubation.

TAKE TIME FOR SOLITUDE AND RELAXATION

Where are you when you get your best ideas? Over the past twenty years, I've asked thousands of people this question. The most frequent answers: "resting in bed," "walking in nature," "listening to music while driving in my car," and "relaxing in the shower or bath." Almost no one claims to get their best ideas at work.

What happens when you walk in the woods, rest in bed, or luxuriate in the shower that isn't happening in the workplace? Solitude and relaxation. Most people experience their breakthrough ideas when they are relaxed and by themselves.

Although Da Vinci loved exchanging ideas with others, he knew that his most creative insights came when he was alone. He wrote, "The painter must be solitary ... For if you are alone you are completely yourself, but if you are accompanied by a single companion you are half yourself."

Nurture Sfumato by taking time for solitude. Take a little time, at least once or twice a week, to go for a walk or just sit quietly by yourself.

"TAKE A LITTLE RELAXATION"

Many of us spend our days working hard in a focused, "left-brained" fashion. We sometimes get so involved in projects that we begin to lose perspective. You can increase your enjoyment and effectiveness when working or studying by taking breaks every hour or so. Modern psychological research shows that when you study or work for an hour, and then take a complete break for ten minutes, your recall for the material you have been working on is higher at the end of the ten-minute break than it was at the end of the hour. Psychologists call this phenomenon the Reminiscence Effect. In his *Treatise on Painting*, Da Vinci counseled "… it is well that you should often leave off work and take a little relaxation because when you come back to it you are a better judge …" Follow the maestro's advice and build the occasional ten-minute "brain break" into your busy schedule. Try listening to jazz or classical music,

Dr. Candace Pert, author of *Molecules of Emotion*, on the mind of your body: "Your brain is extremely well integrated with the rest of your body at a molecular level, so much so that the term *mobile brain* is an apt description of the psychosomatic network through which intelligent information travels from one system to another." Pert adds, "Every second, a massive information exchange is occurring in your body. Imagine each of these messenger systems possessing a specific tone, humming a signature tune, rising and falling, waxing and waning, binding and unbinding. . . ." Intuition is the art of listening, with an inner ear, to the rhythms and melodies of your own "body music."

creative doodling, meditation, or stretching exercises to promote relaxation and incubation. In addition to hourly breaks, be sure to enjoy some kind of weekly "Sabbath" and to take a true vacation every year.

TRUST YOUR GUT

Bring more attention to your everyday hunches and intuitions. Try writing them down in your notebook and then checking your accuracy. By monitoring your daily intuitions, you hone their accuracy.

Cultivating an accurate, reliable inner guidance system requires listening to your body. Comments such as "My gut tells me otherwise," "I just know it in my bones," "I can feel it in the pit of my stomach," and "I know in my heart of hearts that it must be true" reflect the body-centered nature of intuition.

When you take time for solitude – walking in nature, driving in your car, or just lying in bed – remember to listen to your bones and check in with your heart of hearts. Try the following exquisitely simple exercise, one or two times every day, for accessing the subtle nuances of your intuition:

Enjoy a few deep exhalations.

Soften your belly.

Be receptive.

SFUMATO AT WORK

In the 1980s, the American Management Association published a study concluding that the most successful managers were distinguished by "high tolerance for ambiguity and intuitive decision-making skill." Now, as the pace of change accelerates, "tolerance" for ambiguity is no longer sufficient; ambiguity must be embraced and enjoyed.

In *The Logic of Intuitive Decision Making*, Professor Weston Agor reported his discovery, made through extensive interviews, that senior executives overwhelmingly pointed to a failure to heed their own intuition as the prime cause of their worst decisions. As we begin the twenty-first century, information threatens to overwhelm us with sheer volume. Intuition is more important than ever.

The bottom line: Embrace ambiguity and trust your gut.

Arte/Scienza

The Development of the Balance between Science and Art, Logic and Imagination. "Whole-Brain" Thinking.

*A*re you familiar with the research into the left and right hemispheres of the cerebral cortex? If so, do you know your "brain-dominance profile"? In other words, are you a more artistic, intuitive, right-hemisphere thinker? Or do you feel more comfortable with the step-by-step logic of the left?

The terms *left-brained* and *right-brained* came into popular parlance through the Nobel prize-winning research of Professor Roger Sperry. Sperry discovered that in most cases, the left hemisphere of the cerebral cortex processes logical, analytical thinking while the right hemisphere processes imaginative, big-picture thinking.

Although our schools often pay lip service to the idea of the balanced Renaissance individual, in practice we suffer from a pandemic of "half-witted" thinking. In the words of Professor Sperry, "Our education system, as well as science in general, tends to neglect the non-verbal form of intellect. What it comes down to is that modern society discriminates against the right hemisphere." The result is that individuals with left-hemisphere dominance tend to do well in school but often fail to develop their creative capacities, while individuals who are right-hemisphere dominant often feel guilty for the way they think and are frequently mislabeled as "learning disabled."

Seekers of balance are inevitably drawn to a study of Leonardo. A significant part of our fascination with him is his stature as the supreme "whole-brain" thinker.

Art historian Kenneth Clark begins his essay on the relationship between Leonardo's science and art by emphasizing the interdependence of the disciplines: "It is usual to treat Leonardo as a scientist and Leonardo as a painter in separate studies. And no doubt the difficulties in following his mechanical and scientific investigations make this a prudent course.

Nevertheless, it is not completely satisfactory, because in the end the history of art cannot be properly understood without some reference to the history of science. In both we are studying the symbols by which man affirms his mental scheme, and these symbols, be they pictorial or mathematical, a fable or a formula, will reflect the same changes." Historian of science George Sarton reflects from a different perspective but reaches similar conclusions: "Since the growth of knowledge is the core of progress, the history of science ought to be the core of general history. Yet the main problems of life cannot be solved by men of science alone, or by artists and humanists: we need the cooperation of them all. Science is always indispensable but never sufficient. We are hungry for beauty, and where charity is lacking nothing else is of any avail." Sarton adds, "[Leonardo's] outstanding merit is to have shown by his own example that the pursuit of beauty and the pursuit of truth are not incompatible."

So, was Leonardo a scientist who studied art, or an artist who studied science? Clearly, he was both. His scientific studies of rocks, plants, flight, flowing water, and human anatomy, for example, are expressed in beautiful, evocative, expressive works of art, not dry technical drawings. At the same time, the plans for his paintings and sculptures are exquisitely detailed, painstakingly analytical, and mathematically precise.

As Jacob Bronowski, author of *The Ascent of Man,* comments, "[Leonardo] … took an artist's vision into science. He understood that science, as much as painting, has to find the design of nature in her detail … he gave science what is most needed, the artist's sense that the detail of nature is significant. Until science had this sense, no one could care – or could think that it mattered – how fast two unequal masses fall and whether the orbits of planets are accurately circles or ellipses."

For Leonardo, art and science were indivisible. In his *Treatise on Painting* he cautions potential adepts: "Those who become enamoured of the art, without having previously applied to the diligent study of the scientific part of it, may be compared to mariners who put to sea in a ship without rudder or compass and therefore cannot be certain of arriving at the wished for port."

Leonardo emphasized, for example, that the ability of the artist to express the beauty of the human form is predicated on a profound study of the science of anatomy. Lacking an appreciation born of a detailed analysis of bone structure and muscular relationships, the would-be artist was liable to draw "wooden and graceless nudes that seem rather as if you were looking at a stack of nuts than a human form, or a bundle of radishes rather than the muscles ..." He also noted, "Be sure you know the structure of all you wish to depict." Yet Kenneth Clark contends that Leonardo's science was predicated on his art: "It is often said that Leonardo drew so well because he knew about things; it is truer to say that he knew about things because he drew so well."

While championing rigor (one of his mottoes was *"Ostinate rigore!"* – Obstinate rigor!), attention to detail, logic, mathematics, and intense practical analysis, Leonardo also urged his students to awaken the power

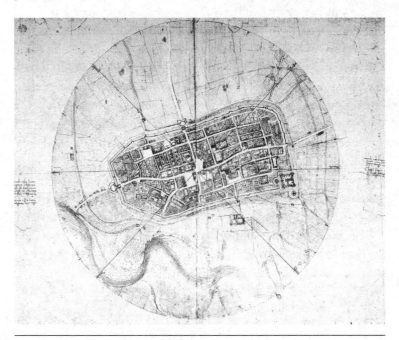

Map of Imola *by Leonardo da Vinci. Leonardo's ability to see the whole picture and the details allowed him to make remarkably accurate maps.*

The Role of the Artist in Leonardo's Time

At the time of Leonardo's birth, the artist was an anonymous craftsman with the social staus of a laborer. Artists worked in a setting more like a factory than a modern studio and were paid wages by the hour. Most of their products were collaborative efforts that remained unsigned. In pre-Renaissance Europe, all creativity was vested in the divine and the idea of human as creator was blasphemous.

In the course of Leonardo's lifetime, the artist's role transformed dramatically. Artists began to undertake work based on their own interests rather than the specific dictates of a patron. They began to sign their paintings and to write autobiographies, and biographies were written about them. Raphael, Titian, and Michelangelo became superstars in their own time, wealthy, respected, venerated.

The seeds of this remarkable transformation were planted by Leonardo's precursor, Leon Battista Alberti, in whose day arithmetic, geometry, astronomy, music, grammar, logic, and rhetoric were accepted, among the intellectual elite, as the noble disciplines, the foundations of knowledge. Painting was not included, but Alberti saw that the emerging mathematically based disciplines of proportion and perspective could provide the common ground for painting and the noble disciplines. Leonardo seized this idea and extended it. His formulation of painting as a science placed his beloved practice of "knowing how to see" first among the liberal arts. Da Vinci's urgings to "go straight to nature," to be an original, what he called an *"inventore,"* served to transform not only the role of the artist but the very concept of genius.

of imagination in what was, then, an unprecedented way. Offering what he called "a new and speculative idea, which although it may seem trivial and almost laughable, is none the less of great value in quickening the spirit of invention," he urged students to stare at stones, smoke, embers, clouds, and mud, and cultivate their ability to see in these mundane forms "the likeness of divine landscapes ... and an infinity of things." Such insight, he writes, "comes about as it does with the sound of bells, in whose clanging you may discover every name and word that you can imagine."

"Study the science of art and the art of science."
– LEONARDO DA VINCI

This instruction represents more than just advice to stimulate an artist's imagination; it is a breakthrough in the evolution of human thought. Da Vinci gave birth to a tradition that resulted in the modern discipline of "brainstorming." Prior to Da Vinci the concept of "creative thinking" as an intellectual discipline didn't exist.

ARTE/SCIENZA AND YOU

While all the principles in this book can help you balance your hemispheres and awaken your latent Da Vincian capabilities, you can concentrate on that balance by using one simple, tremendously powerful method for cultivating a synergy between Arte and Scienza in your everyday thinking, planning, and problem solving. The method is called mind mapping.

Mind mapping is a whole-brain method for generating and organizing ideas, originated by Tony Buzan, and largely inspired by Da Vinci's approach to note taking. You can use mind mapping for personal goal setting, daily planning, and interpersonal problem solving. It can help you at work, with your kids, or with any pursuit. The most marvelous application of mind mapping, however, is that through regular practice it trains you to be a more balanced thinker, à la Leonardo.

Let's set the stage for learning to mind map by considering the method that most of us learned for generating and organizing ideas: the outline.

ARTE/SCIENZA AT WORK

Ned Hermann, founder of the Whole Brain Corporation, developed a test to determine hemispheric dominance. In his workshops, Hermann has been known to take those who test out as "ultra-left" and "ultra-right," and give them a special assignment. They are allowed two hours to complete it. The ultra-left-brained group returns exactly on time, having completed a typewritten report, with all the i's dotted and t's crossed. Beautifully organized, their report is painfully boring and uninspired. The ultra-right-hemisphere group involves itself in a philosophical debate on the meaning of the assignment. They return at different times with ideas scratched on scrap paper, disorganized and generally useless.

The two groups are then combined into one, with a facilitator guiding them as they work together on another task. They return on time with a balanced, organized, creative product. The lesson: Effectiveness demands the creation of balanced brain teams.

More often than not, however, individuals tend to polarize by hemispheric style. The left-brain dominants in the finance department gather by their coffee machine, look over at the right-brained marketing people, and think, "Those flaky dreamers have their heads in the clouds. They don't understand the bottom line like we do." Meanwhile, at the right-brained watercooler, the right-brainers are eyeing the left-brainers and thinking, "What tiny minds those bean counters have. They don't see the whole picture like we do."

Individuals often fall into a similar trap internally. Left-brainers think, "I'm sorry, I'm left-brained. I can't possibly be creative or imaginative." And right-brainers make the mistake of programming themselves: "Well, I'm right-brained – I can't possibly come to meetings on time."

Since 1978 I've worked with thousands of managers at all levels. Some are analytical, serious, thorough planners; others are intuitive, playful, spontaneous improvisers. The very best are those who balance analysis and intuition, seriousness and play, planning and improvisation, Arte and Scienza.

The traditional outline begins with "Roman numeral I." Have you ever spent an inordinate amount of time waiting for idea Roman numeral I? Perhaps you finally get it after twenty minutes or so and continue your outline down to point IIId, when you realize that point IIId should be point IIb. You cross it out and draw an arrow. Now your outline is getting messy. And we all know that outlines must be *neat*. Frustrated, you start to doodle or daydream. Your repressed "right hemisphere" is attempting to express itself, but doodling makes your outline even messier, and you feel guilty for daydreaming. Beset and beleaguered by this internecine cortical strife, you crumple up your paper and try to begin again.

Although valuable as a tool for presenting ideas in a formal, orderly fashion, *outlining is useful only after the real thinking has been done*. If you try to generate your ideas by outlining, you will find that it slows you down and stifles your freedom of thought. It is just plain illogical to try to organize your ideas before you've generated them.

Moreover, outlining and other linear note-making systems exclude your brain's capacity for color, dimension, synthesis, rhythm, and image. By imposing one color and one form, outlining guarantees monotony. Outlining uses only half of your mind, and half a mind is a terrible thing to waste.

Mind mapping frees you from the tyranny of premature organization, which stifles your generation of ideas. Mind mapping liberates your conceptual powers by balancing generation and organization while encouraging the full range of mental expression.

Think about the last book you read or the last seminar you attended. Imagine that you have to write a report on that book or seminar. Begin recalling the information. As you do, observe the process of your mind at work.

Does your mind work by constructing whole paragraphs or by presenting ordered outlines to your mind's eye? Probably not. Chances are that impressions, key words, and images float into mind, one associating with the next. Mind mapping is a method for continuing this natural thinking process on paper.

Pages like this one from Leonardo's notebooks helped inspire the creation of modern mind mapping.

Leonardo urged artists and scientists to "go straight to nature" in the search for knowledge and understanding. If you contemplate the structure of a tree or a plant like the star-of-Bethlehem, you can see that it is a network of life, expanding in all directions from its trunk or stem. Take a helicopter ride over a major city; it is a sprawling structure of interconnecting centers and pathways, main arteries connecting with side roads. Our water table, global telecommunication system, and solar system are similarly linked networks. The structure of communication in nature is nonlinear and self-organizing; it works through networks and systems.

Perhaps the most amazing natural system of all is right inside your skull. The basic structural unit of brain function is the neuron. Each of our billions of neurons branches out from a center, called the nucleus. Each branch, or dendrite (from *dendron*, meaning "tree"), is covered with little nodes called dendritic spines. As we think, electrochemical "information" jumps across the tiny gap between spines. This junction is called a synapse. Our thinking is a function of a vast network of synaptic patterns. A mind map is a graphic expression of these natural patterns of the brain.

It should not be too surprising, therefore, that the note-taking styles of many of history's great brains – such as Charles Darwin, Michelangelo, Mark Twain, and of course, Leonardo da Vinci – feature a branching,

The metaphor of left and right hemispheres of the cerebral cortex.

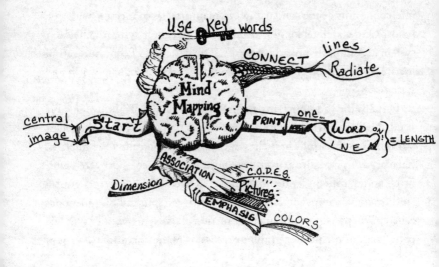

Mind Map on the Rules of Mind Mapping.

organic structure complemented by lots of sketches, creative doodles, and key words.

How right- or left-brained are you? Before you set out to learn to mind map your way to whole-brain thinking, spend a few minutes reflecting on your own "hemispheric proclivities." Which of the statements opposite apply to you?

The first ten statements contain a classic description of someone who is more left-brained. The second ten statements contain characteristics associated with a more right-brained person. Of course, most people are more complex than this simple model suggests. Nevertheless, the metaphor of left and right is a useful tool for thinking about balance.

Whatever your hemispheric tendencies happen to be, the key to fulfilling your full potential is the continuing discovery of balance.

Arte/Scienza:
Self-Assessment

- ❏ I like details.
- ❏ I am almost always on time.
- ❏ I am skilled at math.
- ❏ I rely on logic.
- ❏ I write clearly.
- ❏ Friends describe me as very articulate.
- ❏ Analysis is one of my strengths.
- ❏ I am organized and disciplined.
- ❏ I like lists.
- ❏ I read a book starting at page one and go through in order.

- ❏ I am highly imaginative.
- ❏ I am good at brainstorming.
- ❏ I often say or do the unexpected.
- ❏ I love to doodle.
- ❏ In school I was better at geometry than algebra.
- ❏ I read a book by skipping around.
- ❏ I prefer to look at the big picture and leave the details to someone else.
- ❏ I often lose track of time.
- ❏ I rely on intuition.

ARTE/SCIENZA:
APPLICATIONS
AND EXERCISES

LEARN THE RULES OF MIND MAPPING

At the end of the *Treatise on Painting*, Leonardo wrote, "These rules are intended to help you to a free and good judgement: for good judgement proceeds from good understanding, and good understanding comes from reason trained by good rules, and good rules are the children of sound experience, which is the common mother of all the sciences and arts."

The rules of mind mapping are "intended to help you to a free and good judgement." They are "the children of sound experience," having been extensively tested and refined over the past thirty years.

All you need to begin mind mapping is a topic, a few colored pens, and a large sheet of paper. Follow these rules:

1) Begin your mind map with a *symbol* or a *picture* (representing your topic) at the *center* of your page.
Starting at the center opens your mind to a full 360 degrees of association. Pictures and symbols are much easier to remember than words and enhance your ability to think creatively about your subject.

2) Write down key words.
Key words are the information-rich "nuggets" of recall and creative association.

3) Connect the key words with lines radiating from your central image.

By linking words with lines ("branches"), you'll show clearly how one key word relates to another.

4) Print your key words.

Printing is easier to read and remember than writing.

5) Print *one* key word per line.

By doing this, you free yourself to discover the maximum number of creative associations for each key word. The discipline of one word per line also trains you to focus on the most appropriate key word, enhancing the precision of your thought and minimizing clutter.

6) Print your key words on the lines and make the length of the word the same as the line it is on.

This maximizes clarity of association and encourages economy of space.

7) Use colors, pictures, dimension, and codes for greater association and emphasis.

Highlight important points and illustrate relationships between different branches of your mind map. You might, for instance, prioritize your main points through color coding, highlighting in yellow the most important points, using blue for secondary points, and so forth. Pictures and images, preferably in vivid color, should be used wherever possible; they stimulate your creative association and greatly enhance your memory.

MAKE YOUR OWN MIND MAP

As you experiment with mind mapping, its advantages will become increasingly obvious. Mind mapping allows you to start quickly and generate more ideas in less time; you'll find that thinking, working, and problem solving become a lot more fun. All outlines tend to look the same, but every mind map is different. Perhaps the greatest advantage of mind mapping is that by nurturing your unique, individual self-expression it guides you to discover your own originality. Regular practice of mind mapping will help you become an *"inventore."*

This simple mind-mapping exercise will help you get started:

1) Begin with a large sheet of blank white paper and six or more colored pens. You may want to use phosphorescent highlighters for extra color. Of course, one pen or pencil and a small sheet of paper will work in a pinch.

Although you can make mind maps on the backs of matchbooks, in the palm of your hand, or on Post-it notes, it's best to use a big sheet of paper; flip-chart size is recommended. The bigger the paper, the greater the freedom to express your associations.

Place the paper horizontally in front of you. A horizontal disposition makes it easier for you to keep all your key words upright and easy to read.

2) Let's say that the topic for this mind map is the Renaissance.

+ Start your mind map by drawing a representative image in the middle of the paper.
+ Draw it as vividly as you can, using more than one color.
+ Have fun and don't worry about the accuracy of your drawing.

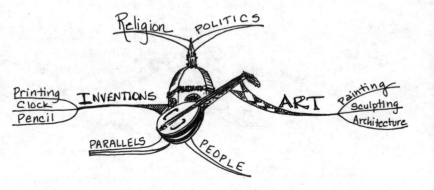

3) Now print key words or draw images on lines radiating out from your central image. (Remember to print *on* the lines, *one* key word or image per line, and keep the lines connected.)

✦ Generating ideas in key-word form is easy. For example, as you think about the Renaissance, one key word might be *art*, which might trigger other key-word associations, like *painting, sculpture, architecture*. Another key branch could be *inventions*, triggering associations such as *printing, clock, pencil*. Other main branches might include *people, politics, religion, parallels*.

✦ If you feel stuck, choose any key word on your mind map and immediately print your first association with that word – even if it seems ridiculous or irrelevant. Keep your associations flowing and don't worry about making sure that every word is "right."

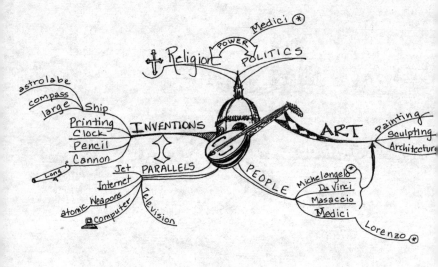

4) When you feel you have generated enough material through free association, look at the result: all your ideas spread across one page.

+ As you examine your mind map, you will see relationships that help you organize and integrate your ideas.
+ Look for words that appear repeatedly throughout the map. They often suggest major themes.

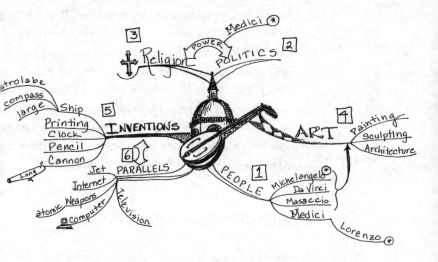

5) Connect related parts of your mind map with arrows, codes, and colors.

+ Eliminate elements that seem extraneous. Pare your mind map down to just the ideas you need for your purpose.
+ Then put them in sequence, if necessary. This can be accomplished with numbers or by redrawing the mind map in clockwise order.

How do you know that your mind map is finished? Theoretically, a mind map never ends. As Da Vinci emphasized, "Everything is connected to everything else." If you had the time, energy, inclination, enough colored pens, and a big enough piece of paper, you could go on linking all your knowledge and ultimately all human knowledge. Of course, if you are planning a speech or studying for an examination, you probably don't have time to link all human knowledge. The simple answer is that your mind map is finished when the information you have generated meets your objectives for the task at hand.

PRACTICE YOUR MIND-MAPPING SKILLS

Although mind mapping is an invaluable tool for simplifying complex tasks such as strategic planning, presentation preparation, meeting management, test preparation, and systems analysis, it is probably best to

Some tips for keeping your mind map neat, easy, and organized. Keep your central image in the center of the page and limit its size. Use angled and curved lines as necessary to keep all your key words upright and easy to read. Use just one word per line and be sure to *print* the key words. Make the lines a bit thicker at their origin and print your letters at least one-quarter inch in height so they are easy to read. You can print some letters even larger for emphasis. Make each word the same size as the line underneath it. This saves space and allows you to see connections more clearly. If possible, use large sheets of paper. This helps to avoid crowding and encourages you to think big. Do not be concerned if your first draft seems disorganized. You can make a second or third draft for further clarification.

make your first few mind maps on relatively simple, lighthearted subjects. Choose one of the following topics to begin practicing your mind-mapping skill, solo. Take about twenty minutes for this first practice map.

+ **Mind Map Your Next Day Off** – Begin with a simple drawing that represents a free day (e.g., a smiling sun, a calendar page). Print key words and draw images that express some things you might like to do on your next day off. Remember to put key words and images on lines radiating out from your central symbol.

+ **Mind Map Your Dream Vacation** – Explore the delightful fantasy of a dream vacation using a mind map. Start with a symbol of your paradise in the center (e.g., ocean waves, snow-covered mountains, the Eiffel Tower), and then branch out with key words and images that represent the elements of your ideal holiday.

+ **Mind Map a Perfect Evening for a Friend** – Use a mind map to explore the design of a perfect evening for someone you love. Start with an image in the center that represents your friend. Then, using key words or images, branch out with all your thoughts for your friend's happiness. Remember, let your mind work by association instead of trying to put things down in order. Just generate ideas for your friend's delight. Then after you have come up with a multitude of possibilities, you can go back and put them in order.

Review your mind map of your day off, dream vacation, or perfect evening. Check your mind map to see how well you followed the rules:

- Did you create vivid, multicolored images?
- Did you remember to use just one word per line?
- Did you print your key words?
- Did you keep your lines connected?

If you departed from the rules, redo your map correctly.

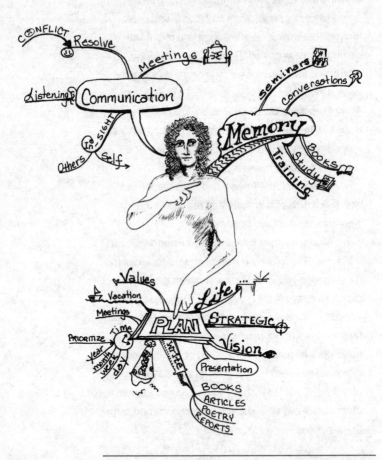

As you can see, there are many possible uses of mind mapping. The two final exercises in this chapter guide you to use this thinking tool in ways that are particularly inspired by the maestro.

MAKE A MIND-MAPPING MIND MAP

Okay, now that you are warmed up, try making a mind map on all possible uses of mind mapping. Start with an image in the center of the page that represents the concept of mind mapping for you. Then branch out, putting printed key words or images on connected lines. Aim to generate at least twenty *specific* possible applications of mind mapping in your personal and professional life. After you have completed your mind map, highlight what you think might be the most valuable applications. Then look at the Applications Map on the previous page for some of the most popular uses of mind mapping.

MAKE A MEMORY MIND MAP

Leonardo's incredible ability to learn and create was predicated on his cultivation of memory, what he called "learning by heart." After careful observation from multiple perspectives, Leonardo drew a visual image of his subject. Then, late at night or early in the morning, as he lay in bed, he would review and vivify the image in his mind's eye. Then he compared his mental image to his best drawing until he could hold the perfect image in his mind.

Mind mapping is a tremendously powerful tool for learning things by heart. Try the following exercise, based on Leonardo's method, for committing something to memory:

- Think of something you would like to remember – perhaps the content of a book you particularly enjoy; a presentation you plan to give; or all the material for a final exam at school or in college.

- Make a comprehensive mind map of your subject, emphasizing vivid images of your most important points. You may, depending on the volume and complexity of your material, need to do multiple drafts to organize, integrate, and clearly express your subject.

- When you complete your "master mind map," put it aside. Take a blank sheet of paper and, without referring back to the original, attempt to re-create your master map from memory. Do this until you can re-create your original in detail.

- When you are resting in bed, picture your master map in your mind's eye. Practice visualizing until your mental image matches your master map.

- Now give your presentation or take your test with *perfect recall* of your material.

MAKE A CREATIVITY MIND MAP

Mind mapping is a wonderful tool for awakening your creativity and, in Leonardo's words, "quickening the spirit of invention." Think of an idea you would like to explore, or a question or challenge that requires some fresh thinking. Get a large sheet of blank paper and in the center draw an abstract image of your topic. Now, just as the maestro suggested free-associating in response to "certain walls stained with damp or at stones of uneven color," free-associate with your abstract image, recording your associations on the branches of your

ARTE/SCIENZA FOR PARENTS

Many of my clients and friends with more than one child report that their kids have different brain "styles," and that if they are not careful, they will tend to pass on the prejudices of their own dominant mode. As a "left-dominant" parent commented, "You know, I've been a fool. I have two kids; one is just like me – very good at math and figures, disciplined and focused. My other kid is totally different – a real dreamer, very artistic but all over the place. Last night I realized that I have been discriminating against my more right-brained child. If I was more open to him and encouraged him to share his way of looking at things with his brother and me, then we would all be better off."

Just as we build "balanced-brain teams" in the workplace, it is also important do so at home. Many parents unwittingly pass on their cortical prejudices to their children. Support your kids in developing the skills of Arte and Scienza together. If your child shows a preference for right-brain thinking, tackle history lessons by acting out scenes from the past. Approach mathematics by writing out theorems and equations in bold colors. Help your child be on time by making a color-coded, picture-filled calendar. If your child's orientation is more left-brained, help her to develop balance by emphasizing art, drama, and music appreciation. Whatever your child's brain dominance, she will become more balanced if you encourage her to use mind maps; focus especially on nurturing your child's ability to "learn by heart" by making memory mind maps of schoolwork.

map. If you let your mind go, you will, in the maestro's words, "be able to see ... an infinity of things, which you will be able to reduce to their complete and proper forms."

If you think of an idea that seems "off the wall," put it in your mind map and keep going. Absurd and unusual associations often lead to creative breakthroughs. Remember that even the greatest genius of all time was concerned that his "new and speculative idea ... may seem trivial and almost laughable." But he did not let that stop him, and neither should you.

+ After you have generated an abundance, if not an infinity, of associations, take a break for incubation.
+ Then come back to your mind map, and generate another wave of associations.
+ After another break, review the big picture of your associations, looking for connections and emerging themes.
+ Next "reduce them to their complete and proper forms." In other words, pare your map down to express your most cogent insights; reorder the branches to reflect a new organization of your thoughts.

After applying the mind-map method of "learning by heart," a twelve-year-old boy from Soweto, South Africa, wrote: "Before ... I did not think I was very smart. Now I know I have a wonderful brain. Now my school is much easier!" A manager from a Japanese computer company used mind mapping to generate ideas for a strategic plan and wrote, "Thank you very much, for finally, you wake up my brain." A chemical engineer from a Fortune 500 company used this approach to create a new patentable invention; the poet laureate of Great Britain uses it to incubate new poems. You can use it too, for strengthening your memory, balancing your brain, and "quickening your spirit of invention."

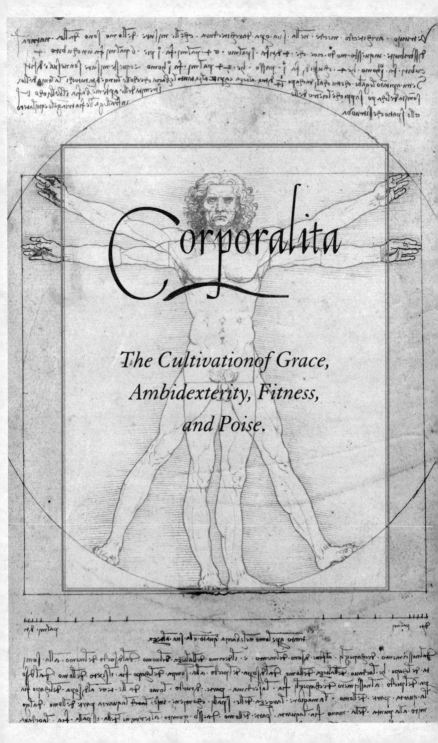

Corporalita

The Cultivation of Grace,
Ambidexterity, Fitness,
and Poise.

What is your image of the body type of a genius? Did you grow up, as I did, with the stereotype of the skinny, "four-eyed," brainiac nerd? It's amazing how many people associate high intelligence with physical ineptitude. With a few exceptions, the great geniuses of history were gifted with remarkable physical energy and aptitude, none more so than Da Vinci.

Leonardo's extraordinary physical gifts complemented his intellectual and artistic genius. Vasari extols his "great physical beauty … and more than infinite grace in every action." Among the citizens of Florence, Leonardo was renowned for his poise, grace, and athleticism. His skill as an equestrian was

> "Handsome and with a splendid physique, he seemed a model of human perfection."
> – Goethe on Da Vinci

of a very high level. And his strength was legendary. Witnesses describe Leonardo stopping horses at full gallop by catching their reins and bending horseshoes and door knockers with his bare hands! As Vasari records, "His great physical strength could check any violent outburst; with his right hand he could bend the iron ring of a door knocker or a horseshoe as if it were made of lead." Vasari adds, "His great personal strength was joined to dexterity …"

A number of scholars have suggested that Leonardo's passion for anatomy was a reflection of his own extraordinary physique. Dr. Kenneth Keele, author of "Leonardo da Vinci, the Anatomist," refers to him as "a unique genetic mutation" and emphasizes that his "approach to the

---

The Canon of Proportion: *This is Leonardo's drawing of the ideal proportions of the human figure based on De Architectura by Vitruvius from the first century B.C. It is used internationally as an icon of human potential.*

> "*Death in old men, when not from fever, is caused by the veins … which thicken so much in the walls that they become closed up and leave no passage for the blood.*"
>
> – LEONARDO DA VINCI

anatomy of the human body was significantly influenced by his own remarkable physical attributes." Walking, riding, swimming, and fencing were the maestro's preferred forms of regular exercise. In his anatomical notebooks he reasoned that arteriosclerosis causes accelerated aging and is the result of lack of exercise. A vegetarian and accomplished chef, Da Vinci believed that a thoughtful diet was a key to health and well-being. Da Vinci also cultivated the balanced use of both sides of his body, painting, drawing, and writing with both hands. He was psychophysically ambidextrous.

Da Vinci believed that we should accept personal responsibility for our health and well-being. He recognized the effect of attitudes and emotions on physiology (anticipating the discipline of psychoneuroimmunology) and counseled independence from doctors and medicines. His philosophy of medicine was holistic. He viewed sickness as "the discord of the elements infused into the living body" and viewed healing as "the restoration of discordant elements."

Leonardo urged, "Learn to preserve your health!" and offered the following specific advice on maintaining well-being:

"To keep in health these rules are wise:

+ Beware of anger and avoid grievous moods.
+ Rest your head and keep your mind cheerful.
+ Be covered well at night.
+ Exercise moderately.
+ Shun wantonness, and pay attention to diet.
+ Eat only when you want and sup light.
+ Keep upright when you rise from the dining table.
+ Do not be with the belly upwards or the head lowered.
+ Let your wine be mixed with water, take a little at a time, not between meals and not on an empty stomach.

- ✦ Eat simple (i.e., vegetarian) food.
- ✦ Chew well.
- ✦ Go to the toilet regularly!"

CORPORALITA AND YOU

What is your personal approach to cultivating fitness and developing mind/body coordination? What is your image of your own body? How much are you influenced by external factors – such as magazine articles, the fashion industry, images on television, other people's opinions – in determining your own body image? Whatever your God-given strengths or weaknesses, you can dramatically improve the quality of your life through a comprehensive approach to Corporalita. Begin by considering the self-assessment on the next page.

Corporalita: Self-Assessment

- ❏ I am aerobically fit.
- ❏ I am getting stronger.
- ❏ My flexibility is improving.
- ❏ I know when my body is tense or relaxed.
- ❏ I am knowledgeable about diet and nutrition.
- ❏ Friends would describe me as graceful.
- ❏ I am becoming more ambidextrous.
- ❏ I am aware of the ways in which my physical state affects my attitudes.
- ❏ I am aware of the ways in which my attitudes affect my physical state.
- ❏ I have a good understanding of practical anatomy.
- ❏ I am well coordinated.
- ❏ I love to move.

CORPORALITA: APPLICATION AND EXERCISES

DEVELOP A FITNESS PROGRAM

Da Vinci's life was an expression of the ancient classical ideal of *"mens sana in corpore sano,"* a sound mind in a sound body. Modern scientific studies confirm many of Da Vinci's recommendations, practices, and intuitions. Although it is a bit difficult to picture the maestro in a modern aerobics class, a personal fitness program is, nonetheless, a cornerstone of physical health, mental acuity, and emotional well-being. To actualize your potential as a Renaissance man or woman, maintain a balanced fitness program that develops aerobic capacity, strength, and flexibility.

Aerobic conditioning: Leonardo guessed that arteriosclerosis was a cause of premature aging, and that it could be prevented by regular exercise. Dr. Kenneth Cooper and many other modern scientists have confirmed the maestro's intuition. Cooper, the originator of the concept of aerobics, found that regular moderate exercise has profoundly beneficial effects for the body and mind. Aerobic ("with oxygen") exercise strengthens your cardiovascular system, improving blood and therefore oxygen flow to your body and brain. Your brain is, on average, less than 3 percent of your body's weight, yet it uses more than 30 percent of your body's oxygen. As you become aerobically fit, you double your capacity to process oxygen.

Da Vinci was highly critical of the physicians of his day. He wrote, "Every man wishes to make money to give to the doctors, destroyers of life: they therefore ought to be rich." And he counseled, "... shun physicians because their drugs are a kind of alchemy ... he who takes medicines is ill-advised."

A regular program of aerobic exercise leads to significant improvements in alertness, emotional stability, mental acuity, and stamina. For an individual who is "out of shape" it generally takes six weeks of exercising for at least twenty minutes, four times a week to yield marked benefits. (Consult your physician for guidance on beginning your own program.) The secret of a successful aerobic training program is to find activities that you enjoy. Brisk walking, running, dancing, swimming, rowing, or martial arts training can be combined to create your ideal program.

Strength training: Leonardo's legendary ability to bend horseshoes with his bare hands and stop runaway horses in their tracks is probably outside the grasp of even the most ambitious denizen of the weight room. Nevertheless, moderate strength training is a valuable part of a balanced approach to fitness. Weight training tones and strengthens muscles and promotes the resilience of connective tissue and bone. Recent research suggests that strength training helps prevent muscle wasting and osteoporosis in the elderly. And it is also the most efficient way to burn excess body fat. To begin your own strength-training program, find a good coach or trainer and seek guidance on developing and maintaining proper form.

Flexibility exercises: Vasari tells us that Leonardo's remarkable strength was "joined to dexterity." You can increase your dexterity with regular flexibility training. Practice simple stretching exercises before and after aerobic and strength workouts and upon arising. Proper stretching prevents injury and benefits your circulatory and immune systems. The secret to a good stretch is to take your time, bring your full awareness to the process, and allow easy release of muscle groups in harmony with extended exhalations. Never bounce or try to force a stretch. You can learn how to get the most from your stretches in a dance or martial arts class or, ideally, by studying yoga.

DEVELOP BODY AWARENESS BY STUDYING PRACTICAL ANATOMY

A healthy diet and aerobic, strength, and flexibility training are key elements in achieving and maintaining well-being; but your fitness regimen is incomplete without a constructive approach to body awareness, poise, and ambidexterity. These elements form the "missing link" in many fitness programs.

In the path of self-development people commonly contemplate the classic question "Who am I?" You can make significant progress in self-realization by asking an even more basic question, "Where am I?" Body image and body awareness play a tremendous role in determining self-image and self-awareness. In the Sensazione chapter you were introduced to a program of exercises for sharpening the five senses: sight,

The Da Vinci Diet

Combined with aerobic conditioning, strength training, and flexibility exercises, a healthy diet will help you live a longer, happier, more balanced life. Although diet fads come and go, there are some fundamental truths of intelligent eating that withstand the tests of time and scientific scrutiny:

+ Seek food that is fresh, natural, and wholesome. Leonardo didn't have to be concerned about avoiding overly processed, additive-injected "junk" foods, but we do.

+ Eat plenty of fiber. Raw and lightly cooked vegetables, grains, beans, and other fiber-rich foods were the mainstay of Leonardo's diet. These foods "brush" and exercise your digestive tract, keeping it active and healthy.

+ Avoid overeating. Leonardo counseled, "Sup light." Learn to stop eating *just before* you are full. You will feel better and probably live longer (numerous experiments by Drs. McCay, Masaro, and others have shown that rats who are slightly underfed live twice as long as those who gorge themselves.)

+ Get enough water. Every traditional Italian table is set with numerous bottles of pure mineral water. Your body is 80 percent water, and it needs a regular resupply to flush away toxins and rebuild cells. So make water-rich foods (vegetables and fresh fruits) an integral part of your daily dining. When thirsty, drink *pure* (distilled or spring) water or fresh fruit/vegetable juice. Avoid swilling colas and other so-called soft drinks. They are filled with additives and empty calories.

+ Minimize your intake of additional salt and sugar. A balanced diet will give you plenty of natural salts and sugars. Too much salt can contribute to hypertension and other maladies; excess sugar distorts your metabolism and loads you up with useless calories. Avoid being seduced by the short-term energy surge that seems to come from a sugary snack; if you pay attention, you'll notice that it is usually followed shortly by a depression of vitality. Aim to wean yourself from sprinkling salt or spooning sugar onto your foods; at the very least, taste your food before adding either.

- Moderate your intake of fats, and minimize saturated fats. Use cold-pressed healthy oils like olive (Leonardo's favorite), canola, and flaxseed, and avoid margarine altogether.
- Eat only "free-range" meats, in moderation. The maestro was a vegetarian. His favorite everyday dish was minestrone soup, composed of vegetables, beans, and rice or pasta. Nevertheless, if you do eat meat, enjoy one serving per day as a recommended maximum. Avoid eating animals that have been fed growth hormones, antibiotics, and other toxins.
- Vary your diet. A varied diet is more likely to be balanced and enjoyable.
- Enjoy a little wine with dinner. Leonardo recommended enjoying wine with food, in moderation; but he decried overuse and drunkenness. Actuarial statistics demonstrate that moderate alcohol consumption (defined as up to two glasses of wine or two beers per day) seems to prolong average life span for two years. There is also significant evidence that moderate daily enjoyment of red wine with food improves circulation and can help prevent heart disease. Of course, as the maestro knew, drinking beyond moderation has the opposite effects, shortening life span and pickling the nervous system.
- Don't eat, *dine*. "Grabbing a bite" while "eating on the run" usually leads to poor dietary choices and much subsequent indigestion. Instead, discipline yourself to sit down and enjoy every meal. Create, as the maestro did, an aesthetically pleasing environment: a nice place setting, flowers on the table, an artful presentation of even the simplest foods. A pleasant atmosphere and an unhurried pace improve your digestion, your equanimity, and the quality of your life.
- Most important, listen to your body before every meal and determine what you actually want to eat. As Leonardo emphasized, "Eating contrary to the inclination is injurious to the health." If in doubt, imagine how you will feel *after* you eat the food in question. Then pause for a few moments before eating and bring your awareness to the present moment. Savor the smell, taste, and texture of every bite. Make every meal an experience of Sensazione.

hearing, smell, taste, and touch. Cultivation of body awareness begins with honing the sixth sense: kinesthesia. The kinesthetic sense is your sense of weight, position, and movement. It tells you whether you are relaxed or tense, awkward or graceful.

You can begin to sharpen your kinesthetic sense and increase your self-awareness by experimenting with the following exercises.

Mirror Observation

Stand in front of a full-length mirror (if you are courageous, do this naked). Avoid judging or evaluating your appearance, just observe your reflection objectively. Does your head tend to tilt to one side or the other? Is one shoulder higher than the other? Does your pelvis rock forward or is it held back? Is your weight distributed evenly on your feet or do you depend on one leg more than the other for support? What parts of your body appear to be overly tense? Are your pelvis, torso, and head in a balanced alignment? Record your observations in your notebook.

Make a Drawing of Your Own Body

In your notebook make a sketch of your whole body. Don't worry about creating a masterpiece, just do a simple five-minute rendering; even a modified stick figure will be fine.

After you've sketched your whole body, color in red the places where you feel the most tension and stress. Then with a black marker, delineate the points in your body where your energy seems blocked, the parts where you feel the least. Next use a green color to indicate the areas of your body that feel most alive, where the energy flows most freely.

Most people have significant areas of red and black. Much of our unnecessary tension and stress is a result of ignorance and misinformation regarding our own natural structure and function. Inaccurate "body maps" result in misuse, exacerbating stress and dulling awareness.

Explore Your Body Map

Return to the mirror, and with the index finger of either hand, point to:

+ the place where your head balances on your neck;
+ your shoulder joints;
+ your hip joints.

Now look at Leonardo's illustration of the human body to begin clarifying your "body map."

Head Balance: The head is poised at the very top of the spine, at the atlanto-occipital joint. Most people locate the balance point of the head too low because they have an unconscious habit of shortening their neck muscles every time they move.

Shoulder Joints: Most people locate the shoulder joint at the point where the upper arm attaches to the torso. They miss the connection of the collarbone and sternum, remaining unaware of the true mobility of this complex of joints. This inaccurate "body mapping" is associated with a tendency to freeze the entire shoulder girdle, causing significant discomfort.

Hip Joints: Just as the shoulder joint must be differentiated from "the shoulders," so the hip joints must be differentiated from "the hips." Watch a toddler bend to pick up a toy and you'll see the natural use of the hip joint. Then observe the average adult bending to pick

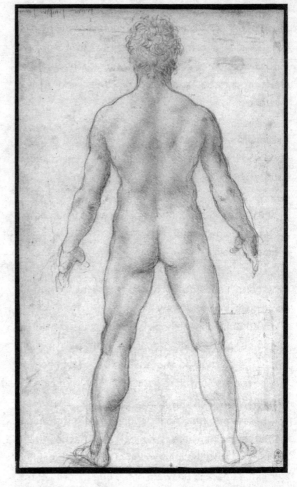

something up and you will see that he or she probably bends at "the waist." Bending from the waist, rather than the hip joints, is a significant cause of lower back pain.

Know Your Spine

Refine your body map a bit further by exploring your assumptions about your spine. How wide do you think your spine is? Draw your estimate of the spine's width in your notebook. Now think about the natural shape of the spine. In your notebook, sketch the shape of a healthy spine. Be sure to complete both sketches before reading any further.

Your spine is wider than you may imagine.

Heavy Thoughts
How much does your head weigh? Jot down your best guess.

Next time you are in the gym pick up a fifteen-pound barbell, or when you visit the supermarket, hoist a fifteen-pound bag of potatoes. That is how much the average head weighs. This fifteen-pound globe contains your brain, eyes, ears, nose, mouth, and balance mechanism. What happens to your whole body if this globe is out of balance? What happens to your awareness and sensory acuity if your head is not properly aligned at the top of your spine? Did you know that 60 percent of your receptors for kinesthetic awareness are located in the neck? What happens to body awareness if the neck muscles are held in contraction to support a poorly balanced head?

Clearly, for the aspiring Renaissance man or woman, head balance is a top priority. You can deepen your appreciation for this question of balance with the following exercise.

Experience the Evolution of the Upright Posture
This exercise was inspired by the work of the great anatomist and anthropologist Professor Raymond Dart, whom I was privileged to interview on a number of occasions. I have led this exercise for many groups over the years including company presidents, martial artists, psychologists, schoolteachers, and police officers.

Although it is particularly fun to do this exercise in a group, you can still get the value by doing it on your own. All you need is some clean, carpeted floor space and a towel.

+ Begin by lying facedown on the floor, with your feet together and your hands resting at your sides. (Put the towel under your face.) Notice that it is now impossible to fall. Rest facedown for a minute or two and contemplate the consciousness of a creature with this kind of relationship to gravity. Experiment with slithering along the floor toward an imaginary morsel of food.

+ Now get ready for an evolutionary leap. You are about to mutate. Slide the back of your hands along the floor beside you until they flip over so that your palms are now on the floor in front of you. Press down with your newly evolved paws to raise your head and upper torso off the ground. Look around and consider the leap in consciousness allowed by your expanded horizon. Experiment with using your paws to help you explore your environment and move toward food.

+ Next evolve to become a mammalian quadruped. Choose your favorite: horse, dog, cougar, gazelle, water buffalo … Move up onto all fours, and just for fun, imitate the gait, sounds, and other behaviors of your chosen animal. How does your range of behavior and potential awareness change in this position?

+ Your next huge evolutionary leap is to rise off your front paws and become a primate. Choose your favorite – chimpanzee, orangutan, gorilla – and enjoy moving around in monkey mode. How do the possibilities for awareness change? Does the changing relationship with gravity affect your options for communication and socialization?

✦ Now rise up to your *full* stature as *Homo sapiens*. What vulnerabilities are inherent in a bipedal, fully upright alignment? What are the implications of your upright posture for the development of intelligence and consciousness? On a day-to-day basis do you observe a relationship between people's posture and poise and their level of awareness and alertness?

Professor Dart, along with most of his colleagues, realized that our potential for consciousness and intelligence is intimately linked to the evolution of our fully upright stature. Yet the pressures of our lives – sitting in chairs, working at the computer, driving through rush hour – lead us to lose touch with this aspect of our birthright. For most of us, poise must be relearned.

RELEARN POISE: STUDY THE ALEXANDER TECHNIQUE

Leonardo was renowned for his effortless, upright poise and grace. The citizens of Florence turned out in numbers just to watch him walk down the street. Vasari enthuses about the maestro's "more than infinite grace in every action." It is almost impossible to imagine Leonardo da Vinci slumping and slouching around.

You can cultivate the Da Vincian qualities of poise, balance, and grace by studying the technique developed by another genius, F. Matthias Alexander. Born in Tasmania in 1869, Alexander was a

Shakespearean actor specializing in one-man shows of tragedy and comedy. His promising career was interrupted by a tendency to lose his voice in the middle of performances.

Alexander consulted the leading doctors, speech therapists, and drama coaches of his day, carefully following their advice. Nothing helped. The average person would have given up and tried another line of work. But like Leonardo, Alexander believed in experience over authority. He resolved to overcome his problem on his own, reasoning that something he was doing with and to himself was causing the problem. But how could he discover the specific cause?

Alexander realized that he must find a way to get objective feedback. He began to observe himself in specially constructed mirrors. After many months of detailed and thorough observation, he noticed a pattern that emerged whenever he attempted to recite:

1) he contracted his neck muscles, thereby pulling back his head;
2) he depressed his larynx; and
3) he gasped for breath.

As he observed further, Alexander noted that this tension pattern was associated with a tendency to:

4) push out his chest;
5) hollow his back; and
6) contract all the major joint surfaces of his body.

Alexander's continued observation confirmed that this pattern was present in varying degrees every time he spoke.

Noticing that this pattern of misuse began to manifest the moment he *thought* of reciting, Alexander realized that he had to "unlearn" this pattern, reeducating his mind and body as a whole system in order to change. He discovered that the key to doing this was to pause prior to action, inhibiting his habitual pattern of contraction, and then focus on specific "directions" he evolved to facilitate a lengthening and expansion of his stature. Alexander described these directions as follows: "Let the neck be free, to allow the head to go forward and up, to let the back lengthen and widen." Creating an Australian version of a Zen koan, Alexander emphasized that these directions were to be projected "all together, one after the other."

Repeated practice of this new method produced astounding results: Alexander not only regained full control of his voice, he also recovered from a number of persistent health problems and became famous on the stage for the quality of his voice, breathing, and stage presence.

People began to flock to Alexander for lessons, among them a group of physicians who had an amateur theatrical company. The doctors began to send their patients with chronic problems to Alexander – people with stress ailments, breathing problems, back and neck pain. Alexander was able to assist these people in a surprising number of instances by helping them to eliminate the habits of inappropriate effort responsible for their maladies.

The doctors were so impressed by Alexander's work that, in 1904, they sponsored his setting sail for London to share his work with the world scientific community. He arrived in London and soon became known as the "protector of the London theater," giving lessons to top

ALEXANDER AND *SAPER VEDERE*

"Knowing how to see" was a crucial aspect of Alexander's genius. His discovery was predicated on painstaking, detailed, amazingly acute observation. But when his sponsors collected funds to send him to England in 1904, they were short of the amount needed by a few hundred pounds. How could Alexander raise this considerable sum? Like Leonardo, Alexander had a passion for horses. Relying on his study of the practical anatomy of the horse, Alexander went to the racetrack, bet a tidy sum on a handsome long shot . . . and won.

actresses and actors of the day. Alexander's work also had a profound influence on a variety of writers and scientists.

Before Alexander died in 1955, he trained a number of individuals to continue his work. For many years the Alexander technique has been taught at the Royal Academy of Dramatic Arts, the Royal Academy of Music, the Juilliard School, and other top academies for musicians, actors, and dancers. Indeed, the technique has become a "trade secret" for people in the performing arts. The Alexander technique is also practiced by professional and Olympic athletes, the Israeli Air Force, corporate executives, and individuals in all walks of life.

The Alexander work begins with a keen level of self-observation. Working in your notebook, keep a diary of the appropriateness of your effort in everyday activities. Watch for inappropriate effort in activities such as sitting, bending, lifting, walking, driving, eating, and talking. Are you stiffening your neck and pulling your head back, raising your shoulders, narrowing your back, bracing your knees, or holding your breath in order to pick up your toothbrush? work at the computer? talk on the telephone? pick up a pen to write? meet someone new? speak in public? hit a tennis, golf, or racquet ball? tie your shoes? turn your steering wheel? bend down to pick something up? take a bite of food?

It is very difficult to observe and change these everyday habits without external feedback. Using a mirror or video can be quite helpful, but the best way to accelerate your progress is to take private lessons with a qualified teacher of the Alexander technique. Alexander teachers are trained to use their hands in an extraordinarily subtle and delicate way to guide you to free your neck, rediscover your natural alignment, and awaken your kinesthetic perspicacity.

In the meantime, you can use the following procedure, inspired by Alexander's work, to begin cultivating everyday poise and balance.

Foster the Balanced Resting State

All you need to benefit from this procedure is a relatively quiet place, some carpeted floor space, a few paperback books, and ten to twenty minutes.

+ Begin by placing the books on the floor. Stand approximately your body's length away from the books with your feet shoulder-width apart. Let your hands rest gently at your sides. Facing away from the books, look straight ahead with a soft, alert focus. Pause for a few moments.
+ Think of allowing your neck to be free so that your head can go forward and up and your whole torso can lengthen and widen. Breathing freely, become aware of the contact of your feet on the floor and notice the distance from your feet to the top of your

head. Keep your eyes open and alive, and listen to the sounds around you.

✦ Maintaining this awareness, move lightly and quickly so that you are resting on one knee. Then sit on the floor so that you are supporting yourself with your hands behind you, feet flat on the floor and knees bent. Continue breathing easily.

✦ Let your head drop forward a tiny bit to ensure that you are not tightening your neck muscles and pulling your head back.

✦ Then gently roll your spine along the floor so that your head rests on the books. The books should be positioned so that they support your head at the place where your neck ends and your head begins. If your head is not well positioned, reach back with one hand and support your head while using the other hand to place the books in the proper position. Add or take away books until you find a height that encourages a gentle lengthening of your neck muscles. Your feet remain flat on the floor, with your knees pointing up to the ceiling and your hands resting on the floor or loosely folded on your chest. Allow the weight of your body to be fully supported by the floor.

✦ To reap the benefit of this procedure, rest in this position for ten to twenty minutes. As you rest, gravity will be lengthening your spine and realigning your torso. Keep your eyes open to avoid dozing off. You may wish to bring your attention to the flow of your breathing and to the gentle pulsation of your whole body. Be aware of the floor supporting your back, allowing your shoulders to rest as your back widens. Let your neck be free as your whole body lengthens and expands.

- After you have rested for ten to twenty minutes, get up slowly, being careful to avoid stiffening or shortening your body as you return to a standing position. To achieve a smooth transition, decide when you are going to move and then gently roll over onto your front, maintaining your new sense of integration and expansion. Ease your way into a crawling position, and then back onto one knee. With your head leading the movement upward, stand up.
- Pause for a few moments … listen, eyes alive. Again, feel your feet on the floor, and notice the distance between your feet and the top of your head. You may be surprised to discover that the

CORPORALITA FOR PARENTS

Put your hand on a baby's back and sense the wholeness, flexibility, and vibrant aliveness under your fingertips. Little children are naturally poised. They move with amazing grace and coordination. What happens to this poise as they get older? Well, most kids are fine through first grade. Look back at your own first-grade photo and you will see that most of the children are beautifully upright. But look at the postures of third and fourth graders; you'll witness the beginnings of slumps, contortions, and tensions of all kinds. And for many kids, the teenage years are a permanent megaslump. Now go to a mall or church or anyplace you can observe families. Watch parents and children walking together and you will see striking similarities in their habits and quirks of posture and movement. Although we can't protect our kids from all of life's slump-inducing burdens and contortion-inspiring tensions, we can aim to provide a positive model of poise by embodying it ourselves.

distance has expanded. As you move into the activities of your day, imagine moving with the grace of a figure painted by the maestro.

For best results, practice the Balanced Resting State twice a day. You can do it when you wake up in the morning, when you come home from work, or before retiring at night. The procedure is especially valuable when you feel overworked or stressed and before or after exercise. Regular practice will help you develop an upright, easy poise that encourages balance and grace in everything you do.

CULTIVATE AMBIDEXTERITY

When Michelangelo was working on the Sistine Chapel, he astounded observers by switching his paintbrush from one hand to the other as he worked. Leonardo, a natural left-hander, cultivated this same ambidexterity and regularly switched hands when working on *The Last Supper* and other masterpieces. When I interviewed Professor Raymond Dart and asked him for his recommendations on the development of human potential, he responded, "Balance the body, balance the brain. The future lies with the ambidextrous human!" Dart emphasized that the right hemisphere of the cerebral cortex controls the left side of the body, and the left hemisphere controls the right side of the body. He suggested that coordinating the two sides of the body would promote the coherence and balance of the two hemispheres.

Begin your investigation of ambidexterity by exploring the power of your nondominant hand. Try the following exercises:

THE VISIBLE EXPRESSION OF GRACE

"Movement, to be perpetuated in art, must be of a special kind. It must be the visible expression of grace. Although Renaissance writers left no formal definition of that word, they would all have agreed that it implied a series of smooth transitions. It was to be found, perfectly exemplified, in flowing gestures, floating draperies, curling or rippling hair. An abrupt transition was brutal; the graceful was continuous. Leonardo inherited this tradition of movement and grace in the parts, and extended it to the whole."

Kenneth Clark's comments on grace in art reflect the qualities cultivated by the Alexander technique in daily life: grace, continuity, and wholeness, embodying "smooth transitions" in everyday movements such as sitting to standing or standing into walking.

Reverse crossing – Practice interlocking your fingers and crossing your arms and legs in reverse of your normal pattern. See if you can wink your nondominant eye and roll your tongue over to *both* sides.

Use your nondominant hand – Try using your nondominant hand for a day, or part of a day to start. Turn on the lights, brush your teeth, eat your breakfast with your *other* hand. Record your feelings and observations in your journal.

Experiment with writing – Try signing your name with the *other* hand. Write out the alphabet. Then do some "stream of consciousness" writing on a topic of your choice (you may discover that writing with your nondominant hand will offer you a different way of thinking about things, a way that helps you access your intuition).

Experiment with writing and drawing with both hands simultaneously – After you have a little practice writing with your nondominant hand, experiment with writing and drawing with both hands at once. If possible, try this on a chalkboard. Draw circles, triangles, and squares. Then sign your name with both hands at the same time.

Experiment with mirror writing – You will be surprised how easy it is to learn; all it takes is a little practice. Use the sample below to guide you.

Take a cross-lateral refresher – To refresh your attention when learning, working, or struggling with a creative challenge: Reach behind your back and touch your right foot with your left hand and then your left foot with your right hand. Do this ten times. Or raise your left knee to touch your right hand, and then your right knee to touch your left hand. Do this ten times.

[mirror-writing sample, handwritten]

LEARN TO JUGGLE

Learning to juggle is a marvelous way to develop ambidexterity, balance, and mind-body coordination. Da Vinci biographer Antonina Valentin confirms that the maestro was a juggler. The art was part of the pageants and parties that he designed for his patrons and went hand in hand with his love of conjuring. Moreover, the basic juggling pattern that you will learn is a *fantasie de vinci* – a knot or infinity symbol.

Get three balls (tennis balls are fine) and try the following:

1. Take one ball and toss it back and forth, from hand to hand, in a gentle arc just above your head.
2. Take two balls, one in each hand. Toss the ball in your right hand just as you did with one ball; when it reaches its high point, toss the ball in your left hand in exactly the same manner. Focus on smooth, easy throws and let both balls drop.
3. Same as step 2, only this time catch the first toss. Let the second one drop.
4. Same as step 2, only this time catch them both.
5. Now you are ready to try three balls. Take two balls in one hand and one in the other. Toss the front ball in the hand that has two. When it reaches its high point, throw the single ball in your other hand. When it reaches its high point, throw the remaining ball. Let them all drop!
6. Same as step 5, only this time catch the first toss.
7. Same as step 5, only this time catch the first two tosses. If you catch the first two balls and remember to throw the third, *you will notice that*

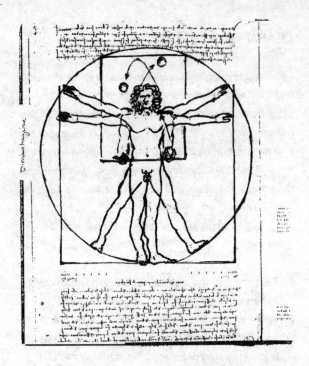

there is only one ball remaining in the air, and you can already do one ball. Catch the third ball and you will experience your first juggle. Celebrate!

Of course, once you achieve your first juggle, you will no doubt wish to experience multiple juggles. As you continue to practice, focus on the ease and direction of your throws, and relax when the balls drop. If you keep your attention primarily on *throwing* and continue to breathe easily, your success will be inevitable.

CORPORALITA AT WORK

The state of your body influences your mind. If your body is stiff and rigid, or collapsed and limp, your mind will often follow suit. Our language is full of phrases that demonstrate an understanding of this relationship, such as: "She won't change her *position* on this issue," "They've taken an aggressive *stance* on this point," and from the Bible, "They stiffened their necks so they would not hear the word of the Lord."

The word *corporation* comes from the root *corpus,* meaning "body." Most corporate bodies are overly stiff and dominated by unconscious habit. In many meetings and brainstorming sessions, for example, people sit around for hours, in more or less the same position, trying to generate new ideas and solve problems. And then they wonder, "Why are we stuck?"

Many organizations are introducing brief, sitting massage sessions, yoga, and aikido classes to help their people discover greater physical and mental flexibility. In addition to these disciplines you can try the following exercise to enliven your next planning meeting or brainstorming session (if you are alone, you can do it in front of a mirror). The object is to move as many body parts as possible, in new ways, at the same time. The exercise leads you to change habitual body-mind positions by moving in a way that you have never moved before.

Find a partner and stand opposite from her. You are going to copy the movements that your partner makes. Your partner begins, for example, by raising her right hand and patting her head, then dropping her hand back to her side. Copy the movement, and keep doing it, while you wait for your partner to introduce the next movement. For the next movement your partner might tap her left foot with her left hand. Copy this movement while *continuing* with the previous one. Next your partner shimmies her shoulders. Copy this while continuing the two previous movements. Then your partner adds a sound like a chicken noise or the theme from *The Twilight Zone.* Copy the sound and continue the previous movements. Then she rotates her head around in a big circle, and so on.

Aim to do at least five different movements at once. Make them as unusual and absurd as possible. Then switch roles and lead your partner to make movements even sillier than the ones you just finished making. Change partners and do it all again. This exercise always raises the level of laughter and fun dramatically. It shakes up old patterns, liberates lots of energy, and wakes up the possibility of making new connections.

Connessione

*A Recognition of and
Appreciation for the
Interconnectedness of all
Things and Phenomena.
Systems Thinking.*

W hen you toss a stone into a still pond, the water ripples out in a series of widening circles. Conjure up that image in your mind's eye; ask yourself how one ripple affects another, and where the energy of the ripples goes, and you will be thinking like the maestro. The ever-expanding circle is a lovely metaphor for the principle of Connessione, which is evident in Leonardo's frequent observations of patterns and connections in the world around him:

+ "The stone where it strikes the surface of the water, causes circles around it which spread out until they are lost; and in the same manner the air, struck by a voice or a noise, also has a circular motion, so he who is most distant cannot hear it."

+ "Observe how the movements of the surface of the water resemble that of hair, which has two movements, one of which stems from the weight of the hair and the other from the waves and the curls. In the same way the water has its turbulent curls, a part of which follows the force of the main current, and another obeys the movement of the incidence of reflection."

+ "Swimming in water teaches men how birds fly upon the air. Swimming illustrates the method of flying and shows that the largest weight finds most resistance in the air."

+ "Mountains are made by the currents of rivers. Mountains are destroyed by the currents of rivers."

+ "Every part is disposed to unite with the whole, that it may thereby escape from its own incompleteness."

Many of us have come across some variation of the following rhetorical gambit, designed to inspire readers to think in Connessione terms: "If a butterfly flaps its wings in Tokyo, does it affect the weather in New York?" Contemporary systems theorists are fond of answering this classic question with an enthusiastic "Yes!" Five centuries ago Leonardo, the original systems thinker, noted, "The earth is moved from its position by the weight of a tiny bird resting upon it."

Leonardo frequently noted these extraordinary observations in the margins of his notebooks. Over the years, a number of scholars have criticized Leonardo for the disorder of his notebooks. He never provided a table of contents, an outline, or an index. He scrawled notes in apparently random fashion, switched from topic to topic, and repeated himself frequently. But the maestro's defenders point out that Leonardo's sense of connectedness was so all-embracing that his observations are equally valid however they are related to one another. In other words, he didn't need to organize them by category, or create an outline, because he saw how everything connected to everything else.

Like a poem, the whole of which is greater than the sum of its parts, the following Da Vincian "to-do" list evokes the spirit of Curiosità and Connessione:

Show how clouds form and dissolve,
how water vapor rises from the earth to the air,
how mists form and air thickens,
and why one wave seems more blue than another;
describe the aerial regions,
and the causes of snow and hail,
how water condenses, and hardens into ice,
and how new figures form in the air,
and new leaves on the trees,
and icicles on the stones of cold places. . . .

One of Leonardo's dragons.

One secret of Leonardo's unparalleled creativity is his lifelong practice of combining and connecting disparate elements to form new patterns. Vasari records an incident from Leonardo's childhood, when he was asked to paint a peasant's shield. Eager to devise an image that "would terrify anyone who encountered it," young Leonardo gathered and collected in his room an assortment of "crawling reptiles, green lizards, crickets, snakes, butterflies, locusts, bats, and other strange species of this kind, and by adapting various parts of this multitude, he created a most horrible and frightening monster with poisonous breath that set the air on fire."

Vasari adds that when Leonardo unveiled this creation to his father, who had commissioned it, Ser Piero was sufficiently shaken and amazed at Leonardo's miraculous talent to give a different shield to the grateful peasant so he could sell his son's work for one hundred ducats to a Florentine merchant (who subsequently sold it to the duke of Milan for three hundred ducats).

Many years later Leonardo wrote a brief guide called "How to Make an Imaginary Animal Appear Real." He advised: "If therefore you wish to make one of your imagined animals appear natural – let us suppose it to be a dragon – take for its head that of a mastiff or setter, for its eyes those of a cat, for its ears those of a porcupine, for its nose that of a greyhound, with the eyebrows of a lion, the temples of an old cock, and the neck of a water tortoise." When he was living in the Belvedere at the Vatican, Leonardo once took a live lizard and crafted a horn, beard, and wings for it. He kept it in a special box and, according to Vasari, "showed it to his friends to make them flee in fear."

Leonardo's dragons are a wonderful metaphor for his creative recipe of combination and connection. He studied the essence of beauty in thousands of human faces and then combined the different elements he observed to create perfect visages in his painting. His insights into acoustics sprang from connections he made to his observations of water. On one page of his notebook Leonardo compares the rate and direction of travel of rays of light, the force of percussion, the voice of an echo, the lines of a magnet, and the movement of odor.

Many of his inventions and designs arose from the playful, imaginary combinations he made of different natural forms. Although the seriousness and intensity that Leonardo brought to his studies cannot be overemphasized, he was, as his love of jokes, riddles, and boxed dragons demonstrates, extremely playful. As Freud commented, "Indeed, the great Leonardo remained like a child for the whole of his life … Even as an adult he continued to play and that was another reason he often appeared uncanny and incomprehensible to his contemporaries." Leonardo's seriousness drove him to penetrate the essence of things, and his playfulness allowed him to make unprecedented, original connections.

For Leonardo, Connessione began with his love of nature and intensified through his investigation of human and animal anatomy. His studies of comparative anatomy included dissections of horses, cows, pigs, and many other animals. He noted distinctions and drew connections between the tongue of a woodpecker and the jaw of a crocodile. He related the legs of a frog, the foot of a bear, the eyes of a lion, and the pupils of an owl to those of man. Clearly, his studies went far beyond what was needed to provide a painter with the knowledge required for accurate representation. Leonardo studied the human body as a whole system, a coordinated pattern of interdependent relationships. As he describes it, "… I will speak of the functions of each part in every direction, putting before your eyes a description of the whole form and substance of man …"

Leonardo referred to his studies of anatomy as a "cosmografica del minor mondo," a "cosmography of the microcosm." His appreciation for the natural proportions of the body were reflected in his architectural and

LEONARDO AND EASTERN PHILOSOPHY

Despite speculation by a few scholars that Leonardo may have ventured to the East, there is no concrete historical evidence of such a journey. Nevertheless, the maestro articulated concepts that are at the core of much Asian wisdom. Bramly compares some of his writings to Zen koans. *Mona Lisa* is his supreme statement of the principle of yin and yang. He was the first Western painter to make a landscape the central focus of a work of art, something that was done regularly in the East. Leonardo's vegetarianism and advocacy of nonattachment to material things are reminiscent of Hinduism and were extremely unusual in cinquecento Florence or Milan. He also expressed, in Western terms, echoes of the Buddhist doctrine of the void: "Nothingness has no center, and its boundaries are nothingness." He added: "Among the great things which are found among us the existence of Nothing is the greatest … its essence dwells as regards time between the past and the future, and possesses nothing of the present. This nothingness has the part equal to the whole and the whole to the part, the divisible to the indivisible, and it comes to the same amount whether we divide it or multiply it or add to it or subtract from it …"

city planning studies. His understanding of the body formed the metaphor for his insights into the earth as a living system. He wrote:

> Man was called the microcosmos by the ancients, and surely the term was well chosen: for just as man is composed of earth, water, air, and fire, so is the body of the earth. As man has bones as support and framework for flesh, so the earth has rocks as support for the soil; as man carries a lake of blood in which the lungs inflate and deflate in respiration, so the body of the earth has the ocean which waxes and wanes every six hours in a cosmic respiration; as the veins emanate from the lake of blood and are ramified throughout the human body, in the same way, the ocean fills the body of the earth with an infinity of veins of water.

Foreshadowing by five hundred years physicist David Bohm's theory of the holographic universe (which posits that the "genetic code" of the universe is held in every atom just as a strand of DNA holds the entire genetic code of an individual), Leonardo wrote, "Every body placed in the luminous air spreads out in circles and fills the surrounding space with infinite likenesses of itself and appears all in all and all in every part." He added, "This is the real miracle, that all shapes, all colors, all images of every part of the universe are concentrated in a single point." Bohm's thesis includes the concept of an "implicate order," a "deep structure" of connectedness that links the universe together. In 1980 Bohm wrote, "Everything is enfolded into everything." Five centuries earlier Leonardo had noted, "Everything comes from everything, and everything is made out of everything, and everything returns into everything ..."

Armed with vision, logic, imagination, and an unrelenting desire to know truth and beauty, Leonardo probed the infinite subtleties of nature. Yet the more Leonardo learned as a disciple of experience, the deeper the mysteries became, until he finally concluded that "nature is full of infinite causes that experience has never demonstrated." Where science reached its limits, art took the lead, explains Bramly, writing that Leonardo was "so overwhelmed and dumbfounded by the mysteries he could

Study of The Deluge.

Hair.

The Star of Bethlehem.

Whirlpool.

contemplate but not penetrate, … [that] he set aside his scalpel, compass, and pen and he took up his paintbrush once more."

And so, we must turn to the maestro's paintings and drawings for his supreme expressions of Connessione. The astute eye will see connections that span his body of work; his insight into a universal pattern or "implicate order," for example, can be detected in details of works as diverse as Verrocchio's Baptism (in the hairs on the angel's head), *The Virgin and Child with St. Anne* (in the grouping of figures), the *Mona Lisa* (in the landscape), and his depictions of the Deluge (in the torrents of water).

Many scholars have drawn countless links between Leonardo's natural philosophy and his art, but it is best to discover them for yourself. Let this thought from Plato inspire you:

"For he who would proceed aright … should begin in youth to visit beautiful forms … out of that he should create fair thoughts; and soon he will of himself perceive that the beauty of one form is akin to the beauty of another, and that beauty in every form is one and the same."

CONNESSIONE AND YOU

As someone who has read this far in this book the chances are pretty good that, like Leonardo, you are a seeker of connections. Physically, we seek health (the word *health* comes from the Old English root *hāl*, meaning "whole"), affection, and the ecstasy of sexual union. Emotionally, we yearn for a sense of belonging, intimacy, and love. Intellectually, we look for patterns and relationships, seeking to understand systems. And spiritually, we pray for Oneness with the Divine.

This chapter aims to give you practical tools for weaving an ever more beautiful tapestry of Connessione in your world. But first, contemplate the self-assessment on the next page.

Connessione:
Self-Assessment

- ❏ I am ecologically aware.
- ❏ I enjoy similes, analogies, and metaphor.
- ❏ I frequently make connections that other people don't see.
- ❏ When I travel, I am struck more by people's similarities than their differences.
- ❏ I seek a "holistic" approach to diet, health, and healing.
- ❏ I have a well-developed sense of proportion.
- ❏ I can articulate the systems dynamics – the patterns, connections, and networks – in my family and workplace.
- ❏ My life goals and priorities are formulated clearly and integrated with my values and sense of purpose.
- ❏ I sometimes experience a sense of connectedness with all Creation.

CONNESSIONE:
APPLICATION
AND EXERCISES

CONTEMPLATE WHOLENESS

What does wholeness mean to you? Experiment with expressing your concept of wholeness in a drawing, gesture, or dance. Do you experience wholeness in daily life? How about disconnection? Describe the difference. What are the different parts or elements that make up your character? Do you experience conflicts between the different parts of your self? In other words, do your mind, emotions, and body ever disagree? If so, which part tends to dominate? Describe some of the dynamics of your head, heart, and body, then try diagramming them.

Do a stream of consciousness writing session on Leonardo's observation that "every part is disposed to unite with the whole, that it may thereby escape from its own incompleteness." How does this apply to you?

FAMILY DYNAMICS

Contemporary psychology emphasizes the importance of understanding the "systems dynamics" of your family to better understand yourself. In your search for wholeness and self-knowledge you can gain valuable insight by contemplating the following questions about your family:

> To Leonardo, a landscape, like a human being, was part of a vast machine, to be understood part by part and, if possible, in the whole. Rocks were not simply decorative silhouettes. They were part of the earth's bones, with an anatomy of their own, caused by some remote seismic upheaval. Clouds were not random curls of the brush, drawn by some celestial artist, but were the congregation of tiny drops formed from the evaporation of the sea, and soon would pour back their rain into the rivers.
>
> – KENNETH CLARK

+ What roles does each person play?
+ How are the roles interdependent?
+ What are the benefits of the distribution of family roles? What are the costs?
+ What happens to the dynamics under stress?
+ What patterns have been handed down over generations?
+ What are the primary outside forces that affect the family dynamics?
+ What were the dynamics like one year ago? Seven years ago? How have they changed? What will they be like in a year? In seven years?
+ How do the patterns of functioning you learned in your family affect the way you participate in other groups?
+ As you generate insights based on the questions above, try drawing a diagram that represents your family as a system.

The Body Metaphor
Use Leonardo's favorite metaphor – the human body – to further explore the dynamics of your family system.
Ask:

CONNESSIONE AT WORK

The movement toward creating "learning organizations" and "total quality" is an attempt to apply Connessione thinking to organizations. Peter Senge, author of *The Fifth Discipline: The Art and Practice of the Learning Organization*, emphasizes that complex, rapidly changing systems demand that we cultivate "… a discipline for seeing wholes … a framework for seeing interrelationships rather than things, for seeing patterns of change rather than snapshots." In a delightfully Da Vincian turn of phrase Senge adds, "Reality is made up of circles, but we see straight lines."

You can strengthen your perception of circles and your ability to function as a leader in creating a "learning organization" by applying the principle of Connessione to the organizations in which you are involved. Choose an organization, and ask the same questions as in the "Family Dynamics" exercise (if you choose a large organization, you can substitute "department," "task force," or "business unit" for "person"). Then experiment with drawing a diagram that represents the systems dynamics of your organization. Finally, view your organization or corporation from the perspective of the body metaphor questions.

- Who is the head?
- Who is the heart?
- Is the head in balance with the body?
- What is the quality of our nourishment?
- How well do we digest and assimilate nourishment?
- How effectively do we process waste?
- How is our circulation? Are our arteries sclerotic?
- What is our backbone?
- What are our sharpest senses? Our dullest?
- Does the right hand know what the left hand is doing?

- What is our state of health? Do we have chronic maladies, natural growing pains, or a life-threatening disease?
- Are we working to become more fit, strong, flexible, and poised?

MAKE DRAGONS

The ability to see relationships and patterns, and make unfamiliar combinations and connections, is the core of creativity. Leonardo's wonderful dragons, and many of his innovations and designs, arose from the fanciful connections he made between seemingly unrelated things. You can develop your Da Vincian powers by looking at things that at first glance seem unrelated, and finding different ways to link them.

For example, what connections can you make between:

A bullfrog and the Internet?

The frog's feet are webbed; the Internet links you to the World Wide Web.

An Oriental rug and psychotherapy?

Oriental rugs have complex repeating patterns and so does your psyche.

Get the idea? Aim to generate three or four connections for each of the following. This exercise is a great warm-up for individual and team brainstorming sessions. Have fun.

Experiment with making connections between the following:

+ An oak leaf and a human hand
+ A laugh and a knot
+ A bowl of minestrone soup and the United States
+ Mathematics and *The Last Supper*
+ A pig's tail and a bottle of wine
+ A giraffe and coleslaw
+ Sketches of the Deluge and rush-hour traffic
+ A porcupine and a computer
+ Samurai warriors and the game of chess
+ Gershwin's "Rhapsody in Blue" and rain
+ A tornado and curly hair
+ The global economy and a portobello mushroom
+ Juggling and your career
+ The star of Bethlehem and the principle of Connessione

To understand the systems in your world, think about how they perform in extreme circumstances. You can learn the most about your family dynamics, for example, during weddings, serious illnesses, births, and funerals. The *real* vision and values of an organization become apparent after a particularly bad financial report, ethical crisis, or unexpected change in the marketplace.

IMAGINARY DIALOGUES

Hillary Clinton was ridiculed by the press a few years ago for her imaginary dialogue with Eleanor Roosevelt. But "talking" with an imaginary role model is a time-honored and very effective way to gain insight and perspective. It

GOING TO EXTREMES TO MAKE CONNECTIONS

How does *The Last Supper* relate to Da Vinci's study of the Deluge? The maestro once sat with a dying man, comforting him as he experienced a peaceful and easy death. Moments after the old man exhaled for the last time, Leonardo began an autopsy, fascinated by the anatomy of such a peaceful departure. In his quest for truth, and his search to understand the essence of natural systems, Leonardo went to extremes. His anatomical studies of the act of coitus, his dinner party for deformed and grotesque characters, his remarkably composed sketch of the hanging of Bandinelli, the phantasmagorical war machines, all demonstrate his intuitive knowledge that to understand a system, one must explore it, or imagine it, under extreme conditions. Leonardo's *Last Supper* is distinguished from many that preceded it, by focusing on the most extreme drama – the precise moment that Christ proclaims, "One of you shall betray me." His studies of the Deluge, the end of the world by flood, represent the forces of nature conspiring to the extreme of destruction.

was recommended by the great Italian poet Petrarch and practiced enthusiastically in the Academy of Lorenzo de' Medici.

Choose a problem you wish to work on or an issue you want to understand in more depth. In addition to contemplating the maestro's views, you can also imagine the perspective that might be offered by any of your role models, "anti–role models," or perhaps one of the great minds from history. You can have even more fun and further stimulate your creativity by imagining discussions on your problem or issue between different characters, past or present, real or imaginary. Imagine a dialogue on your issue by, for example:

- Michelangelo's David and Leonardo's Saint John
- Winona Ryder and Margaret Thatcher
- The "canon of proportion" figure and Jane Austen
- Muhammad Ali and Mona Lisa
- NPR's Susan Stamberg and Niccolò Machiavelli
- Miles Davis and Verrocchio
- Christ and Buddha
- Bill Gates and Lorenzo the Magnificent
- Any combination of characters you like

ORIGIN-ALL THINKING

In the Sensazione chapter I recommended pausing before dining, bringing your awareness into the present moment. In addition to enhancing your experience of the taste of your food, this practice provides a regular opportunity for attunement with the principle of Connessione. Before you take your first bite, reflect on the origins of the meal you are about to enjoy. For example, last night for dinner a friend and I enjoyed a big bowl of linguine with garlic, olive oil, black pepper, and pecorino cheese accompanied by a salad of crisp romaine lettuce, fresh tomatoes, parsley, and roasted red peppers dressed with olive oil, lemon juice, garlic, and more pecorino. This typical Tuesday night dinner was made extra special by a couple of glasses of Falesco Montiano 1995, a luscious Italian merlot imported by Leonardo LoCasio. Before enjoying our meal, we paused to give thanks and reflect on the origins of the blessing we were about to receive. The following mind map represents some of our thoughts on the sources of our dinner:

Thinking about the origins of things is a great way to appreciate Connessione. The modern Renaissance

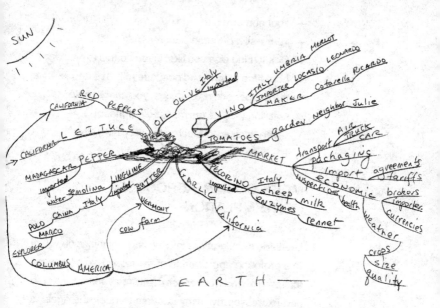

genius Buckminster Fuller was known for enthralling audiences with his amazing improvisational presentations. Instead of preparing a lecture, Fuller would invite his audience to suggest a topic – anything at all. In one typical session, a college student suggested that Fuller speak about a Styrofoam cup. Fuller kept his audience spellbound for the next two hours as he discussed the origins of the cup: the chemical engineering advances that led to the invention of Styrofoam, the economic and social forces related to its manufacture, and their cultural and environmental implications.

In addition to reflecting on the origins of your food, choose any of the following objects and consider all the elements involved in its creation:

+ This book
+ The clothes you are wearing now
+ Your watch

- ✦ Your computer
- ✦ Your wallet or purse
- ✦ Or anything else you like. If you do this exercise from time to time and continue to probe and explore the deeper origins of things, you cannot help realizing that, as the maestro emphasized, "everything is connected to everything else."

MICROCOSM/MACROCOSM CONTEMPLATION

Leonardo's explorations into the origin of things drew him to a profound appreciation of the relationship between microcosm and macrocosm. This relationship, intuited and expressed by many cultures through the ages, is receiving serious attention from contemporary science. Heisenberg, Mandelbrot, Prigogine, Pribram, Sheldrake, Bohm, Chopra, Pert, and many others have set the stage for a modern scientific understanding of the ancient dictum "As above, so below." This understanding invites a deep experience of Connessione. As neuroscientist Candace Pert emphasizes, "As above, so below. To think otherwise is to suffer, to experience the stresses of separation from our source, from our true union."

As you center yourself by bringing your awareness to the flow of your breathing, pause, and contemplate your connection to the microcosm and the macrocosm. Start by appreciating the coordinated working of your digestive, endocrine, epithelial (skin), musculoskeletal, nervous, circulatory, and immune systems. Then imagine the harmonious activity of the tissues and organs that form these systems: the bone, intestines, muscle, stomach, blood, nerves, pancreas, liver, heart, and kidneys. Next move down to the cellular level, appreciating the billions and billions of cells that form your organs and tissues. Go deeper, to the molecular level; imagine the molecules linking together in different combinations to form all your cells. Imagine the play of the atoms that make up your molecules. Then bring your appreciation to subatomic level, composed of approximately .001% matter and 99.999% space.

All these subsystems conspire to make you possible. And you are a subsystem of a family, social, professional, and economic network. Create an image in your mind's eye of your role in these networks. Think of your connections with systems of information flow: the cables, satellites, fiber networks, and computer chips that conspire to link you with millions of other minds through your telephone, fax, computer, television, radio, and reading material. See yourself in the context of geopolitical systems, as a resident of a city or town, part of a state, province, or region that is a subsystem of a nation. Then visualize your role in the ecosystem of your bioregion and planet. See your planet through the eyes of the astronauts, as an element of the solar system, part of a galaxy in an expanding and contracting universe composed of approximately .001% matter and 99.999% space.

CONNESSIONE MEDITATION

The sometimes frantic pace of our lives can, of course, lead us to lose touch with the microcosm and the macrocosm. It is hard to remember cosmic truths when you are rushing to meet a deadline, cleaning up after your kids, or fighting your way through rush-hour traffic.

Connessione for Parents

As you gain insight into your family patterns and systems through the Family Dynamics and Body Metaphor exercises, ask: How can I apply my emerging understanding of family systems to be a more conscious, loving parent? How can I avoid passing on to my children the unresolved issues and unconscious vestiges of the family dynamics with which I was raised?

On a more lighthearted note, the exercises Make Dragons and Imaginary Dialogues are easily adapted for children; and they are great for cultivating kids' creativity. The Origin-all Thinking exercise is particularly valuable in nurturing your child's sense of "everything connecting to everything else."

The following simple meditation offers another way to bring the experience of Connessione to your life every day.

Find a quiet place and sit down with your feet squarely on the floor, spine lengthening up. Close your eyes and bring your attention to the flow of your breathing. Be aware of the feeling of the air against your nostrils as you inhale. Exhale through your nose and feel the air flow out. (If your sinuses are stuffy, it's okay to breathe out through your mouth.) Keep your attention on the flow of your breathing, without trying to change it. Sit for ten to twenty minutes, just following your breath. If your mind wanders, bring it back to the immediate sensation of the breath.

For most people, this meditation yields a significant experience of calm and well-being. Breathing is always happening *now*, and our worries and anxieties are usually associated with concerns about the past or future. Moreover, the cycle of breath links you to the rhythms of creation, the ebb and flow of the tides, the shift from night to day. You share the air you breathe with all living things. Your loved ones, your dog or cat, Republicans and Democrats – we all breathe the same air. Old men sighing in Azerbaijan, newborn girls crying in Myanmar, corporate raiders laughing in Wall Street suites, teenagers shouting on the beach in Malibu, lovers screaming in ecstasy, and beggars wailing in Calcutta – we all share the same air.

Sitting quietly and meditating on the flow of breathing for twenty minutes will do you a world of good. But twenty minutes aren't always easy to find. So whenever you remember, in the course of your day, bring your awareness to your breathing. On busy days aim to pause once or twice and be fully present for seven breaths. When you are very busy, aim to be conscious for at least one full breath in the course of your day. These little oases of consciousness help connect you to yourself, to nature, to creation.

> " He discovered . . . God in the miraculous beauty of light, in the harmonious movement of the planets, in the intricate arrangement of muscles and nerves inside the human body, and in that inexpressible masterpiece the human soul."
> – SERGE BRAMLY ON LEONARDO'S SPIRITUALITY

TIME LINE – RIVER OF LIFE

History books frequently offer time lines of significant events, chronicling a significant era or the life of a major figure. Making a personal time line is a marvelous tool for seeing the big picture of your life. Make a time line for your life, including all the events you deem significant, personally and globally.

After you have sketched out the time line of your existence, experiment with imagining your life as a river. Visualize a source, perhaps the snow crystals on a mountain. Your destination, for this life, is the ocean.

Describe the dams, levees, eddies, whirlpools, rapids, and waterfalls of life so far. What are the major confluences with other rivers and bodies of water? How deep is your river? How pure? Does it ever freeze, almost dry up, or overflow its banks? How much flows underground? Is it teeming with life, providing sustenance for those who dwell on its shores? Look at the course of your life. Leonardo noted, "In rivers, the water you touch is the last of what has passed and the first of that which comes: so it is with time present."

Use your power of choice, in this present moment, to direct the course and quality of the river of your life.

"THINK WELL TO THE END"

It is hard to believe Vasari's claim that on his deathbed, Leonardo was filled with repentance and apologized to "God and man for leaving so much undone." We do know, however, that in moments of despair the maestro wrote, *"Dimmi se mai fu fatto alcuna cosa?"* "Tell me if anything was ever done?" Although he left much undone, even Leonardo, as he died in the arms of the French king, could not have imagined the scope of his own legacy.

Leonardo was the ultimate "idea man." Although his practical skills in all areas are unsurpassed, his greatest strength was not to be found in implementation. Nevertheless, as he aged and became aware of his own mortality, he increasingly emphasized the importance of setting clear goals and following through to completion. In his later years he wrote repeatedly, "Think well to the end" and "Consider first the end." He even drew a representation of his personal goals.

You can set and achieve your goals more effectively with the help of a simple acronym – make all your goals SMART.

S – Specific: Define exactly what you want to accomplish, in detail.

M – Measurable: Decide how you will measure your progress and, most important, how you will know that you have achieved your goal.

A – Accountability: Make a full commitment to be personally responsible for achieving your goal. When setting goals with a team, be certain that accountability is clear.

R – Realistic and Relevant: Set goals that are ambitious but achievable; as Leonardo noted, "We ought not to desire the impossible." Check that your goals are relevant to your overall sense of purpose and values.

T – Time Line: Create a clear time line for the achievement of your goals.

Before you embark on the final exercise, which will include guidance for setting SMART goals for your life, let's set the stage by "thinking well to the end." Consider the legacy you would like to leave. In your notebook, write your ideal eulogy from the perspective of family, friends, professional associates, and members of your community. How would you like to be remembered?

MAKE A MASTER MIND MAP OF YOUR LIFE

One of the aims of *Think Like Da Vinci* is to provide you with tools to live your life as a work of art. To help you realize this goal, try the following exercise for making a work of art about your life.

In this final exercise you will look at your life – your goals, values, priorities, and purpose – from a Connessione perspective. It is all too easy to go through life without *comprehensively* considering what we want. Of course, we all think about our careers, relationships, and finances from time to time. And many people devote significant time to crafting visions, goals, and strategies at work. But rarely, if ever, do we contemplate all our personal goals and how they fit together.

The advantages of making a master mind map of your life are:

✦ By setting down all your goals, priorities, and values on one piece of paper, you can see the Connessione, or lack thereof, in your life.

- As you clarify your understanding of how everything in your life connects to everything else, you will be better able to overcome the discoordinations, conflicts, and "blind spots" that interfere with the achievement of your goals and dreams.
- By representing your goals and priorities in key words and images, you will bring together your powers of Arte and Scienza to energize your creative vision.

To get the most from this potentially life-changing exercise, I recommend that you devote a minimum of an hour a day over the course of seven days. The seven days do not have to be consecutive, but you should aim to complete the whole exercise within three weeks. Set up your equivalent of the maestro's studio: instead of brush and canvas, you will use colored felt-tip pens and large sheets of blank white paper. Work to the sounds of inspiring music and fill the air with your favorite aromas.

Day One: Sketch the Big Picture of Your Dreams
- *Create Your Own "Impresa"* (*impresa*: emblem) – An impresa was the personal "logo" of scholars, nobles, and princes during the Renaissance. Make up your own personal impresa, or logo. Take your time and allow a resonant image to emerge from within. This impresa will become the central image of your life mind map.
- *Make a "Sprezzatura" Map of Your Goals* (*sprezzatura*: nonchalance) – Sketch your impresa in the center of a large sheet of blank paper. On lines radiating out from this central image, print a key

word or sketch a symbol for each of your life's major areas, such as: people, career, finances, home, possessions, spirituality, fun, health, service, travel, learning, and self. (Express these life areas in any terms you like; feel free to add, delete, or change the categories suggested here.) Make this first version a sprezzatura or nonchalant sketch of the "big picture" of your life. Ask yourself, "What do I want?" in each of these areas.

Look at your first casual draft and ask: "Have I expressed all the areas that are important to me? If I could have, do, or be anything at all, what would it be?"

Day Two: Explore Your Goals

Begin by drawing your impresa in the center of a fresh sheet of paper. Now do a more organized mind map of your life goals, with vivid, multicolored images for each of your major life areas. Radiating from each of your main branches (Finances, Health, etc.), print key words or draw other images that begin to express your goals for each branch in more detail. Explore each branch in depth:

+ **People** – What relationships are most important to me? What qualities would my relationships have ideally?
+ **Career** – What is my ultimate career goal? What are my interim goals? What would my ideal job or career be?
+ **Finances** – How much money do I need to support all my other goals and priorities?
+ **Home** – What is my ideal living environment?
+ **Possessions** – What stuff is important to me?

- **Spirituality** – What kind of relationship would I like to have with God? How can I become more susceptible to grace?
- **Health** – What shape would I like to be in? What is the quality of energy I want?
- **Fun** – What would give me the greatest delight?
- **Service** – What contributions do I dream of making to others?
- **Travel** – Where do I want to go?
- **Learning** – If I could learn anything at all, what would it be?
- **Self** – What kind of person would I like to be? What qualities would I like to cultivate?

Use all your senses to create a vivid image of what you want in each area. You may wish to make a separate mind map for some or all of your major life goals. Then recombine them into your emerging master life mind map.

Day Three: Clarify Your Core Values

Your goals represent your response to the question "What do I want?" Your understanding of your values arises from considering "Why do I want it?" Look at each of your goals, contemplating the questions "Why do I want this?" "Why is it important?" and "What will the realization of this goal bring to my life?"

Ask yourself: "How much of what I want is determined by my conditioning: the messages I have internalized from parents, priests, and pundits? How much of what I want is determined by my reaction to or rebellion against my conditioning? How much of what I really want springs from my essence, independent of conditioning or reaction?"

The Beginning of a Life Mind Map.

As you contemplate the deeper motivations underlying your goals, your core values begin to come into focus. This exercise is designed to accentuate that focus. The following list contains some key words that represent values. (Please add your own key words to the list at any time.) Read through the whole list and notice your response to each key word. Which ones resonate most strongly? Select your top ten, and then rank them in order of importance to you.

achievement	honesty	playfulness
adventure	humility	pleasure
authenticity	humor	power
awareness	imagination	recognition
beauty	independence	religion
charity	insight	respect
community	integrity	responsibility
compassion	justice	security
competition	kindness	sensitivity
creativity	knowledge	serenity
discipline	leadership	spirituality
diversity	learning	spontaneity
ecology	love	stability
excellence	loyalty	status
excitement	money	subtlety
expression	nature	teaching
family	novelty	time
fashion	order	tradition
freedom	originality	truth
friendship	passion	winning
fun	patriotism	wisdom
generosity	perfection	working
growth		

Reflect on your list of ten values. How are your values mirrored in your goals? What areas of your life provide the truest expression of your values? What areas lead you away from what you value?

Next create an image or a symbol that represents each of your core values.

Day Four: Contemplate Your Purpose

Some people seem to be born with a clear sense of purpose. Leonardo, for example, always organized his life around the quest for truth and beauty. Most of us, however, require a lot of contemplation to understand the meaning and purpose of our lives. The secret of discovering your life's purpose is to hold the question "What is my purpose?" in your mind and heart until enlightenment strikes. While you are waiting, try the following to make yourself more susceptible to enlightenment:

+ Do a stream of consciousness writing session on "What my purpose is *not!*" This will help you define the "negative space" around what *is* your purpose.
+ Experiment with writing a "Statement of Purpose" in twenty-five words or less. Just give it your best shot. Then rewrite it once a month until you feel a frisson of focused energy through your whole body when you read it.
+ You know you've got it when all your cells say: "Yes!"

Leonardo's Values and Advice for Living

In addition to his artistic and scientific wisdom, Leonardo offered observations, insights, and advice on a wide range of topics including ethics, human relations, and spiritual fulfillment. As you put together your master life mind map, you may wish to consider some of the maestro's guidance for living.

On Materialism and Ambition
"Neither promise yourself things nor do things if you see that when deprived of them they will cause you material suffering."

"Happy is the estate that is seen by the eye of its lord."

"To the ambitious, whom neither the boon of life, nor the beauty of the world suffice to content, it comes as penance that life with them is squandered, and that they possess neither the benefits nor the beauty of the world."

"He who possesses most is most afraid to lose."

On Ethics and Personal Responsibility
"Justice requires power, insight and will."

"You can have neither a greater nor a lesser dominion than that over yourself."

"He who does not punish evil commends it to be done."

"He who walks straight rarely falls."

"Man is worthy of praise and blame solely in respect of such actions as it is within his power to do or abstain from." (Leonardo borrowed this thought from Aristotle.)

On Relationships
"Ask advice of him who governs himself well."

"The memory of benefits is frail as against ingratitude."

"Reprove a friend in secret but praise him before others."

"Patience protects from insult as clothes protect from the cold."

On Love
"To enjoy – to love a thing for its own sake and for no other reason."

"The love of anything is the fruit of our knowledge of it, and grows as our knowledge deepens."

And Leonardo was fond of quoting the ancient Latin saying "*Amor vincit omnia*," "Love conquers everything."

Day Five: Assess Current Reality

Review the major areas of your life, assessing your current status as objectively as possible. For added perspective, solicit feedback from someone you trust. Ask:

+ **People** – What are my relationships like now?
+ **Career** – What is the current state of my career?
+ **Finances** – What is my financial status? What are my assets, debts, income, and earning potential?
+ **Home** – What is my living situation now?
+ **Possessions** – What stuff do I have?
+ **Spirituality** – What relationship do I have with God?
+ **Health** – What kind of shape am I in? What is the quality of my energy now?
+ **Fun** – Am I enjoying life?
+ **Service** – What contributions do I make to others?
+ **Travel** – Where have I been?
+ **Learning** – What are the biggest gaps in my education?
+ **Self** – What kind of person am I now? What are my strengths and weaknesses?
+ **Values** – What is the difference between the values I would like to have and those that, judging from my actions and behavior, I actually have now?

Day Six: Look for Connections

Make a new mind map that includes all your goals, and branches for Values and Purpose. Draw your impresa and other images with care. Make them as vivid and beautiful as possible. After expressing your life goals, values, and purpose on one large piece of paper, put your emerging masterpiece mind map on the wall at home or in the office. Then contemplate the following questions:

+ Are there any key words that appear repeatedly in my mind map? Do they suggest a theme?
+ Are my goals relevant to my purpose and values?
+ Is my life in proportion – do my goals, values, and purpose all fit together and support one another? The maestro wrote: "Proportion is not only to be found in number and measure, but also in sounds, weights, times and places, and in every power that exists." Ask: How does my career affect my health and energy level? How does my health and energy level influence my relationships? How do my relationships express my spirituality? What is the connection between my spirituality, finances, and possessions? How do my finances influence my attitude toward learning and travel? Am I seeking a balance between altruism and fun?
+ What are my priorities?
+ Does my current mode of working, relating, learning, loving, relaxing, and budgeting time and money contribute to the achievement of my goals and the fulfillment of my purpose?

When you complete your assessment of the connection and proportion of your goals and your life now, seek to answer the following questions: Where are the greatest gaps between what I want and what I've got? Am I "on course" for realizing my most important goals? What "course adjustments" do I need to make to bring my life in balance?

Now the most important question for artists of life: **Am I willing to hold the creative tension between my ideals and my current reality?** Of course, it is much easier to hold that tension if you have a strategy for closing the gap.

Day Seven: Strategize for Change

You define your goals and vision by contemplating the question "What do I want?"

You clarify your values and purpose by contemplating the question "Why do I want it?"

You craft a strategy by answering the question "How will I get it?"

Working backward from your ideal eulogy, go through your goals and consider the resources and investments you will need for realizing each one.

+ Now translate your life mind map into a five-year plan. Then do a one-year version.
+ When you have completed your one-year mind map plan, review your goals and make sure they are smart. Then create an affirmation for each of your major life areas.
+ Now decide the steps you will take this week, today, toward realizing each of your goals.
+ At the beginning of each week, invest twenty to thirty minutes, and make a mind map of your weekly goals, priorities, and plans. If you like you can color-code each of your major life areas. This gives you instant visual feedback on your success in balancing your priorities.
+ Look at the whole picture of your weekly plan. Is your week a balanced rainbow or a monochromatic blur? Have you planned enough time for nurturing

your relationships, your health, your personal and spiritual development?

+ As you survey your weekly map, ask how each activity you have planned supports the realization of your purpose and values.

+ Finally, each day, make a mind map of your daily plan. If you can devote just ten to fifteen minutes at the start of your day, or the evening before, to mind mapping your goals and priorities, you'll be better able to take a Connessione approach to your everyday challenges.

Da Vinci Review

Look at your life mind map from the perspective of the Seven Da Vincian Principles:

Curiosità – Am I asking the right questions?

Dimostrazione – How can I improve my ability to learn from my mistakes and experiences? How can I develop my independence of thought?

Sensazione – What is my plan for sharpening my senses as I age?

Sfumato – How can I strengthen my ability to hold creative tension, to embrace the major paradoxes of life?

Arte/Scienza – Am I balancing Arte and Scienza at home and at work?

Corporalita – How can I nurture the balance of body and mind?

Fix Your Course to a Star

The most carefully crafted strategies rarely work out exactly according to plan. But the best improvisers do not just "wing it," they start with a well-made plan and then adapt gracefully to changing circumstances.

You are the captain of your own ship, but you can't control the weather. Sometimes life brings us smooth sailing; other times we get squalls, hurricanes, and tsunamis. Leonardo counseled, "He who fixes his course to a star changes not." Fix your course to a star, and be ready to navigate through storms and around uncharted icebergs.

Since 1975, I've watched thousands of people around the world use mind mapping to clarify and realize their goals. I've been refining the process over the years and, of course, applying it to my own life. In 1987, when I was thirty-five, I put extra energy into my master mind map, with a special focus on what I aimed to create by the time I was forty. Grace smiled, and almost everything I visualized – professionally, financially, and personally – came true. When I was forty, I went through the whole exercise again, focusing particularly on the next five years, and again my dreams pretty much came true. Now I am forty-five and going through the process again.

Of course, the master mind-mapping process hasn't magically protected me from the disappointments, angst, and grief that are part of everyone's life; I've had my share of squalls, hurricanes, and even the occasional tsunami. But this process has proved invaluable to me, as I hope it will for you, in keeping on course for a star.

Connessione – How do all the above elements fit together? How does everything connect to everything else?

Scan through the self-assessment questions in each of the above chapters and ask yourself how your answers may have changed since you began this book.

Conclusion

Leonardo's Legacy.

n a rare expression of personal feeling, redolent of the great Platonic metaphor of the cave, Leonardo once wrote, "Drawn by my eager wish, desirous of seeing the great confusion of the various strange forms created by ingenious nature, I wandered for some time among the shadowed cliffs, and came to the entrance of a great cavern. I remained before it for a while, stupefied, and ignorant of the existence of such a thing, with my back bent and my left hand resting on my knee, and shading my eyes with my right, with lids lowered and closed, and often bending this way and that to see whether I could discern anything within; but this was denied me by the great darkness inside. And after I stayed awhile there arose in me two things, fear and desire – fear because of the menacing dark cave, and desire to see whether there were any miraculous thing within."

The essence of Leonardo's legacy is the inspiration for wisdom and light to triumph over fear and darkness. In his never-ending quest for truth and beauty, art and science were married through the ministry of experience and perception. His unique synthesis of logic and imagination, of reason and romance, has challenged, inspired, and baffled scholars through the ages. History's greatest master of science and art has achieved the status of myth. In an age of specialization and fragmentation, Leonardo da Vinci shines forth as a beacon of wholeness, reminding us of what it can mean to be created in the image of our Creator.

The nymph Matelda from Dante's Paradiso *by Leonardo da Vinci. Dante wrote a phrase in the* Paradiso *delightfully applicable to the magnetic fascination experienced by students of the maestro: "Who might have confined me in such sweet bonds?"* "Che mi ligasse con si dolci vinci?"

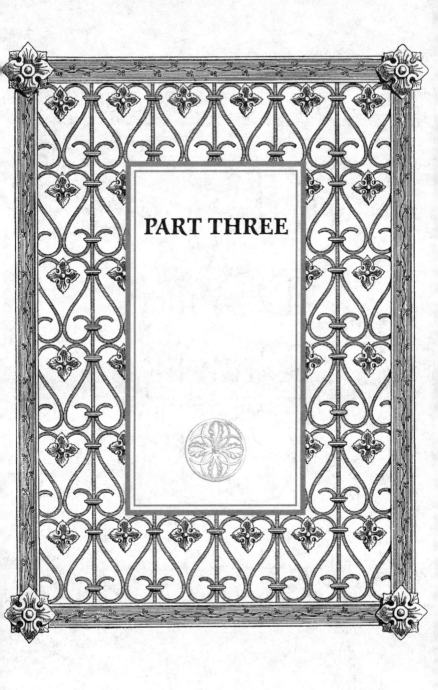

PART THREE

The Beginner's
Da Vinci
Drawing
Course

*L*eonardo emphasized that drawing was the foundation of painting and of learning how to see. For the maestro, drawing was much more than illustration, it was the key to understanding creation and creativity. So for aspiring Da Vincians, learning to draw is the best way to sharpen your ability to see and create.

Many people are reluctant to experiment with drawing because they are convinced that they are "not artistic." I know because I was one of them. In my elementary school, "art class" was held twice a week. I hated it. I wasn't particularly talented and cringed when the teacher criticized my awkward attempts to draw an airplane or a house. I grew up with the conviction "I can't draw, I'm not artistic," and for many years this was a self-fulfilling prophecy. Then, as part of my own Renaissance training program, I started taking drawing lessons. I discovered, as I trust you will, that drawing is fun and that it offers a wondrous expansion of perspective on life.

The following seven assumptions will prepare you for maximum enjoyment and accelerated progress:

"O admirable necessity! O powerful action! What mind can penetrate your nature? What language can express this marvel? None, to be sure. This is where human discourse turns toward the contemplation of the divine."
– LEONARDO ON THE MIRACLE OF THE HUMAN EYE

1. *You can draw.* If you can see, you can draw. Drawing is simple, natural, and fun. Just like any other skill, it requires a desire to learn, focused attention, and practice.

2. *The purpose of drawing is discovery.* Leonardo's drawings are reflections of his experiments in seeing. They are attempts to

discover the nature of things. Approach your experiments in drawing with this delightful anticipation of discovery.

3. *Drawing is for you.* Leonardo did not draw to please others. He drew because he loved it. And judging from the fact that most of his drawings were contained in his voluminous, unpublished notebooks, he valued the process of drawing more than the finished product. As you learn to draw for yourself, you will find that you draw deeper insights and joy from the process.

4. *It is possible that you don't really know what things look like.* To discover something new, you must be willing to loosen your grip on the old. One of the strongest impediments to drawing is the representative "looks-like code" we've developed for what things are. "I know this like the back of my hand" is code for "I no longer look at this, because I have created an image in my mind that will suffice." But if you take a moment right now and actually look at the back of your dominant hand – your *doing* hand – you may notice something new ... the tiny lines across the skin forming small asymmetrical webbing patterns. Or a minute scar or mole, or the vein patterns under the skin, and how they move around the bones as your fingers move. Perhaps you'll see subtle gradations of color that you hadn't appreciated before. Now look at your nondominant hand. Can you see any differences between your two hands? These are the elements we miss when we hit the "replay" button in our minds rather than see in immediate experience as Da Vinci did.

5. *You should put your "art critic" aside for the drawing exercises.* Your inner "art critic" can be very useful when deciding which of your works to include in your next exhibition, but for the beginner criticism is premature. Moreover, experienced artists know that suspension of criticism is essential to the creative process. As you experiment with the following exercises, suspend judgment on the quality of your drawing. Give up the labels "good" and "bad" and just draw.

6. *Instruction helps.* When did you have your last art lesson? Unless you demonstrated special talent, chances are that you had your last art lesson when you were ten or eleven years old. Can you imagine if we treated other subjects in this manner? "Sorry, you don't show any special talent for history, so we're cutting you off at the Middle Ages." Most drawing techniques are simple and easy to learn, but they do require at least a soupçon of instruction. So the recipe for a successful Da Vinci drawing course is: You provide a positive experimental attitude; add focused attention, practice, and the unique elements of your self-expression, and this chapter will offer a simple, step-by-step series of instructions that will guide you to develop your skill and delight.

7. *Drawing is a lifelong process of seeing freshly.* "Established" artists are always seeking freshness and "beginner's mind." If you haven't drawn for quite some time, then the "artist" in you is still young, fresh, and unjaded. Your "beginner's mind" will make this exploration process that much more fun. Be patient with yourself, and remember that today's drawing is a marker for tomorrow's progress.

TOOLS OF THE TRADE

You may have many of these "ingredients" around you already. Otherwise, a visit to your local art-supply store will get you set up. Gather together the following:

Paper
+ **Newsprint** is ideal for fast sketches.
+ **A large sketch pad** will serve you well for the rest of the exercises. The bigger the better.
+ **Your notebook** – Leonardo knew that inspiration was everywhere, so he carried a blank-paged notebook at all times. Many of the exercises that follow will lead you beyond the walls of your work space and into the world at large. You never know when inspiration will strike, but as you practice the exercises, you will find that it strikes more frequently. So, as Leonardo did, carry your notebook everywhere.

Drawing Implements
+ **Graphite:** Different degrees of softness will make finer or softer lines. Try three different grades of pencil: 2B, 3B, and another of your choice. Test them out and see which is most appealing to you.
+ **Conté crayons:** Conté crayons are composed of graphite or pigment, clay, and water, all mixed into a paste, pressed into sticks, then baked. They come in four major colors: Sanguine (four shades of red), Bistre (sepia), white, and black (soft, medium, and hard grades). Conté crayons work well on many types of paper. They produce rich tones and

smooth lines. The effect is similar to that of Leonardo's red-chalk self-portrait.

+ **Charcoal:** Charcoal makes for rich, dark lines that smudge nicely for atmospheric effects.
+ **Pens:** These range from ballpoint, mechanical, and felt-tipped to various drawing-nibbed pens, similar to fountain pens. Try a sampling: Felt-tipped markers can be fun and easy for quick sketches (make sure they are water-soluble). Choose a ballpoint pen you like. And find a fountain pen or a drawing dip pen with a couple of different nibs. The drawing pen will be closest to Da Vinci's experience. (You will need some ink for your drawing dip pen; seek the advice of the art-supply store clerk.)

+ **Brush:** Usually this would be considered an advanced tool, but sometimes the flow of a brush is irresistible. So keep a nice brush or two handy (along with watercolor or ink). Remember, anything that makes a line is a tool for self-expression; so lipstick on a mirror, a toe in the sand, and an airplane in the sky are all "tools of the trade."
+ **Your favorite:** Experiment with pencils, Conté crayons, charcoal, crayons, pastels, brush-tipped markers, or calligraphy pens. It is important to play with different media to discover what you like best.

Undrawing Implements

+ **Eraser:** A white rubber eraser is efficient and clean. Don't plan on using this much. The pink one at the end of a pencil is actually a handy tool for smudging hard lines … play with it and see.
+ **Liquid paper:** Don't bother.
+ **Finger:** Another great smudging tool to keep handy.

+ A straightedge is helpful in laying out perspective.
+ A T square will help you construct neat angles.

PREPARATION

CREATING A BRAIN-NOURISHING ENVIRONMENT

Leonardo's studio was a sensory treasure trove filled with music, flowers, and beautiful scents. In the manner of the maestro, find a peaceful, beautiful, well-lit haven for your drawing practice.

DRAWING WITH THE BODY/MIND

Drawing is a body/mind activity. You will learn faster and have more fun if you do one or two body/mind warm-ups before drawing. All the exercises that you learned in the Corporalita chapter are valuable in preparing to draw. Juggling and the other ambidexterity exercises and the Balanced Resting State procedure are particularly useful in tuning your body/mind for drawing. Also useful are the Eye Palming, Focus Near and Far, and "Soft Eye" exercises from the Sensazione chapter and the Connessione Meditation from the Connessione chapter.

In addition, try the following drawing warm-ups. Notice how each of them "opens" you to drawing in a different way.

Warm-up 1: Whole-Body Rainbows

What parts of your body do you use to draw?

Most people look down at their hand and say, "My hand." But that's just the tip of the iceberg. The most satisfying and expressive drawing is done with the active engagement of the entire body. Your hand is connected to your whole arm, the arm to the torso, supported by your feet on the floor. To awaken the active engagement of your whole body in drawing, try the following:

✦ Begin by drawing small circles in space with each of your fingers.
✦ Then move your hands in circles around the wrist.
✦ Next make bigger circles with your forearms.
✦ And finally, make giant swinging arm circles.
✦ Now make all these circles again, only this time imagine lines of color streaming up from the ground, through your torso, out through your fingertips. Fill the entire universe with magnificent rainbows.

Warm-up 2: Self-massage

Sit comfortably and enjoy a few easy full breaths. Now start to massage your dominant hand. Massage the fingers, knuckles, palm, and wrist, and then work your way up the forearm, elbow, upper arm, toward the shoulders. Explore the deep structure of bone, muscle, and sinew. Then do the same with the other side. Finish with a gentle massage of your face, neck, and scalp, bringing special focus to releasing any tensions in your forehead and jaw.

Sketches from one of the maestro's notebooks.

Warm-up 3: Scribble

Who says we have to do it right the first time? We do, in our heads. Scribbling exercises help us let go of that belief in the body:

+ Get a fresh sheet of paper and scribble the shapes, lines, and textures of your feelings of the moment. If you hold any anxiety, express it on the page free-form. Keep going until your page is carrying your tensions, and your body is relaxed and free to draw.
+ For advanced scribbling, play your favorite music and scribble to it.

ACTUAL DRAWING

A SIMPLE STARTING POINT: PATTERNS WE KNOW

Take a moment to look at anything – this book, an object hanging on your wall, something outside your window – anything at all. As you look, see if you can find triangles, circles, squares, lines, curves, or dots. Are there any shapes that *cannot* be broken down into these core forms?

A delightful secret that will help you appreciate the essential simplicity of drawing is: *Everything* you see is composed of circles, triangles, squares, lines, curves, and dots (not necessarily in that order). Da Vinci scholar Martin Kemp describes Leonardo's conviction that "… the organic complexity of living nature, right down to its minutest nuances of mobile form, is founded upon the inexhaustibly rich interplay of geometrical motifs in the context of natural law."

Make triangles, circles, and squares a theme for a day's observation. Then take lines, curves, and dots on another day. Note the way these shapes come into play in daily life: in people's faces, architecture, furniture, art, and nature. Record your observations in your notebook.

Meantime, take a piece of paper and quickly draw these shapes:

(Notice how "perfect" they are not… *this isn't a course in mechanical drawing; our shapes will be organic.)*

(A "square" is anything with four angles.)

All drawing involves combinations of these simple core elements.

NEW WAYS OF SEEING

We think we know how to see, but as Leonardo said, "People look without seeing …"

Seeing for drawing means looking at things as if you've never seen them before. Rather than relying on recognition and objectification – e.g., "That's an apple" – for drawing purposes an artist suspends the concept "apple" and sees the qualities of a subject in a more elemental way: as shapes, hues, and textures.

Here are a few exercises for exploring this way of seeing.

Seeing Exercise 1: Upside-down Drawing

Upside-down drawing frees us from habitual perceptions. Look at the lines and shapes following. Copy these lines and shapes as you see them, on a fresh piece of paper.

The rules are:

a) *Keep thinking you do not know what this is as you draw.*

b) *Don't turn the book upside down until you are finished.*

c) *You're not finished yet.*

d) *Take a stretch break in which you look around freshly with "soft" eyes.*

e) *After you have copied everything you see, turn your paper around and discover what you have drawn.*

Seeing Exercise 2: Opposite-handed Drawing

Now, again with your nondominant hand, go back and draw the Leonardo da Vinci portrait once more. Notice the effect on your perception, awareness, and sensitivity as you draw upside down and (or with) your "other hand." If these exercises lead you to a slightly unfamiliar feeling, then you are entering into the world of the artist.

What did you notice from the first time to the second?

Use your nondominant hand to draw the above image:

The rules are:

a) *As you draw, name what you are seeing/drawing out loud.*

b) *Don't switch hands.*

Seeing Exercise 3: Light and Dark

One of Leonardo's great contributions to art was the development of chiaroscuro, the use of contrast between light and dark for dramatic emphasis.

Prior to the Renaissance, artists generally emphasized light, to the exclusion of shadow. For the beginning artist this is still an easy mistake to make. In art as in life, it is necessary to delve courageously into the shadows of the darker palette. And it is from the richness of its shadow, and the darkness that surrounds it, that a figure takes form, dimensionality, and depth. As the maestro emphasized, "Shadows have their boundaries at certain determinable points. He who is ignorant of these will produce work without relief; and the relief is the summit and the soul of painting."

These simple exercises will deepen your appreciation for "chiaroscuro" in everyday life.

+ **Look for shadows.** Make shadows a theme for a day. Notice how the quality of shadow changes throughout the day with the movement of the sun. Record your observations in your notebook.
+ **Get impressions of dark and light.** Take a walk in the park, or sit at your favorite café watching people come and go. As you watch the world go by, squint your eyes so that everything becomes "impressionistic." Aim to see the world purely in terms of light and dark, as though your eyes were movie cameras making black-and-white films.

The secret of perceiving light and dark is looking for darkness. As you ask "What is dark?" light appears in relief. With a little practice you will become accustomed to looking at the world in this way.

Seeing Exercise 4: Kaleidoscopic Configurations
As in the light/dark exercise, start in an interesting environment with squinting eyes. But this time, ask the

questions "What shapes does red come in around here?" "How about blue?" "Green?" And so on …

As you seek the color/shapes, the world around you will take on a delightfully sculptural, colorful, and kaleidoscopic quality. Enjoy it.

Seeing Exercise 5: The Artist's Frame

The universe seems infinite; yet the page is finite, and this can sometimes seem limiting. But as an artist, you will learn to use the definition a page provides to your advantage.

Make an L shape with each of your hands by extending your thumbs ninety degrees from your index fingers. Use these angles to make an imaginary frame. As you spy potential "subjects" for observation and drawing, practice looking at them through the "frame" of your hands.

Experiment by making the frame larger or smaller, and shifting it to the right, to the left, up, or down. Enjoy your power to choose and frame your focus.

Seeing Exercise 6: Editing and Magnetizing

Leonardo's masterful use of ambiguity magnetizes our attention to his subject. Later Cézanne used his own version of this "magnetizing" process by rendering indistinct that which was not his subject. This may be the greatest power of the artist: the power to choose the area of focus, and to edit, retire, obscure, or otherwise render secondary anything else.

"Frame" a subject, this time without using your hands. As you do, let everything that is not the subject of choice begin to fade; "mute" all surrounding color and forms. Cast a fine veil around all that is not the focus of your attention.

Let your eyes become soft. As you "blur out" all the surroundings, you open yourself to a new intimacy with your subject.

CONTOURS: OUTSIDE-IN DRAWING

The contour is the outside form, the "topography" of your subject.

Contour Exercise 1: Touch-drawing

Look at a nearby object. Choose something like a plant, a book, a cup, or a chair.

+ First trace the surfaces of your object with your index finger.
+ Then, with your arm outstretched, move your finger, this time just *imagining* that you are touching the object's surfaces.
+ Next, without using your physical finger at all, *imagine* that your gaze is your finger, and your finger-gaze is touching the outer edge of the object. This is more than an outline, because the object is three-dimensional; so you are actually mapping the surface of your subject with your touch-gaze (this "outer edge" is the contour).
+ Now you are ready to touch-draw. Trace the outer edge of your object with your finger-gaze, but this time the tip of your pencil on the paper is an "extension" of your imagined touch-gaze.

The Rules Are:
+ Keep your eyes only on the object as you map it with your finger-gaze.

- Move your gaze around the contour very slowly.
- Keep your pencil tip moving on your page at the same speed as your eyes move along the contour.
- Consider only the point that you are touch-drawing at the moment, without thought of any future or past part of your drawing.
- Develop the conviction that you are actually touching the object with your gaze.
- Do not lift your pencil or look at the page until you've finished the contour.

While the finished drawing will probably not look like the object, it will reveal hidden qualities of texture and depth. This touch-drawing exercise is a kinesthetically rich introduction to *contour*.

Contour Exercise 2: Remember Your Hand?

Earlier we considered the notion of "knowing something like the back of your hand." Then we explored the hand itself. So by now you really know your hand, right? Good. Now, without looking at your hand, close your eyes and re-create it in your mind's eye. Then, with a fresh sheet of paper, draw the contour of your hand from memory.

Once finished, notice how the picture compares with the actual item. Avoid thinking in terms of good or bad. Just ask: How are they similar? How are they different?

Contour Exercise 3: Touch-draw Your Hand

Now observe your nondominant hand. Imagine that your slow, searching gaze is your touch. Touch-draw your hand. Remember, your touch-drawing is a three-dimensional sensory mapping process (more than just an outline). Also do not be misled by shadows; when you "touch" the subject, it will feel the same to your touch

As the maestro suggested, pause periodically and look at your drawing, and your subject, from a distance. Look at what you are doing in a mirror, and from a different angle. Notice changes in your perception and then return to drawing.

whether it is in light or shadow. Follow the rules of touch drawing as in Contour Exercise 1.

Contour Exercise 4: Hand Contour

Now you are ready for a contour drawing of your hand. This is just like touch drawing, except this time you look back and forth between subject and paper. And you will lift your pencil tip from the paper.

Now try a contour drawing of your original touch drawing subject.

DRAWING MOVEMENT

As Leonardo probed the depths of nature, he saw that everything is changing and moving all the time. His drawings possess an inner dynamism that expresses this fundamental quality of movement, even in objects that appear to be still.

Most of our previous drawing exercises require a slow, thoughtful, meditative approach. In drawing movement, we will shift to a faster, more dynamic approach.

Movement Exercise 1: Falling Objects

+ In this exercise, observe the "essential movement" in an object as it falls. Drop tissues, a scarf, napkins, leaves, or a feather … and watch them fall. Ideally, sit by a waterfall for a few hours or just run a bath and watch the water come out of the faucet. Make "falling objects" a theme for a day. Aim to discover at least three new observations about falling bodies. Record your observations in your notebook.

- ✦ Then experiment with drawing the "tracks" of the movement of a falling object. Imagine feeling these tracks in your own body. Leonardo suggested the following: "Make some silhouettes out of cardboard in various forms and throw them from the top of the terrace through the air; then draw the movements each makes at the different stages of its descent." Marcel Duchamp's *Nude Descending a Staircase* was inspired by this Da Vincian exercise in seeing.

Movement Exercise 2: Still Movement

With reckless abandon, draw the essence of a still object such as a bow, a drapery, a napping dog, or an old shoe.

Artist's rendition of a ringing telephone.

Movement Exercise 3: Motion in People

Find a nice spot to sit in a public place – train stations and airports are ideal – and watch people move. Practice the following exercise suggested by the maestro: "… Keep a sharp lookout for figures in movement … and note down the main lines quickly: that is to say putting an O for the head and straight or bent lines for the arms and the same for the legs and trunk."

Motion drawing of the author telling a story.

Figures in movement: Main Lines.

SHADING & "MASSING": INSIDE-OUT SUBSTANCE

A mark on a piece of paper is a two-dimensional phenomenon. The artist's challenge is to turn two dimensions into three or more. Shading and massing are keys to this transformation.

Shading Exercise 1: Light on a Sphere

Draw a few circles on your page and experiment with different angles of light and shade as follows:

Shading Exercise 2: Apple in the Sun

This exercise works with an apple, or any basic form.

For an object to convey that it has "realistic substance," the shadows must make sense in relation to light. Remember how in the light/dark seeing exercise you squinted your eyes and began to distinguish between shades of light and dark? Now it is time to apply that awareness to your apple.

Place the apple on a simple surface near you. (It could be on a plain-colored plate, a piece of paper, a table, a cloth – anything not distracting.) Now, allowing yourself to look back and forth between subject and page, make a contour outline of the form of the apple on the plate.

(You will notice that even if it is the same apple as before, it never looks the same from any other angle, under any other light; so there is really no such thing as doing the exact same thing twice.)

Now look to see where and what is the major source of light (sometimes there are more than one; choose the dominant source, and if possible, turn the others off). Once again squint your eyes to distinguish the light and dark on the apple. Got it? Confirm that the dark (shadow) is opposite your light source. If it is not, look again.

✦ On your paper, indicate where the light is coming from with a little sun. With a soft pencil, begin shading the dark parts of your apple. Shading is an additive process, so shade in thin "layers" as Da Vinci did.

As you shade, keep returning to your light/dark squinting. It will help clarify how dark the shadows really are.

Shading Exercise 4: Value Chart

In drawing, value does not refer to how much money this little baby's going to bring at auction. Rather, value refers to depth of shade.

At the bottom of your page, make a rough value chart similar to the one on the next page:

| LIGHTEST | MEDIUM-LIGHT | MEDIUM | DARKEST |

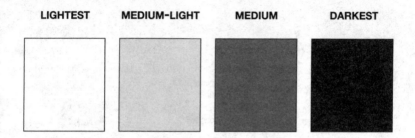

Shading Exercise 5: Sphere Values

Go back to your shaded drawing of a sphere. Review the value chart, and by squinting at your sphere and the chart, note how your shading corresponds to values of Lightest, Medium-Light, Medium, or Darkest. For example, in the following shaded figure, the different "levels" of darkness can roughly be broken down into these four value categories. This exercise will develop your ability to distinguish among different values and reduce shading into simple groupings. Later you can add more refined value variation.

Shading Exercise 6: More Fruit

Collect a couple of apples and pears. (The smooth texture will keep the focus on drawing shadows rather than on surface patterns.) Next arrange them on a plate. Decide on the light source, and mark it with a little sun at the edge of your page. Look at the overall pattern of fruits on the surface. Are any overlapping? When you squint your eyes, which ones stand out? What are the patterns of the different values?

Now "frame" your picture. Then, using contour and shading, draw the still life before you. (Remember to break occasionally and view your work from a distance.)

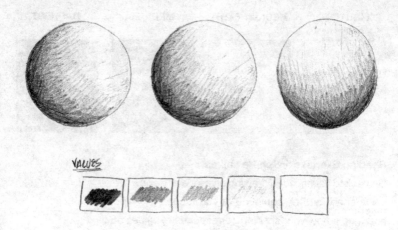

VALUES

MASSING YOUR FORCES

The shading techniques you have just learned are very effective, but to convey the fullness of things from the inside out they must be complemented by a special secret of depth creation. This secret of depth creation is "massing," also known as modeling. Massing is a way of conveying a visceral sense of "bulk." Without it, figures appear to be "wearing" their depth like makeup, rather than feeling like objects of substance.

Mass Exercise 1: Very Red Apple

To get the most from this exercise, pretend you are a four-year-old who has just found a red crayon.

Then find a bright red apple. Place it at a comfortable distance in front of you on a well-lit spot. Imagine that you are building a reservoir of that same color red in your own imaginary inkwell … let it keep filling with color until the color red seems absolutely juicy and bursting with life. Now take a red marker or crayon and draw a red dot on your paper.

Simple still life.

Think of the apple as a living substance; with your red color you are searching for its core. Now start "filling" the apple with color from the inside out. Make the reddest parts really red, and let the outer edges, which don't seem to "contain" as much color, reflect that as well. This exercise provides the foundation experience for massing.

Mass Exercise 2: Sculpting

In this exercise we seek the sensation of a sculptor modeling with clay. So imagine you are the sculptor, and you've put approximately the right amount of clay where it belongs to sculpt your subject. Now you shape your sculpture by pressing into the clay wherever the form has a hollow, molding and shaping the curves of the form.

Choose a subject, preferably a live one (such as a dog, cat, husband, wife, child, or friend). Draw the form of your subject using the flat edge of a black Conté crayon, rather than a tip or an end, as we have before.

Where the form goes in, let the crayon press more heavily onto the page (yielding a darker shade); and

Massing a sleeping dog.

where the form moves out, closer to you, let the crayon rise lightly, only just touching the page. Imagine that you are "molding" this drawing.

Mass Exercise 3: Anatomy of an Apple

This is an advanced Da Vincian fruit experiment that aims to inform us, scientifically, what is at the core of an apple, and how that mass is structured to give the apple form.

Take three bright, luscious apples. Pick up each one and turn it in your hand, feeling its weight, texture, and balance. Observe its color as if through a magnifying glass. Notice the patterns on the surface. How is each apple different? Make notes in your notebook of your observation. Then notice the arcs of each contour. Notice the subtle variations that make this apple unique and unlike the common "apple image" that pops into your mind when you think "apple."

Now that you are intimate with your apples, we are ready for the autopsy. It's time to dissect (a.k.a. "slice") the apples to examine the inner structure. Slice one apple in half horizontally, another vertically, and the third diagonally for three different perspectives.

Next arrange the apple pieces on a plate. Place the plate on a surface, and prepare to draw this "core" study. Note the light source. Squint to measure value. Note how the surfaces create different "planes" for the light reflection. Now you are ready for your core still life.

After you complete your core still life, draw a whole apple. Let your drawing reflect your understanding of the apple from the inside out.

PERSPECTIVE

Shading and massing build depth and dimension, and perspective puts them in context.

Perspective Exercise 1: Distant Horizons
The maestro invested many hours in observing the distant horizon. He noted:

+ "Among objects of equal size that which is most remote from the eye will look smallest."
+ "Of several bodies, all equally large and equally distant, that which is most brightly illuminated will appear to the eye nearest and largest."
+ "A dark object will appear bluer in proportion as it has more luminous atmosphere between it and the eye, as may be seen in the color of the sky."

Before Leonardo, objects in the background and foreground were usually depicted with similar dimension, value, and color. Begin your exploration of perspective by studying the far horizon and then working forward. Make perspective a theme for a day and record your observations.

Perspective Exercise 2: Overlap

Which comes first? The one in front. The object that overlaps another appears to be in front. This principle is so basic, we might miss it. This simple observation makes the visual communication of relationship between objects unquestionably clear. For example, the following four frames contain the same four lightly drawn boxes. They could be in any positional relation to one another. However, by simply tracing the boxes with different overlaps, some will appear to recede, while others will appear to move forward.

First trace the outline of one particular box. Then trace in the lines of a second box (omitting any lines that appear to fall "behind" the first box). Then trace in the third, then the last box in a similar fashion.

In the next frames, make a different box the closest forward in each picture. Notice that overlap dictates size. It does not even matter that one box is the smallest or largest; depending on its relational position, it might just appear closer or further away.

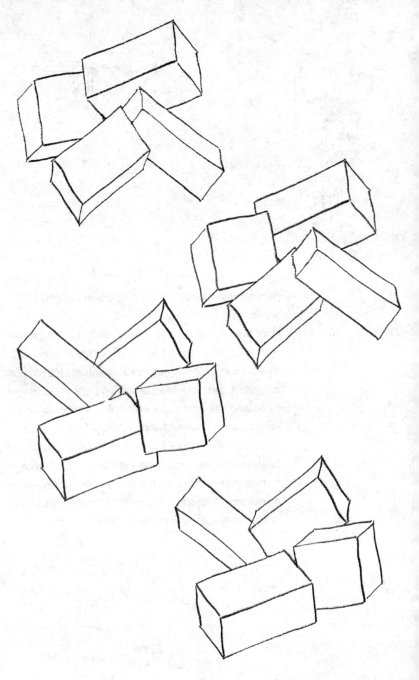

Perspective Exercise 3: My Paper's in the Way of My Subject

Once you've "framed out" your subject, it can be a little perplexing to keep the same perspective over time, especially since the surface you are actually drawing on may be lying flat on a table, or slanted on an easel. Forget where and how your paper or canvas is actually situated. Rather, *always* imagine that your paper or canvas is set up vertically between you and the objects you are drawing. Imagine you are actually seeing *through* the paper or canvas and simply tracing them. So when you are drawing something, always refer back to that imaginary paper or canvas between you and your subject.

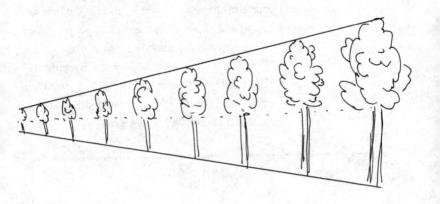

Perspective Exercise 4: Small – Far . . . Big – Near

When looking at people from a great distance, we've all noticed how small they can appear to become. We use this size variation automatically to gauge distance. In the overlap exercise we learned that relative position can convey a lot of information. But once we know the sequence of objects, size becomes the next most informative factor. For example, in the picture above, what happens as the trees get smaller?

The following exercises will introduce the crux of perspective: the horizon line (a.k.a. your eye level) and the vanishing point.

Perspective Exercise 5: Horizon – Eye Level

With your straightedge, draw a horizontal line across your paper and label it "eye level." Experiment by drawing it at different heights on your page.

Establishing the eye level is essential, because as drawings become more complex, the eye level might be covered by mountains, buildings, or trees; yet everything in a picture is drawn relative to eye level.

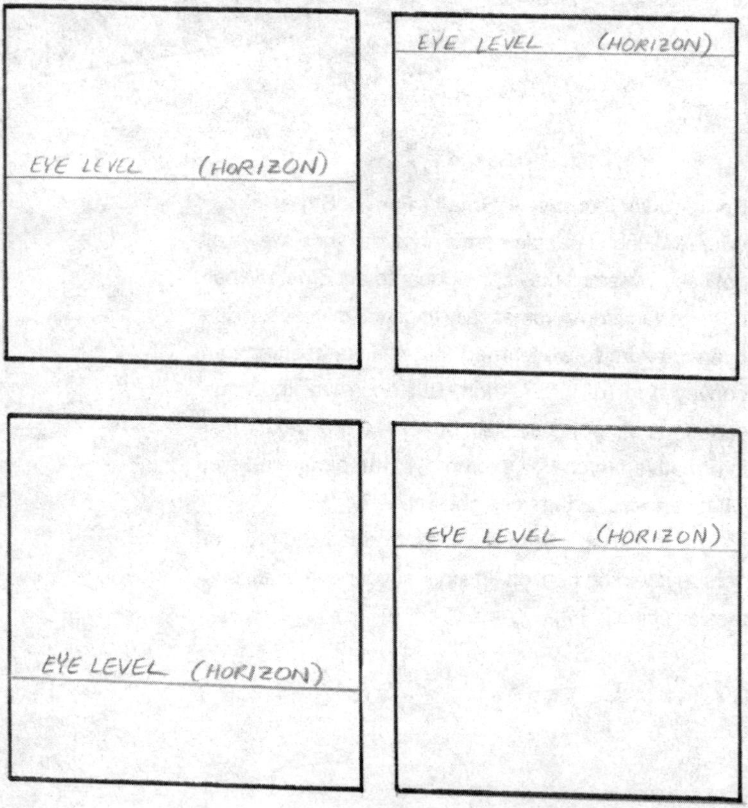

EYE LEVEL (HORIZON)

EYE LEVEL (HORIZON)

EYE LEVEL (HORIZON)

EYE LEVEL (HORIZON)

Perspective Exercise 6: Vanishing Point

Now go back to your eye levels and, with a Conté crayon, place a dot near the center. Label that dot "VP" for vanishing point.

From that dot, draw a straight line to each bottom corner of your paper. You will notice you have what appears to be a wide opening street. Notice the difference the eye levels make on the impression of the street.

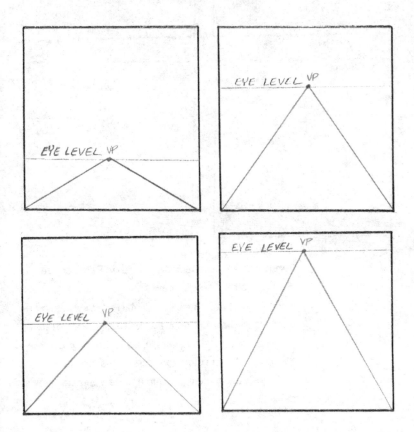

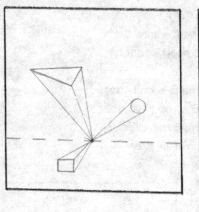

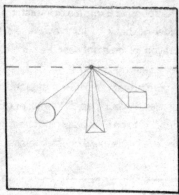

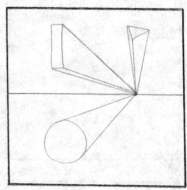

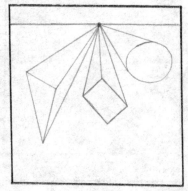

Perspective Exercise 7: A Square on Perspective

With your straightedge, draw a soft, dotted horizon line. Choose and dot a vanishing point. Next draw a triangle, a square, and a circle in the frame. Keeping the vanishing point in mind, make the triangle, square, and circle three-dimensional in the direction of the vanishing point.

Step back to see if your figures seem to "make sense."

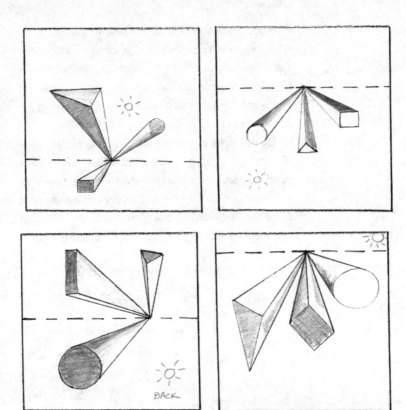

On your best example, choose a light source and label it with a little sun. Take a moment to "feel" the direction of the light, as if you were the object you will shade. With a soft graphite pencil, shade the three-dimensional figures with shadows away from the light source (remember to shade in light layers).

When you are comfortable with the above, you may want to practice and experiment with other shape variations.

Perspective Exercise 8: An Interesting Street

As before, with your straightedge, draw a horizon line. Dot a vanishing point (VP). From the VP draw lines to the bottom and top corners of the frame: Now, in descending order, draw a row of simple trees along the street you've begun.

On the other side of the street, similar to the three-dimensional triangle, square, circle exercise, make a couple of "square" buildings. Remember that all vertical (up and down) lines will be exactly parallel. Also note that there should be an imaginary roofline to the vanishing point, so that will be your guide for descending size.

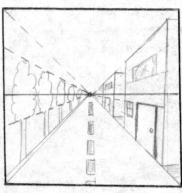

LAYERS OVER DISTANCE

VALUE CHANGE – DISTANCE

Perspective Exercise 9: Landscape

Practice looking at landscapes to deepen your appreciation of perspective. Experiment with sketches in your notebook.

DRAWING BY HEART

Heart Drawing Exercise 1: Face Memory – You

From memory, without looking in a mirror, draw your face. Sign it. Date it. Smile.

Heart Drawing Exercise 2: Face Memory – a Friend

Think of someone close to you. In your mind's eye, conjure that person's face, and begin to observe it as an artist. Notice the core shapes and the relationship of one feature with another. What features are most outstanding? Where do you see symmetry and asymmetry?

Think in contours. Are the cheeks prominent? Do they recede quickly? Are the eyes deep set? Where are the rises and falls in the face? Imagine you touch it with your mind's gaze, and follow along the contours of the face.

Remember to keep your mental gaze flowing around the whole face; do not get "lost" in one feature.

Now make a drawing of the face from memory.

Next take an opportunity to study your friend's face. Make a note of what was "missing" from your memory. Each memory drawing will make your subsequent observation richer and more refined.

Leonardo's *Study of Profiles* from the Windsor Collection.

Heart Drawing Exercise 3: A Nose for Study

Leonardo suggested the following exercise in "knowing how to see": "… first learn by heart the various kinds of heads, eyes, noses, mouths, chins, throats, and also necks and shoulders. Take as an instance noses: they are of ten types: straight, bulbous, hollow, prominent either above or below the center, aquiline, regular, simian, round and pointed. These divisions hold good as regards profile. Seen from in front, noses are of twelve types: thick in the middle, thin in the middle, with the tip broad, and narrow at the base, and narrow at the tip, and broad at the base, with nostrils broad or narrow, or high or low, and with the openings either visible or hidden by the tip. And similarly you will find variety in the other features; of which things you ought to make studies from nature and fix them in your memory."

Following the maestro, take faces as a theme for a day. Then on a subsequent day take noses as a theme. Sketch the different types in profile and from the front. Then do the same with eyes, mouths, etc.

Heart Drawing Exercise 4: Face Study

After you have studied faces and features for a while, try a study of the face of a friend, preferably the friend whose face you drew from memory in the earlier exercise. Try the following steps:

Look at your friend as though you are seeing her for the first time.

View her face in terms of geometry. Look for triangles, circles, and squares. Note lines, curves, and dots.

If your friend consents, gently stroke her face with your fingertips, exploring the contour and texture.

Then step back and do a slow touch-draw of her face.

Next study the shadows and shadings. Do a quick

When you wish to know anything well by heart which you have studied, follow this method: When you have drawn the same thing so many times that it seems you know it by heart, try to do it without the model: but have a tracing made of the model upon a thin piece of smooth glass and lay this upon the drawing you have made without the model. Note well where the tracing and your drawing do not tally, and where you find that you have erred bear it in mind in order not to make the mistake again. Even return to your model in order to copy the part where you were wrong so many times as to fix it in your mind.

– Leonardo da Vinci

FRANCESCO SFORZA CONTE DI PAVIA
figlio di Gio: Galeazzo Sforza e d'Isabella
d'Aragona pronepote di Lodovico Sforza il moro
disegnato

da LEONARDO da VINCI.

Study of the Face of Francesco Sforza.

sketch that reflects the values you observe.

Now, with a soft Conté crayon, make a quick abstract
"sculptural" drawing of your friend's face. Draw out the
depth and richness of what you see.

Penultimately, make a quick sketch of your friend's
face using your nondominant hand.

Finally, make a drawing that combines everything you
have learned from the face study exercise.

Heart Drawing Exercise 5: Self Study

Apply all the steps in exercise 4 to a study of your own
sweet face in the mirror.

The Beginner's Da Vinci Drawing Course is designed to inspire a lifelong
love affair with the art of "knowing how to see." Drawing, in the manner
of the maestro, is making love with the world through your eyes. Savor
the seduction of color, the lustiness of mass, the romance of light and dark.
Practice, experiment, surrender, breathe, and have fun. To get the most
from your relationship with your drawings, sign, date, and save each one.
Your drawings will form a fascinating record of your evolving vision of
the world.

Re-creation of the model of the Sforza horse based on sketches by Leonardo da Vinci.

LEONARDO DA VINCI
CHRONOLOGY: LIFE AND TIMES

1452	15 April	Birth of Leonardo
1453		Fall of Byzantium
1469		Birth of Machiavelli/Death of Piero de' Medici – Lorenzo (Il Magnifico) and Giuliano assume leadership in Florence
1473		Birth of Copernicus/Leonardo admitted to the painters' guild
1475		Birth of Michelangelo
1480		Birth of Magellan
1481		Leonardo works on *The Adoration of the Magi*
1483		Birth of Raphael
1488		Birth of Titian
1490		Leonardo establishes his own workshop
1492		Columbus in New World
1497		Leonardo works on *The Last Supper*
1498		
1499		Sforza equestrian model destroyed
1500		
1504		Michelangelo's *David* completed; Leonardo consulted as to the best position for its display
	9 July	Death of Leonardo's father, leaving ten sons and two daughters
1506		*Mona Lisa* completed
1507		
1508		
1512		Michelangelo completes Sistine Chapel ceiling
1513		
1516		Leonardo leaves Italy for Amboise
1519	23 April	Leonardo's last will and testament
	2 May	Death of Leonardo

RECOMMENDED READING

CURIOSITÀ

Adams, Kathleen. *Journal to the Self.* New York: Warner Books, 1990.
Filled with marvelous exercises for increasing self-knowledge.

Fuller, Buckminster. *Critical Path.* New York: St. Martin's Press, 1981.
Insights from a modern *uomo universale.*

Goldberg, Merrilee. *The Art of the Question: A Guide to Short-Term
Question-Centered Therapy.* New York: John Wiley & Sons, 1998.
A therapist's masterful application of Curiosità.

Gross, Ron. *Peak Learning.* Los Angeles: Jeremy P. Tarcher, 1991.
A handbook for lifelong learners.

Progoff, Ira. *At a Journal Workshop.* New York: Dialogue House, 1975.
Progoff is the modern pioneer in the use of journaling as a tool for
personal growth.

DIMOSTRAZIONE

Alexander, F. M. *The Use of the Self.* New York: Dutton, 1932.
An inspiring story of learning from experience.

McCormack, Mark. *What They Don't Teach You at Harvard Business
School.* New York: Bantam, 1984. Dimostrazione in the business
world.

Seligman, Martin. *Learned Optimism.* New York: Knopf, 1991. How to
learn resilience in the face of adversity.

Shah, Idries. *The Wisdom of the Idiots.* New York: Dutton, 1971. A book
about the Sufis, "disciples of experience."

SENSAZIONE

Ackerman, Diane. *A Natural History of the Senses*. New York: Vintage Books, 1991. The *Chicago Tribune* called it "an aphrodisiac for the sense receptors."

Campbell, Don. *The Mozart Effect: Tapping the Power of Music to Heal the Body, Strengthen the Mind, and Unlock the Creative Spirit*. New York: Avon Books, 1997.

Collins, Terah Kathryn. *The Western Guide to Fêng Shui*. Carlsbad, Calif.: Hay House, Inc., 1996.

Cytowic, Richard. *The Man Who Tasted Shapes*. New York: Putnam, 1993. A neurologist's creative investigation of synesthesia.

Gregory, R. L. *Eye and Brain: The Psychology of Seeing* (fourth edition). New York: Oxford University Press, 1990.

Rossbach, Sarah. *Interior Design with Fêng Shui*. New York: Dutton, 1987. A manual for creating "brain-nourishing environments."

SFUMATO

Agor, Weston. *The Logic of Intuitive Decision Making*. Westport, Conn.: Greenwood Press, 1986. Agor makes a strong case for the use of intuition in managing complexity.

Gelb, Michael J. *Thinking for a Change: Discovering the Power to Create, Communicate, and Lead*. New York: Harmony Books, 1996. Introduces the concept of "Synvergent Thinking," an approach to thriving with Sfumato.

Johnson, Barry. *Polarity Management: Identifying and Managing Unsolvable Problems*. Amherst, Mass.: Human Resource Development Press, 1992. Johnson's concept of Polarity Management is a brilliant example of applied Sfumato.

May, Rollo. *The Courage to Create*. New York: Bantam, 1976. A seminal exposition of the central role of creative tension in a creative life.

Arte/Scienza

Buzan, Tony. *Use Both Sides of Your Brain* (third edition). New York: Penguin, 1989. Buzan's classic work, originally published in 1971, established him as the father of "whole-brain" education. An invaluable guide for anyone interested in balancing Arte and Scienza.

Buzan, Tony, and Barry Buzan. *The Mind Map Book: Radiant Thinking*. London: BBC Books, 1993. The bible of mind mapping.

Wonder, Jacqueline. *Whole Brain Thinking*. New York: Ballantine, 1985. Are you more Arte or Scienza? Wonder offers the opportunity to test your brain dominance.

Corporalita

Anderson, Bob. *Stretching*. Bolinas, Calif.: Shelter Publications, 1980.

Conable, Barbara and William. *How to Learn the Alexander Technique*. Columbus, Ohio: Andover Road Press, 1991. The Conables introduced the concept of "body mapping."

Cooper, Kenneth. *New Aerobics*. New York: Bantam, 1970.

Fincher, Jack. *Lefties: The Origin and Consequences of Being Left-Handed*. New York: Putnam, 1977. An amusing and well-researched overview of the relationship between hand and brain.

Gelb, Michael. *Body Learning: An Introduction to the Alexander Technique*. New York: Henry Holt & Company, 1987 (new edition, 1995). A guide to developing the Da Vincian qualities of poise, presence, and grace.

Gelb, Michael, and Tony Buzan. *More Balls Than Hands: Juggling Your Way to Success by Learning to Love Your Mistakes*. New York: Prentice Hall, 2003. A unique approach to applied ambidexterity and learning how to learn.

CONNESSIONE

Kodish, Susan and Bruce. *Drive Yourself Sane: Using the Uncommon Sense of General Semantics*. Englewood, N.J.: Institute of General Semantics, 1993. An approachable work on systems thinking and general semantics.

Lao-Tzu. *Tao Te Ching: A New English Version,* with forward and notes by Stephen Mitchell. New York: Harper & Row, 1988. Taoism mirrors many of the maestro's insights.

Russell, Peter. *The Awakening Earth: Our Next Evolutionary Leap*. A Connessione view of earth and human evolution. London: Routledge & Kegan Paul, 1982.

Senge, Peter M. *The Fifth Discipline: The Art & Practice of the Learning Organization*. New York: Doubleday, 1990. Guides the reader to see and understand patterns, relationships, and systems in business and everyday life.

Wheatley, Margaret. *Leadership and the New Science*. San Francisco: Berret-Koehler Publishers, 1992. Applications of the new physics to understanding organizations.

THE BEGINNER'S DA VINCI DRAWING COURSE

Edwards, Betty. *Drawing on the Right Side of the Brain*. Los Angeles: Jeremy P. Tarcher, 1979. Betty Edwards's book is a classic in the field of whole-brain education.

Gill, Lorraine K. Soon to be published manuscripts on drawing and seeing.

Nicolaides, Kimon. *The Natural Way to Draw*. Boston: Houghton Mifflin, 1941. The best how-to-draw book.

THE RENAISSANCE AND THE HISTORY OF ART AND IDEAS

Burke, Peter. *The Italian Renaissance: Culture and Society in Italy*. Princeton, N.J.: Princeton University Press, 1987.

Burkhardt, Jacob. *The Civilization of the Renaissance in Italy*. New York: Boni, 1935.

Durant, Will. *The Story of Civilization*. New York: Simon & Schuster, 1935.

Gombrich, E. H. *The Story of Art* (sixteenth edition). London: Phaidon Press, 1994. If you are going to read just one book on the history of art, this should be it.

Hibbert, Christopher. *The House of Medici: Its Rise and Fall*. New York: William Morrow, 1974.

Janson, H. W. *History of Art*. Englewood Cliffs, N.J.: Prentice Hall, 1982.

Jardine, Lisa. *Worldly Goods: A New History of the Renaissance*. New York: Doubleday, 1996. The role of "material culture" in the Renaissance.

Manchester, William. *A World Lit Only by Fire: The Medieval Mind and the Renaissance*. Boston: Little, Brown and Co., 1992. One of the most lively, engaging history books you will ever read.

Schwartz, Lillian (with Laurens Schwartz). *The Computer Artist's Handbook*. New York: Norton, 1992. An art book for the information age. Includes the author's groundbreaking studies of the *Mona Lisa* and *The Last Supper*.

Tarnas, Richard. *The Passion of the Western Mind: Understanding the Ideas That Have Shaped Our World View*. New York: Ballantine Books, 1991. Tarnas concludes that the Western psyche is on the verge of an unprecedented epochal transformation: "a triumphant and healing ... reconciliation between the two great polarities, a union of opposites: a sacred marriage between the long-dominant but now alienated masculine and the long-suppressed but now ascending feminine."

Tuchman, Barbara. *A Distant Mirror: The Calamitous 14th Century*. New York: Ballantine Books, 1978.

Vasari, Giorgio (translated by Julia Conway Bonadella and Peter Bonadella). *The Lives of the Artists*. Oxford: Oxford University Press, 1991.

I have used various Vasari translations, but the Oxford University edition is the most recent.

LEONARDO DA VINCI

Beck, James. *Leonardo's Rules of Painting: An Unconventional Approach to Modern Art*. New York: The Viking Press, 1979.

Bramly, Serge. *Discovering the Life of Leonardo da Vinci*. New York: Harper Collins, 1991. The best biography.

Clark, Kenneth. *Leonardo da Vinci*. London: Penguin Books, 1993 (new edition with revision and introduction by Martin Kemp).
A compelling account of the development of the artist.

Costantino, Maria. *Leonardo*. Leicester, U.K.: Magna Books, 1994. The best illustrations.

Freud, Sigmund. *Leonardo da Vinci: A Study in Psychosexuality*. New York: Vintage Books, 1961. In a famous passage from the notebooks Leonardo interrupts his observations of the flight of the vulture to offer a rare personal recollection: "It seems that it had been destined before that I should occupy myself so thoroughly with the vulture, for it comes to my mind as a very early memory, when I was still in the cradle, a vulture came down to me, opened my mouth with his tail and struck me many times with his tail against my lips." With this memory and a few other reliable facts as his point of departure, Freud offers an analysis that is essential reading for those who wish to understand Leonardo (and Freud). Freud's analysis of Da Vinci is not, as is often supposed, an attempt to reduce genius to pathology. Rather, it is one genius's respectful and sensitive attempt to deepen our understanding of another.

Merezhkovsky, Dmitry. *The Romance of Leonardo da Vinci*. New York: Garden City Publishing Co., 1928.

Philipson, Morris. *Leonardo da Vinci: Aspects of the Renaissance Genius*. New York: George Brazilier, Inc., 1966. Thirteen scholars on the maestro. Philipson's brief introduction – "The Fascination of Leonardo da Vinci" – is a most elegant summary of the maestro's legacy.

Reti, Ladislao, ed. *The Unknown Leonardo*. New York: McGraw-Hill, 1974. Includes articles entitled "Leonardo and Music" and "Horology"; fantastic illustrations throughout.

Richter, Irma A., ed. *The Notebooks of Leonardo da Vinci*. Oxford: Oxford University Press, 1952. "World Classics Edition," 1980. The daughter of Jean Paul Richter has made the maestro's work even more accessible.

Richter, Jean Paul, ed. *The Notebooks of Leonardo da Vinci*. New York: Dover Publications, Inc., 1970. (First published in London in 1883 under the title *The Literary Works of Leonardo da Vinci*.)

Stites, Raymond. *The Sublimations of Leonardo da Vinci*. Washington, D.C.: Smithsonian Institution Press, 1970.

Vallentin, Antonina. *Leonardo da Vinci: The Tragic Pursuit of Perfection*. New York: The Viking Press, 1938.

THE NATURE OF INTELLIGENCES AND GENIUS

Boorstin, Daniel. *The Creators: A History of Heroes of the Imagination*. New York: Random House, 1993.

Briggs, John. *Fire in the Crucible*. Los Angeles: Jeremy P. Tarcher, Inc., 1990. An aesthetician's first-class research into the nuances of genius.

Buzan, Tony, and Raymond Keene. *Buzan's Book of Genius (And How You Can Become One)*. London: Stanley Paul, 1994. A systematic examination of the nature of genius with practical exercises for developing intelligences.

Dilts, Robert. *Strategies of Genius* (volumes 1–3). Capitola, Calif.: Meta Publications, 1995. Dilts, a pioneer in neurolinguistic programming, offers brilliant insights into the minds of Aristotle, Walt Disney, Sigmund Freud, and others, including Leonardo da Vinci.

Gardener, Howard. *Creating Minds: An Anatomy of Creativity Seen Through the Lives of Freud, Einstein, Picasso, Stravinsky, Eliot, Graham, and Ghandi*. New York: Basic Books, 1993.

Gardener, Howard. *Frames of Mind: The Theory of Multiple Intelligences*. New York: Basic Books, 1983.

Pert, Candace. *Molecules of Emotion*. New York: Scribner, 1997. A leading neuroscientist's engaging personal account of her pioneering work in illuminating the inseparability of body, mind, emotion, and spirit.

Restak, Richard M. *The Brain: The Last Frontier*. New York: Warner Books, 1979. A thorough, easy-to-read discussion of brain science.

Von Oech, Roger. *A Whack on the Side of the Head* (revised edition). New York: Warner Books, 1990. The modern classic on thinking creatively.

LIST OF ILLUSTRATIONS

Leonardo da Vinci. *The Last Supper*. S. Maria delle Grazie, Milan, Italy. Photo: Alinari/Art Resource, NY.

Leonardo da Vinci. *Study for Sforza Monument*. Royal Library, Windsor, Great Britain. Photo: Scala/Art Resource, NY.

Boltraffio. *Portrait of Ludovico il Moro*. Photo: Alinari/Art Resource, NY.

Leonardo da Vinci. *Drawing of The Virgin and Child with St. Anne*. Photo: Scala/Art Resource, NY.

Anonymous. *Portrait of Niccolò Machiavelli*. Uffizi, Florence, Italy. Photo: Alinari/Art Resource, NY.

Portrait of Cesare Borgia. Accademia Carrara, Bergamo, Italy. Photo: Alinari/Art Resource, NY.

Peter Paul Rubens's rendition of *The Battle of Anghiari* by Leonardo da Vinci. Louvre, Paris, France. Photo: Giraudon/Art Resource, NY.

Jean Clouet. *Francis I of France*. Louvre, Paris, France. Photo: Alinari/Art Resource, NY.

Leonardo da Vinci. *Landscape dated August 5, 1473, # 8p*. Gabinetto dei Disegni e delle Stampe, Florence, Italy. Photo: Scala/Art Resource, NY.

Raphael. *Detail of Plato and Aristotle. School of Athens*. Stanze di Raffaello, Vatican Palace, Vatican State. Photo: Alinari/Art Resource, NY.

Leonardo da Vinci. *Sketches of war machines (vol. 73 1860 6 16 99)* British Museum, London, Great Britain. Photo: Alinari/Art Resource, NY.

Leonardo da Vinci. *Bombards Firing Shrapnel, Shells*. Codex Atlanticus 9v-a. Photo: Art Resource, NY.

PART TWO

Curiosità

Leonardo da Vinci. *Study of flowers*. Accademia, Venice, Italy. Photo: Alinari/Art Resource, NY.

Leonardo da Vinci. *Flying machine – sketch from Codex Atlanticus*. Biblioteca Ambrosiana, Milan, Italy. Photo: Art Resource, NY.

Leonardo da Vinci. *Drawings of birds. E-fol 22-V 23-R.* Bibliotheque de L'Institut de France, Paris, France. Photo: Giraudon/Art Resource, NY.

Page from Leonardo da Vinci's notebooks. The Royal Collection © Her Majesty Queen Elizabeth II.

Sfumato

Leonardo da Vinci. *Virgin of the Rocks.* Louvre, Paris, France. Photo: Alinari/Art Resource, NY.

Leonardo da Vinci. *Two Heads (No. 423).* Gabinetto dei Disegni e delle Stampe, Florence, Italy. Photo: Scala/Art Resource, NY.

Leonardo da Vinci. *Saint John the Baptist.* Louvre, Paris, France. Photo: Giraudon/Art Resource, NY.

Leonardo da Vinci. *Mona Lisa (La Gioconda).* c. 1503-1006. Oil on panel, 97 x 53 cm. Louvre, Paris, France. Photo: Giraudon/Art Resource, NY.

Lillian Schwartz. *Juxtaposition of Leonardo's Self-portrait and Mona Lisa.* Copyright © 1998 Computer Creations Corporation. All rights reserved. Reprinted by permission.

Arte/Scienza

Leonardo da Vinci. *Map of Imola.* Photo: Scala/Art Resource, NY.

Mind Mapping. Illustration: Nusa Maal

Hemispheres. Illustration: Nusa Maal

Mind Map on the Rules of Mind Mapping. Illustration: Nusa Maal

Mind Map Applications. Illustration: Nusa Maal

Corporalita

Leonardo da Vinci. *Drawing of ideal proportions of the human figure according to Vitruvius's first century A.D. treatise "De Architectura."* Photo: Alinari/Art Resource, NY.

Leonardo da Vinci. *Back View.* The Royal Collection © Her Majesty Queen Elizabeth II.

Mirror writing. Illustration: Joan Gelb.

Leonardo da Vinci Juggler. Illustration: Nusa Maal.

Connessione

One of Leonardo da Vinci's dragons. The Royal Collection © Her Majesty
Queen Elizabeth II.

Leonardo da Vinci. *Floral study, probably a study for the Virgin of the
Rocks.* (Facsimilie, original in the Windsor Collection, Great
Britain). Gabinetto dei Disegni e delle Stampe, Florence, Italy.
Photo: Scala/Art Resource, NY.

Leonardo da Vinci. *Cataclism* (facsimilie). Gabinetto dei Disegni e delle
Stampe, Florence, Italy. Photo: Scala/Art Resource, NY.

Leonardo da Vinci. *Whirlpool.* The Royal Collection © Her Majesty
Queen Elizabeth II.

Leonardo da Vinci. *Study for the head of Leda.* (Facsimilie, original in
the Windsor Collection, Great Britain). Gabinetto dei Disegni e delle
Stampe, Florence, Italy. Photo: Scala/Art Resource, NY.

Mind Map on Dinner. Illustration: Nusa Maal.

The Beginning of a Life Mind Map. Illustration: Nusa Maal.

Conclusion: Leonardo's Legacy

Leonardo Da Vinci. *The nymph Matelda from Dante's Paradiso.* The
Royal Collection © Her Majesty Queen Elizabeth II.

PART THREE

The Beginner's Da Vinci Drawing Course

Da Vinci Drawing Course Illustrations: Nusa Maal.

Leonardo da Vinci. *Studies and Positions of Cats (no. 12363).* Windsor
Castle. Photo: Art Resource, NY.

Leonardo da Vinci. *Profile studies. v. 12276.* Royal Library, Windsor,
Great Britain. Photo: Alinari/Art Resource, NY.

Leonardo da Vinci. *Portrait of Francesco Sforza, son of Gian Galeazzo.*
Gabinetto dei Disegni e delle Stampe, Florence, Italy. Photo:
Scala/Art Resource, NY.

Recreation of the model of the Sforza horse based on sketches by
Leonardo da Vinci. Photo courtesy of Leonardo da Vinci's Horse, Inc.

ABOUT THE AUTHOR

MICHAEL J. GELB, is the world's leading authority on the application of genius thinking to personal and organizational development. He is a pioneer in the fields of creative thinking, accelerated learning, and innovative leadership.

Gelb leads seminars for organizations such as DuPont, IBM, Merck, Microsoft, Nike, and YPO. He brings more than 30 years of experience as a professional speaker, seminar leader and organizational consultant to his diverse, international clientele.

Michael J. Gelb's publications include *Body Learning: an Introduction to the Alexander Technique and Present Yourself! Captivate Your Audience with Great Presentation Skills*. His best selling audio programs include: *Mind Mapping: How to Liberate Your Natural Genius*, and *Work Like Da Vinci: Gaining the Creative Advantage in Your Business and Career*.

A former professional juggler who once performed with the Rolling Stones and Bob Dylan, Gelb introduced the idea of teaching juggling as a means to promote accelerated learning and team-building. He authored *More Balls Than Hands: Juggling Your Way to Success by Learning to Love Your Mistakes*. A fourth degree black belt in the Japanese martial art of Aikido, Gelb is co-author with International Grandmaster Raymond Keene, of *Samurai Chess: Mastering Strategic Thinking Through the Martial Art of the Mind*.

A passionate student of the Renaissance and the nature of genius, Gelb ignited the current fascination with all things Da Vinci. *Think Like Da Vinci: Seven Easy Steps to Boosting Your Everyday Genius* has been translated into 25 languages and has appeared on the Washington Post, Amazon.com, and the New York Times best seller lists. Gelb's 2004 release, *Da Vinci Decoded*, and his recent Sounds True audio program *The Spirit of Leonardo* tap into the seven Da Vinci principles outlined in

Think Like Da Vinci to show readers how to cultivate spiritual intelligence.

Michael Gelb's passion for applying genius thinking to personal and organizational development is also expressed in his HarperCollins release *Discover Your Genius: How To Think Like History's Ten Most Revolutionary Minds.*

In 1999, Michael Gelb shared the Brain Trust Charity's "Brain of the Year" award with former U.S. senator John Glenn. Previous honorees include Prof. Stephen Hawking, Bill Gates, Garry Kasparov and Gene Rodenberry. In 2003, Michael was awarded a Batten Fellowship by the University of Virginia's Darden Business School.

Gelb's latest book is *Innovate Like Edison: The Success System of America's Greatest Inventor* co-authored with Sarah Miller Caldicott, the great grand niece of Thomas Edison.

He lives in Santa Fe, New Mexico.